Promoting Equity for Multilingual Learners With Disabilities

Sara E. N. Kangas

Teachers College Press
Teachers College, Columbia University

Published by Teachers College Press,® 1234 Amsterdam Avenue, New York, NY 10027

Front cover design by Geronna Lewis-Lyte. Photos by Pragyan Bezbo / Unsplash; Pexels; John Nash / Flickr; and ArtRachen01 / iStock by Getty Images.

Library of Congress Cataloging-in-Publication Data is available at loc.gov

ISBN 978-0-8077-8680-2 (paper)
ISBN 978-0-8077-8681-9 (hardcover)
ISBN 978-0-8077-8293-4 (ebook)

Printed on acid-free paper
Manufactured in the United States of America

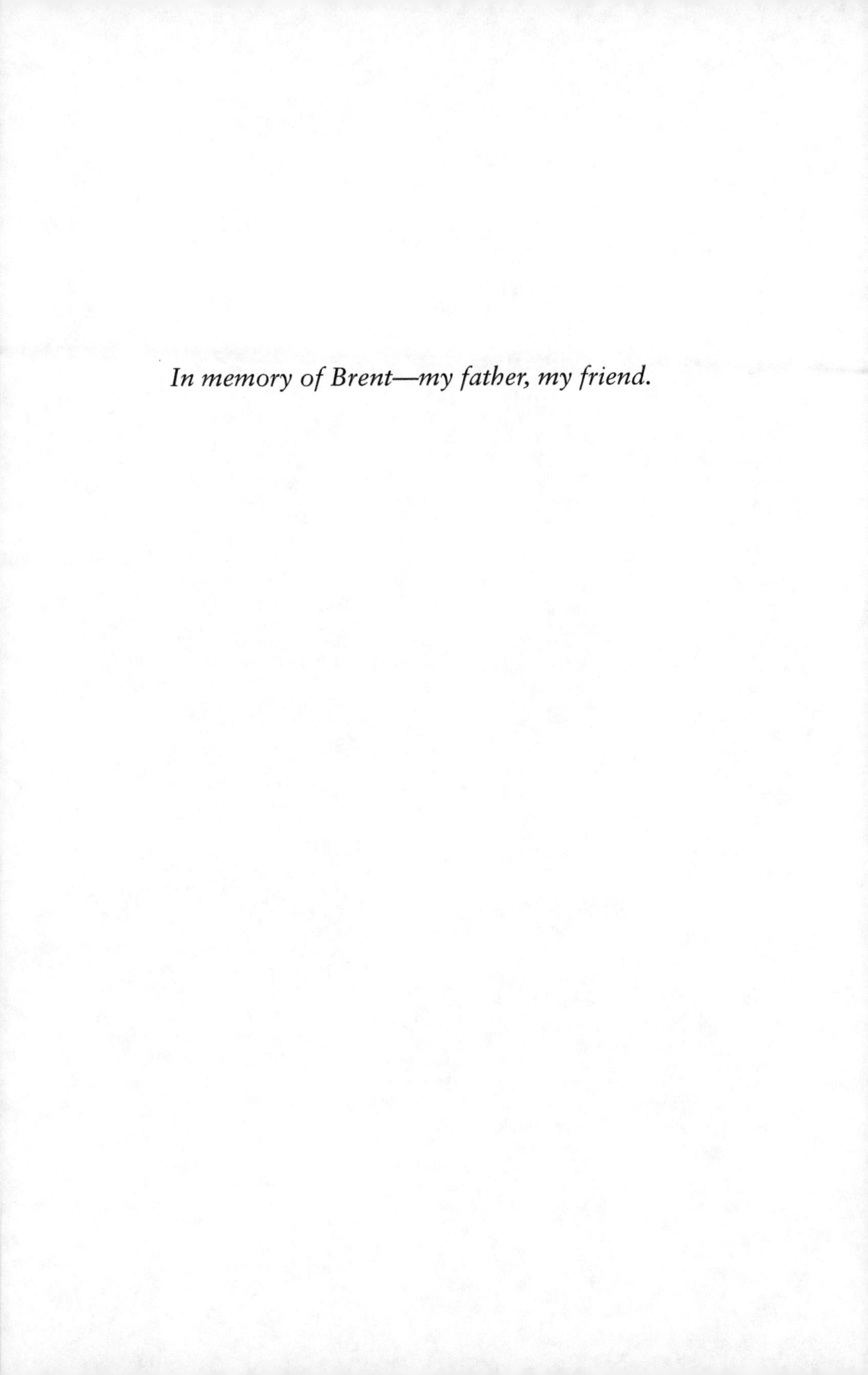

In memory of Brent—my father, my friend.

Contents

Preface

For a while now, I have been wanting to write a book that centers equity for multilingual learners (MLs) with disabilities. Several reasons compel me. First, I have come to see that MLs with disabilities tend to be a "back burner" population of students. Although education stakeholders—teachers, education leaders, teacher educators, and state education agency (SEA) leaders—genuinely desire to support MLs with disabilities and to develop policies and initiatives that open up pathways for their learning, other pressing issues rise to the top. As such issues arise, it is commonly reasoned that when the hurdles are conquered and conditions settle down, attending to MLs with disabilities can then become a priority. But, as we know, ideal circumstances in education are exceedingly rare. Just as one challenge subsides, a new one is there to take its place. Knowing this, this book seeks to elevate the needs of MLs with disabilities, asking readers to consider the proposition that working toward equity for this population is for the now and cannot be penciled in for later.

Second, I am writing this book because I see that regardless of our roles in K–12 education, education stakeholders encounter similar problems of practice at the intersection of language learning and disabilities. I recall sitting in a Zoom meeting in 2020 and hearing SEA leaders discuss the challenges they face among the silos of their departments of education. The problems were familiar: Silos prevent communication and collaboration, stymie holistic changes, and perpetuate compartmentalization of children. I first observed this phenomenon after conducting an ethnographic study on service provision for MLs with disabilities. Teachers in the study grappled with the same everyday consequences of the departmental silos in their districts and schools that these leaders reflected. The mirroring experiences of K–12 teachers and SEA leaders became an observation I could not shake. As I began to consider this premise more fully, I revisited prior research as well as my own studies and experiences to look for other common problems of practice. This inquiry brought me to the central premise of this book: Most problems of practice in the education of MLs with disabilities have the same repeated and predictable causes. As such, if we become familiar with these root causes, we can anticipate their emergence and respond more readily and effectively.

Third, I have observed that disproportionality (i.e., over- and underrepresentation) of MLs in special education is often positioned as the primary injustice facing these students. For the past 40 years, research has emphasized special education referral and disproportionality, and consequently has faltered in keeping pace with the realities of K–12 education; equity for dually identified students extends far beyond this juncture. This book pulls to the center other critical moments in the education of MLs with disabilities that are deserving of attention. By focusing on the entirety of their schooling, this book offers a comprehensive framework for understanding and promoting equity for MLs with disabilities.

Finally, as I finished editing this book, President Trump signed an executive order to dissolve the U.S. Department of Education, terminating numerous staff and drastically reducing certain offices within the department that are most critical to MLs with disabilities (e.g., Office for Civil Rights, the Office of English Language Acquisition). While legal challenges to this executive order have been filed, the fate of the department is uncertain. Amid such a shifting political landscape at the federal level, now more than ever, those who occupy critical roles at the local and state levels of the education system—from classrooms to district offices to state departments of education—matter. Without question, the influence and actions of these stakeholders are the linchpin for an education that is fair and just for MLs with disabilities.

A WORD OF THANKS

When you write a book, so many people contribute to the endeavor: the teachers and students who shared their world with you, the colleagues whose work inspired you, and the friends and family whose love kept you going. Here is my attempt to capture my appreciation for the many individuals who contributed to the content and writing of this book.

Over the years, there have been countless teachers, administrators, and students who have participated in my studies. For teachers and administrators, it often requires courage to take part in a research study, especially when the topic at hand involves MLs with disabilities. Apart from courage, it requires generosity of spirit to share your classrooms, ideas, perspectives, and time with a researcher. I am incredibly thankful for them and for all that they have kindly shared with me. It is through their giving that the ideas in this book have taken form. I am also indebted to the students who talked with me during interviews and tolerated me shadowing their classes. I deeply appreciate the experiences I had with them, their personalities, charm, sense of humor, and sweetness. As I think of them, I am reminded of the importance of the pursuit of equity—for their learning and life opportunities. In recent years, I have also had the pleasure of working with SEA leaders who work in departments and offices of education across the United States. I have been thoroughly heartened by their dedication to MLs, especially those with disabilities, and I am grateful for their perspectives on developing policies for dually identified students and guiding local districts and schools as they support these students.

There are several collaborators to whom I owe a great deal of thanks, as their ideas and experiences have pushed my own thinking along: María Cioè-Peña, Megan Hopkins, Jamie Schissel, and Hayley Weddle. I am also grateful for colleagues in the field whose scholarship on the intersection of language, disability, and race has long been inspiring to me: Patricia Martínez Álvarez, Alfredo Artiles, Alba Ortiz, and the late Janette Klingner. There are colleagues at Lehigh University whose words encouraged me and whose interest in the book gave me a lift: Brook Sawyer, Esther Lindström, Lee Her, and Lia Sandilos. There are also several wonderful doctoral students at Lehigh whose efforts directly supported the content in the book: Xiaodi Li, Molly Ruiz, Dylan Young, and Henry Zink.

I am very grateful for Yasuko Kanno, who was once my dissertation chair but—whether she knows it or not—has become my forever mentor and writing buddy. I owe so much to Yasuko. She is the one who encouraged me to consider doctoral studies in the first place. As a first-generation college student from a working-class family, I thought doctoral studies were well beyond my reach. Yasuko, however, believed in me, and her belief gave me the kick in the pants I needed to begin my PhD. When it came time to finish my dissertation, Yasuko recommended that we exchange writing on a biweekly basis. She would write chapters for her book, and I, chapters for my dissertation. Ten years later, we are still exchanging writing. Without her discerning feedback, support, and kindness, I would not have started—or finished—this book.

Last, I would like to express my love and appreciation for my dear family. Thank you, John, for reading the pages of the book and for keeping me motivated when the writing, at times, became a real slog. To my darling Margot and Inez, I give my deepest thanks; you have filled my heart and days with joy.

THIS BOOK INCORPORATED ELEMENTS FROM THE FOLLOWING PUBLICATIONS

Kangas, S. E. N. (2014). When special education trumps ESL: An investigation of service delivery for ELLs with disabilities. *Critical Inquiry in Language Studies*, *11*(4), 273–306.

Kangas, S. E. N. (2017a). A cycle of fragmentation in an inclusive age: The case of English learners with disabilities. *Teaching and Teacher Education*, *66*, 261–272.

Kangas, S. E. N. (2017b). "That's where the rubber meets the road": The intersection of special education and bilingual education. *Teachers College Record*, *119*(7), 1–36.

Kangas, S. E. N. (2018a). Breaking one law to uphold another: Service provision for English learners with disabilities. *TESOL Quarterly*, *52*(4), 877–910.

Kangas, S. E. N. (2018b). Why working apart doesn't work at all: Special education and English learner teacher collaborations. *Intervention in School and Clinic*, *54*(1), 31–39.

Kangas, S. E. N. (2020). Counternarratives of English learners with disabilities. *Bilingual Research Journal*, *43*(3), 267–285.

Kangas, S. E. N. (2021a). "Is it language or disability?': Confronting an ableist and monolingual filter for English learners with disabilities. *TESOL Quarterly*, *55*(3), 673–683.

Kangas, S. E. N. (2021b). *Supporting ELs with disabilities during remote learning and school reopening*. Council of Chief State School Officers.

Kangas, S. E. N. (2024). *Promoting equitable reclassification of English learners with disabilities*. The Center for Promoting Research to Practice. College of Education. Lehigh University.

Kangas, S. E. N., & Cook, M. (2020). Academic tracking of English learners with disabilities in middle school. *American Educational Research Journal*, *57*(6), 2415–2449.

Kangas, S. E. N., & Cook, M. (2023). Navigating competing policy demands: Dual service provision for English learners with disabilities in middle school. *Language Policy, 22,* 315–341.

Kangas, S. E. N., & Ruiz, M. (in press). Data skepticism and capacity for data-based decisions: The case of reclassifying English learners with disabilities. *Studies in Second Language Acquisition.*

Kangas, S. E. N., & Schissel, J. L. (2021). Holding them back or pushing them out?: Reclassification policies for English learners with disabilities. *Linguistics and Education*, *63*, 1–11.

Schissel, J. L., & Kangas, S. E. N. (2018). Reclassification of emergent bilinguals with disabilities: The intersectionality of improbabilities. *Language Policy*, *17*(4), 567–589.

Part I

EQUITY FOUNDATIONS

CHAPTER 1

Introduction

More than 40 years ago, research began to consider whether multilingual learners (MLs), students who are in the process of acquiring grade-level English, were inappropriately identified with disabilities in K–12 schools (e.g., Cummins, 1981; García & Ortiz, 1988; Wilkinson & Ortiz, 1986). These early works questioned the accuracy of special education referrals of MLs, arguing that language acquisition and disabilities were likely conflated during the evaluation processes. Since this juncture, two interrelated issues have garnered the collective attention of K–12 educators, researchers, and policymakers:

1. the disproportionate representation of MLs in special education
2. the importance of distinguishing language learning and disability

Equity is at the crux of these issues. On one hand, if educators do not disentangle language learning and disability during initial special education evaluations, MLs could be wrongly identified with disabilities they do not have, thereby contributing to the overrepresentation of MLs in special education (see Collier, 2011; Hoover et al., 2016; Klingner & Eppolito, 2014; Ortiz et al., 2011). On the other hand, if educators are hesitant to initiate special education referrals out of concern that language learning can resemble particular disabilities, MLs could be overlooked for disabilities they, in fact, have, thus creating issues of potential underrepresentation in special education (see Hibel & Jasper, 2012; Park, 2020). Erring on one side or the other has hefty consequences for MLs, shaping their learning opportunities and their life chances. For this reason, the disproportionate representation of MLs in special education has held the attention of the education community for decades, as reflected in the sustained line of research on this phenomenon (e.g., Artiles et al., 2005; Barrio, 2017; Cuba & Tefera, 2024; Gage et al., 2013; Morgan et al., 2018; Park, 2020; Samson & Lesaux, 2009; Sullivan, 2011; Umansky et al., 2017; Yamasaki & Luk, 2018). In both research and practice, this dedication to examining and preventing disproportionate representation indicates that it is one of the most critical inequities facing MLs.

This book argues, however, that disproportionality in special education is the tip of the iceberg. When taken together, research, federal reports, and policies tell us a startling story: Once students are dually identified as MLs with disabilities,[1] they encounter repeated formidable inequities. Yet aside from special education disproportionality, other equity issues, such as receipt of services, inclusion in general education, and access to rigorous instruction, have remained relatively overlooked in research, practice, and policy. This book centers such underexamined equity issues *after* special education evaluation to depict a broader landscape of equity in the education of MLs with disabilities.

As a researcher and author of this book, I conceptualize *equity* in terms of MLs with disabilities' access to learning opportunities and their educational rights. And I take the stance that equity for MLs with disabilities cannot be achieved by student-level interventions alone but rather requires intervening in obstacles—the systems, practices, and policies that are often too rigid to support the complex needs of MLs with disabilities. Researcher and educational sociologist Adam Gamoran (2021) astutely captured this sentiment when he stated: "If we wish to reduce inequality it will not be enough to identify programs that compensate for such built-in obstacles—we need to overturn the obstacles from the start" (para. 2). This book aims to promote equity by raising awareness of and supporting stakeholders to dismantle the systemic "built-in" barriers in our education system that stifle the learning opportunities and rights of MLs with disabilities. To contextualize the central premise of the book, I provide a contemporary portrait of the demography of MLs with disabilities in U.S. K–12 public schools.

DEMOGRAPHIC OVERVIEW OF MLS WITH DISABILITIES

The Every Student Succeeds Act (ESSA, 2015), with its mandate for districts to disaggregate the performance of MLs with disabilities from the larger ML population, has given us a clearer understanding of both the prevalence and general characteristics of MLs with disabilities. In recent years, MLs with disabilities represent 15.8% of the nation's 5.3 million MLs and 11.7% of the nation's student with disability population (National Center for Education Statistics, 2024; U.S. Office of Special Education Programs, 2022). Contemporary estimates indicate that the ML with disability population increased by approximately 30% from 2012 to 2020 (U.S. Office of Special Education Programs, 2022) or by 50% in the 2006 to 2020 timeframe (Cooc, 2023). Federal reports illuminate that MLs with disabilities are a heterogeneous group, but they are commonly identified with high incidence disabilities, namely specific learning disabilities (SLDs) and speech and language impairments (SLIs). One in every two MLs with disabilities will be identified with an SLD, and one in five will be identified with an SLI (U.S.

Department of Education, n.d). From there, the prevalence of other disabilities decreases significantly, with 7% of MLs with disabilities identified with a disability that falls under the umbrella of other health impairment, 7% with intellectual disabilities, 6.3% with autism, and 2.9% with emotional or behavioral disorders (U.S. Department of Education, n.d). The heterogeneity of MLs with disabilities is not fully captured by such demographic reporting. In my research with schools, many of the MLs in my studies have two or three—or even more—identified disabilities. Further, MLs have diverse backgrounds, linguistic needs, and educational profiles—they may be newcomers and refugees or may have spent the entirety of their lives living and attending schools in the United States. Reporting that focuses on singular labels fails to adequately capture the true diversity of MLs with disabilities.

Overall, the prevalence of MLs with disabilities varies across states and larger regions within the United States as well as across grade-level bands in schools. Addressing the former, in states such as California, Nevada, New Mexico, and Texas, MLs with disabilities constitute over 20% of all students with disabilities, whereas West Virginia and the New England states of New Hampshire and Vermont have the lowest percentages of dually identified students at 0.67%, 0.98%, and 2.1%, respectively (U.S. Office of Special Education Programs, 2022). This reflects larger trends discovered by Cooc (2023), whereby MLs with disabilities are enrolled in highest numbers in the U.S. southwest and west. Addressing the latter, the ML-with-disability population varies by grade level with disproportionately fewer MLs with disabilities in the earliest elementary grades, particularly kindergarten and grade 1 but with marked increases in MLs with disabilities from mid-elementary into secondary grades (Artiles et al., 2005; Hibel & Jasper, 2012; Ortiz et al., 2011; Samson & Lesaux, 2009). As will be explored later in Chapter 2, MLs with disabilities' representation across grades is noticeably uneven, with particular disability categories over- or underrepresented in certain grade bands (Artiles et al., 2005; Samson & Lesaux, 2009; Umansky et al., 2017).

In terms of the first language (L1) backgrounds of MLs with disabilities, there are no nationally available data disaggregating the population by L1; however, in looking at the ML population overall, the U.S. Department of Education (n.d.) reports that the languages commonly spoken by MLs include Spanish (77.1%), Arabic (2.3%), Chinese (2.2%), Vietnamese (1.8%), and Hmong (0.8%). Yet over 14% of all MLs—whether they have disabilities or not—will speak languages outside of the five most common L1s. Taking these linguistic and disability demographics together, MLs with disabilities are not monolithic. This book acknowledges the heterogeneity of MLs with disabilities in terms of their L1 backgrounds, disabilities, race, and immigration status, among others, but it cannot meaningfully address the unique needs of each subgroup of MLs with disabilities nor all the disability categories represented therein. This reflects the unfortunate truth that research is lagging far behind the current needs of our schools. Yet the book gives attention to the nuances and complications that arise in promoting equity for such a heterogeneous student group and the diverse school contexts they attend. Now that we have a clear sense of demographic trends for MLs with disabilities, we turn to the topic of equity.

INEQUITIES EXPERIENCED BY MLS WITH DISABILITIES

Research, federal data, state policies, and our observations of the K–12 system point to an unsettling reality: that equity is compromised for MLs with disabilities in predictable, repeated ways—what I call *patterned inequities*. These inequities conform to three distinct patterns and are pervasive in our education system, manifesting routinely in classrooms, district and school systems, and state policies. In fact, I argue that the inequities that alarm us about the special education evaluation of MLs continue well past this juncture and replicate in other moments of these students' schooling. Even as stakeholders encounter what seem to be new *problems of practice*, those vexing dilemmas encountered in their work relating to MLs with disabilities, I contend that, at the core, they are confronted with a patterned inequity. The book explores the patterned inequities at length in Chapter 2; below is a brief synopsis of the three patterns identifiable in the education system.

Pattern One: Language-or-Disability Filter

This pattern occurs when MLs with disabilities experience difficulties, whether academic, linguistic, behavioral, or social. Informed by Valencia's (1997) notion of deficit thinking, in this pattern, either language or disability is assumed to be the source of the difficulties MLs with disabilities experience in school. While such internal sources, in this case, language or disability, are deemed the origin of MLs with disabilities' problems, external contributors (i.e., systems, processes, and policies) are ignored. This way of making sense of MLs with disabilities' difficulties—which I refer to as the *language-or-disability filter* (Kangas, 2021)—focuses inordinately on language or disability, blinding education stakeholders to the disadvantageous ecologies surrounding students and, in the process, giving way to bias.

Pattern Two: Unitary Identity

The second patterned inequity occurs when MLs with disabilities' intersecting identities are erased in processes, systems, and policies. For MLs with disabilities, this often occurs when they are positioned as if they have a unitary identity, or more simply when they are treated as either MLs *or* students with disabilities—but not both. Rooted in the theory of intersectionality (Crenshaw, 1989, 1991), the book will demonstrate that unitary identity is a routine response to MLs with disabilities that compromises their learning and life opportunities as their intersecting needs remain unmet.

Pattern Three: Specialization Trap

This patterned inequity captures the tendencies of education stakeholders to work narrowly within their professional silos—a phenomenon that I call the *specialization trap* (Kangas, 2017a). Relying on a medical model of disability, education stakeholders take a hands-off approach to addressing the needs of MLs with disabilities that lie outside their respective areas of expertise. This siloed approach reduces MLs with disabilities to a fragment of needs, resulting in disjointed practices as well as bureaucratic errors that constrain these students' learning and life opportunities.

Throughout the book, I will draw from research evidence, theories, and my own experiences as a researcher, teacher educator, and policy consultant to demonstrate how patterned inequities are at work individually and simultaneously in the varied contexts of our K–12 system.

AUDIENCES OF THE BOOK

This book is for education stakeholders—teachers and educational leaders, and the professoriate that trains them—who desire to make their systems and practices more equitable for MLs with disabilities and are looking to translate that desire into concrete action. This book is also intended for education policymakers who wish for laws and policies that better reflect the interests and needs of dually identified students. While *policymaker* is often a catchall term for anyone at the state or federal level who is involved in policy development (Garcia, 2021), this book focuses on the professional staff (e.g., directors, coordinators) employed in departments of education or other state education agencies (SEAs; hereafter called *SEA leaders* or *state leaders*). Finally, researchers who are interested in understanding the educational landscape of MLs with disabilities will also benefit from this book. Each of these education stakeholders plays a critical role in promoting equity in the schooling of MLs with disabilities, and thus, their respective roles, experiences, and contexts are reflected in the content and structure of this text.

STRUCTURE AND FEATURES OF THE BOOK

Structure

The book is organized into three primary sections: systems, classrooms, and policies. These sections are intentional, targeting specific education stakeholders who are each essential to securing an equitable education for MLs with disabilities. Depending on their role in K–12 education, readers may find particular chapters more relevant to their work. The book's structure and arguments take this into account, allowing stakeholders to hone their attention on specific sections.

Inarguably, Chapter 2 is the cornerstone of the book—the preferred place to begin for all stakeholders—as it sets the stage for all subsequent chapters. This chapter lays bare the intricacies of the three patterned inequities; it teases out how inequities MLs with disabilities experience are, in fact, a part of a larger pattern occurring in predictable forms in the K–12 education system, from classrooms to district offices to state departments of education.

Chapters 3 through 5 address equity in educational institutions' systems. These chapters take on four systems that wield a great deal of influence in shaping equitable learning opportunities for MLs with disabilities. These systems are organizational, meaning they attempt to organize students and the supports these students need. Chapter 3 explores the organization of services and organization of students (i.e., the physical placement of pupils) as interrelated phenomena, while Chapter 4 examines the organization of individualized plans and the teams that develop them. Thus, aspiring or inservice educational leaders—principals, district directors of ML and special education, superintendents—as well as teachers and the higher education faculty who train them will find these chapters useful for reimagining school systems for MLs with disabilities.

As a departure from the previous chapters, Chapter 5 attends to teacher education, particularly teacher preparation programs in higher education, as sites from which patterned inequities for MLs with disabilities also emanate and are, thus, a critical point of intervention. My colleagues in teacher education programs will benefit the most from this chapter as they nurture the skills and equity-mindedness of teachers. SEA leaders who develop policies and requirements for teacher licensure will also benefit from the focus of this chapter, as the licensure mandates established by states directly influence the programs and approaches to training offered by teacher preparation programs.

Chapters 6 through 8 explore ways to advance equity in classrooms through transforming teachers' practices and dispositions. These chapters, more specifically, examine high expectations, rigorous instruction, as well as sound data interpretation and use. K–12 teachers, education leaders, and teacher educators will gain the most from these chapters, as the patterned inequities can be ameliorated through adjustments to the ways in which teachers see and respond to MLs with disabilities. Given the centrality of families to any effort to implement equitable practices and policies, readers will find that a commitment to valuing and authentically partnering with parents and other key family members is woven across these and other chapters of this book.

Chapters 9 and 10 are dedicated to equity in policy for MLs with disabilities. Chapter 9 attends to the academic performance standards established by state policies, with a focus on reclassification as one example of such a policy. This chapter examines how achievement policies often marginalize MLs with disabilities. Chapter 10, however, turns to the siloed conditions that state leaders grapple with as they work to develop policies and guidance that reflect the unique needs of MLs with disabilities. With these foci, Chapters 9 and 10 speak directly to state leaders and other policymakers as critical stakeholders in expanding access and equity for MLs with disabilities.

Finally, Chapter 11 concludes the book by arguing that patterned inequities require education stakeholders' awareness and response. This chapter underscores the agency of all education stakeholders, summarizing the pathways they can each pursue to promote equity for MLs with disabilities.

Features

Across most of the chapters of the book, readers will find some reoccurring features. These chapters begin with a discussion of why the topic at hand is consequential to the learning opportunities and educational rights of dually identified students. Following this, readers will encounter "Key Research Findings," which provides an overview of what research has to tell us about the chapter's topic. With this background knowledge, readers will then find "Evidence of Patterns," the section of the chapter that provides readers with findings that indicate the inner workings of patterned inequities in the schooling of MLs with disabilities. The evidence presented in the chapters is drawn from an array of sources, including findings from empirical studies, whether my own or those of other scholars, and my professional experiences as a scholar, teacher educator and trainer, ethnographic researcher, and policy consultant. The chapter then pivots from understanding to responding to patterned inequities. In these sections, entitled "Response to Patterned Inequities," readers will find targeted recommendations for promoting equity in their respective roles for MLs with disabilities. As noted above, depending on the topic of the chapter, the recommendations offered may gravitate toward particular stakeholders. Each chapter concludes with a succinct "Summary" that pulls together the evidence and arguments presented in the chapter. When possible, I provide readers with tools and additional recommended resources that they can use in their efforts to enhance the educational experiences of dually identified students. It is my hope that these common features of the chapters will give readers a clear sense of what obstacles MLs with disabilities face in their education and how readers, in their varied roles as education stakeholders, can be powerful agents of equity.

A FEW THOUGHTS

Books about equity can often be deflating—a wet blanket of sorts that leaves us feeling hopeless. Education stakeholders who have been working with MLs with disabilities, or supporting those who do, know firsthand that promoting equity for this population of students is not for the faint of heart. Rest assured: This book does not merely catalog problems. In the pages ahead, readers will certainly encounter evidence elucidating the inequities that exist for MLs with disabilities, because we need to know what these inequities are if we want to address them. More importantly, though, readers will also find that the book focuses on pathways forward to reduce and ultimately eliminate these inequities in our education system. In focusing on these pathways forward, the book seeks to empower education stakeholders—the teacher, school leader, state education leader, professor, and researcher—with a more nuanced understanding of equity at the intersection of language learning and disability and the strategic options that can promote equity for MLs with disabilities.

CHAPTER 2

Patterned Inequities

This chapter addresses the central question: What do we know about the nature of equity for MLs with disabilities? The answer, I argue, is this: Equity is jeopardized in repeated, similar ways—what I call *patterned inequities*. These inequities are pervasive, cropping up in the work of all education stakeholders and across all education sites. Patterned inequities are also endemic to our work, undergirding many of the problems of practice we grapple with as we attempt to teach MLs with disabilities or to support those who do. In this chapter, I delve into three patterned inequities—language-or-disability filter, unitary identity, and specialization trap—making a case for how these patterned inequities arise, interact, and are perpetuated across the layers of the education system. Later in the chapter, I use disproportionality in special education as a principal example to illustrate the manner in which the three patterned inequities materialize. I conclude the chapter with a summary of patterned inequities' shared characteristics.

PATTERN ONE: LANGUAGE-OR-DISABILITY FILTER

"Is it language or disability?" After more than a decade of poring over and conducting research on MLs with disabilities, I encountered this question more than any other—uttered by countless teachers, education leaders, and policymakers as they try to make sense of the difficulties MLs with and without disabilities encountered. During my research studies on MLs with disabilities, rare would it be for an interview or meeting to go by without teachers articulating the salience of the question in their practice. Despite the currency of the question in our day-to-day practice now, "Is it language or disability?" has a multidecade history. It originally surfaced in Cummins's (1981) examination of special education evaluation, wherein he brought to light the questionable validity of diagnostic assessments used during special education evaluations. Since that time, "Is it language or disability?" has remained at the fore of special education evaluation and referral matters (see Artiles et al., 2005; Artiles & Ortiz, 2002; Klingner et al., 2005), positioned as a critical question all education stakeholders must ask about MLs because certain disabilities can resemble second language (L2) learning. Thus, the

English proficiency of MLs must be taken into account in special education evaluation, lest educators and school psychologists mistake L2 learning for a disability and contribute to MLs' overrepresentation in special education (Collier, 2011; Klingner & Geisler, 2008; Ortiz et al., 2011). Federal laws have reinforced the prominence of the question; in 1999, regulations for the Individuals with Disabilities Education Act (IDEA) mandated that educators rule out emerging English proficiency as the reason for special education evaluation (Assistance to States for the Education of Children with Disabilities, 1999).

As we look around us, it is apparent that the primacy of "Is it language or disability?" has remained intact for over 40 years now. Contemporary publications center this question and its importance for promoting equity in special education referral and multitiered systems of support (MTSS) more broadly (see Haas & Esparza Brown, 2019; McCain & Farnsworth, 2018; Park, 2019; Swanson et al., 2020). Leading organizations across education, such as the Council for Exceptional Children, the National Association of School Psychologists, and the TESOL International Association, offer professional learning sessions and resources on disentangling L2 learning and disabilities.

The sustained effort to sort out language learning and disability has resulted in "Is it language or disability?" becoming arguably *the* question most commonly asked about MLs who are experiencing difficulty in their learning. Through my years of research and teacher training, it is evident that teachers have internalized "Is it language or disability?" as the go-to question in their practice for a spectrum of issues and concerns, whether linguistic, academic, or behavioral. Although the question was traditionally posed about special education referrals, it has now become for educators "an explanatory tool for a wide range of issues they encounter" (Kangas, 2021, p. 675) while teaching and supporting MLs with identified and suspected disabilities.

Take, for instance, an ML with a disability who does not make gains in English language proficiency (ELP). In recent years, scholarship has unearthed the concerning trend that many MLs with disabilities are unable to meet reclassification criteria (see Burke et al., 2016; Umansky et al., 2017), which most commonly include meeting a specified score on the annual standardized ELP assessment (e.g., ELPA21, WIDA ACCESS, etc.). In my research on this phenomenon, educators have attributed the challenges MLs with disabilities experience in reaching reclassification criteria to two primary sources: either L2 learning itself or a disability (see Kangas & Schissel, 2021). In my study that examined the learning opportunities of middle school MLs with disabilities—all of whom had been receiving English as a Second Language (ESL) services since they entered kindergarten—the ML Department tried to suss out whether these students were unable to exit

ESL due to their language or due to their disability. This question drove their decision-making in reclassification, as evidenced by these words from a veteran ESL teacher:

> But what we did this past summer is we took a good, hard look at those [MLs with disabilities] who had been in the [ESL] program say, for three, four years. And we tried to do a real, solid, true evaluation of where they really were. Was it their disability, or was it their language that prevented them or held them back from advancing to another level?

Despite having origins rooted in social justice, I argue, the question has ironically become troubling in everyday education practice, perpetuating inequity for MLs with disabilities. The question has morphed into what I call the *language-or-disability* filter (Kangas, 2021)—a "lens through which educators attempt to understand the academic performance and behaviors of MLs with identified or suspected disabilities by focusing inordinately on language and disability alone" (p. 676). More simply, the language-or-disability filter is a way of seeing and making sense of the educational needs and performances of MLs with disabilities by looking to language or disability as the root cause. The filter compromises equity in two ways. First, the filter operates as a lens to understand *problems* and is not used to make sense of student success or achievement. When an ML with a disability earns an A on a social studies test, the teacher does not sit back and wonder, "Is it language or disability?" In similar fashion, when an ML with a disability makes steady gains in their ELP, the question of language-or-disability is not uttered. These imaginary scenarios demonstrate how the filter is both problem- and deficit-oriented.

Second, the filter is myopic, focusing on students in ways that disregard environmental contributors to educational problems. It is through "relying on the filter as a sense-making tool, we are presupposing that the source of the problem—whatever it may be—is the language or disability that lies within the student" (Kangas, 2021, p. 677). Richard Valencia (1997), an educational psychologist, argued that patterns of thinking that attribute problems in schooling to the capabilities of students constitute what he termed *deficit thinking*. He theorized that for historically minoritized students, internal contributors (e.g., academic and linguistic abilities) are commonly identified as the sources of underperformance, while external contributors (e.g., limitations in the classroom and school) are ignored. Herein is the crux of the patterned inequity for MLs with disabilities: Language or disability are often identified prematurely as the lone sources of underperformance or difficulty in the education of MLs with disabilities, without environmental contributors being sufficiently examined and ruled out. If careful attention is not paid to the role of the environment—classrooms, school structures, and policy contexts—in influencing learning opportunities and outcomes, equity is hampered.

PATTERN TWO: UNITARY IDENTITY

In a recent study, I recall thumbing through the schedules of middle school MLs with disabilities, noticing that ESL classes were conspicuously missing. I wondered whether the students were receiving ESL support—perhaps through a push-in coteaching model not indicated on the schedule—or whether this was reflective of a larger trend in U.S. schools whereby MLs with disabilities lacked access to both language services[1] and special education services (U.S. Departments of Justice & Education, 2015). Upon further inquiry, however, I discovered that the needs stemming from the disabilities of the MLs were considered "more severe" than that of their ELP, and thus, special education services took precedence. By relinquishing ESL support, service provision practices in the school erased the language learning needs of students, ultimately positioning the *multilingual learners* with disabilities as *students* with disabilities. Instances such as these highlight the second patterned inequity—unitary identity—as MLs with disabilities are treated as MLs *or* students with disabilities, not both.

Unitary identity is prominent in service provision, reified in the turf war that occurs when special education and language services compete with one another (Kangas, 2014, 2017b, 2018a). Yet it seeps across other junctures and contexts. As we consult research, theory, and education stakeholders themselves, there is ample, convincing evidence that systems, processes, and policies in education respond to MLs with disabilities in ways that ignore their intersecting identities. In response, scholars have advocated for an intersectional approach to understanding and supporting MLs with disabilities that accounts for the complexity and multiplicity of their needs (Artiles, 2013; Cioè-Peña, 2017, 2021; Kangas, 2017b, 2018a). This approach to supporting students from multiple minoritized statuses is situated within the broader framework of intersectionality.

Intersectionality is often attributed to Crenshaw (1989, 1991), a renowned legal studies scholar, who theorized that both institutions and the policies they produce marginalize individuals who represent multiple minoritized identities by failing to account for the ways in which such intersections create a distinct experience for these individuals. Her argument arose from examining the experiences of African American women who were marginalized by the social movements of the 1960s and 1970s in the United States. As Crenshaw argued, despite the obvious parallels between the aims of women's rights and civil rights movements—to defend and expand the rights of women, in the one case, and of African Americans in the other—neither movement took into account the distinct needs of African

American women, assuming their experiences and needs were identical to those of White women and African American men, respectively. In this way, African American women experienced sexism and racism, as well as "double discrimination," a combined discrimination based on the intersection of gender and race, as Crenshaw (1989) highlights through the following metaphor:

> Consider an analogy to traffic in an intersection, coming and going in all four directions. Discrimination, like traffic through an intersection, may flow in one direction, and it may flow in another. If an accident happens in an intersection, it can be caused by cars traveling from any number of directions and, sometimes, from all of them. (p. 149)

With this intersectional lens, we can begin to see how inequities arise from individual discriminatory norms and their interface.

This metaphor encapsulates the second patterned inequity: MLs with disabilities' intersectional identities are erased, as they are treated like either MLs *or* students with disabilities—but not both. Across education sites, there is, in essence, a "default student" upon whom practices and policies are often based. For MLs with disabilities who are heterogeneous—with multiple minoritized statuses—these default norms are especially worrisome; the intersecting minoritized identities of these students that encompass not only language and disability but very often include racial, socioeconomic, and immigration statuses are likely to be reduced to one identity or another. This is even true in subfields of education, such as ESL, bilingual, and special education, that originated in pursuit of equity and have long histories of safeguarding the rights of children. In ESL and bilingual education, processes, practices, and policies in place very often have MLs *without* disabilities as the default norm. Likewise, we see evidence of a similar response in special education, as its processes, practices, and policies are predicated on monolingual—not multilingual—students with disabilities. For instance, in an overview of court cases and precedents, special education legal expert Perry Zirkel (2021) elucidated the tensions and gaps between special education and ML legal systems, characterizing MLs with disabilities as caught in a "perilous intersection" of laws (p. 59).

From an equity standpoint, unitary identity is troubling in that it erases part of these students' identities and compromises their learning and life opportunities as their intersecting needs remain unmet. Though unitary identity arises from different education sites and practices, such as the ways in which we train teachers and the manner in which we craft policies and guidance for schools, the results vis-à-vis equity are the same: Education systems fall short in thinking of and accounting for the intersecting educational needs of MLs with disabilities, and as a consequence, this group of students experiences a distinct form of double discrimination.

PATTERN THREE: SPECIALIZATION TRAP

The years have ticked by, but I will not forget one ML with a disability: Ahmed. At the time of the study, he was in 3rd grade and was dually identified as an ML with autism. Ahmed had inarguably the most complex combination of supportive services: He had autism support, ESL, speech services, occupational therapy, and social skills support—with each service rotating at different intervals and lasting for variable durations. On any given day, identifying where Ahmed was in the school building and what service he was receiving was a real puzzle. As I observed Ahmed across these services and interviewed those who supported him, I was struck by the lack of coordination and communication for this child, who had a demanding array of needs. Here is a telling example: His former ESL teacher had not had access to his Individualized Education Program (IEP), while his autism support teacher had no time to consult with his ESL teacher. And although Ahmed spent most of the day in a general education setting, his general education teacher reported to me, "I don't really work with him" (Kangas, 2014, p. 295). Throughout interviews with staff and observations of services, a fragmented approach to supporting Ahmed poignantly emerged—one marked by rigid boundaries and siloed efforts to support students. I would later come to call this approach the *specialization trap* (Kangas, 2017a)—the third patterned inequity.

Ahmed's experiences are distressingly unremarkable. Research studies, including my own, indicate that educators are prone to work apart even when they are supposedly working together—much like when young children engage in parallel play, occupying the same physical space but without meaningful interaction. More broadly in education, many publications and professional learning opportunities have attempted to improve teacher collaborations in inclusive settings in which services—whether language or special education—are embedded (see Conderman et al., 2009; Council for Exceptional Children, 2022; Davison, 2006; Dove & Honigsfeld, 2010; Friend et al., 2010; Honigsfeld & Dove, 2010, 2021; Kangas, 2018b; Scruggs & Mastropieri, 2017). In state education departments, too, research findings signal that collaborations need strengthening to enhance ML education, as some ML SEA leaders reported working in silos and feeling like "singletons," having to advocate for the needs of MLs with colleagues from various divisions of the SEAs (Hopkins et al., 2022, p. 605). In my state, Pennsylvania, teacher preparation programs mimic these same trends with pre- and inservice teachers receiving fairly siloed training; in fact, it was not until 2014 that preservice general education teachers were required to have the equivalent of one course in ML education, which arguably is still de minimis.

Across these education sites, we see the third patterned inequity, the specialization trap, at work. This patterned inequity captures the tendencies of education stakeholders (i.e., teachers, educational leaders, policymakers) to work narrowly within their professional silos, "conceptualiz[ing] their work in terms of boundaries corresponding to their own specialization—what they can or cannot do and which students they can or cannot support" (Kangas, 2017a, p. 267). Believing they cannot support MLs with disabilities, educators leave "treating" the disability, language proficiency, or other needs outside of their expertise to their specialist counterparts. This disposition toward supporting students is common in education, stemming from a lack of interdisciplinary training and, more broadly, from a medical model of disability wherein students with disabilities as well as other vulnerable student groups (e.g., MLs, students with interrupted or informal education, etc.), require "treatment" from specialists (Sailor, 2008). However, this disposition becomes a trap, unintentionally preventing students with multiple needs (i.e., academic, linguistic, health, and behavioral needs) from receiving optimal support.

The specialization trap and its underlying medical model remind me of the healthcare my late grandmother received for her multiple complex conditions. She had a cardiologist, hematologist, internist, and general primary care practitioner, and much like Ahmed, she was always shuffling from one specialist to the next. Despite her many appointments and the wealth of expertise held by these medical specialists, the results were fragmented and suboptimal. When the cardiologist changed her medication, for example, it resulted in a string of adverse effects for her other health conditions. During our weekly phone calls, my grandmother would often complain about this approach to her care, saying "No one is looking at the big picture." She was defeated by this approach, longing for integrated care that would enable her overall health to improve.

The pitfalls evident in my grandmother's experience likewise illuminate several unintended ways in which inequities arise from the specialization trap. First, this siloed approach reduces MLs with disabilities to a collection of fragmented needs, resulting in disjointed practices and policies that constrain these students' learning and life opportunities. As MLs with disabilities are positioned as a "set of repositories or vessels, with each teacher and specialist pouring interventions and supports into a separate one," the whole child is lost (Kangas, 2017a, p. 269). The late Nel Noddings (2006), known as an authority on childhood education, argued that in education and other fields, *people* are reduced to *needs*: "In the pursuit of efficiency, we have remade ourselves into a collection of discrete attributes and needs" (p. 8). Second, as education stakeholders are closed off in their silos, bureaucratic errors tend to emerge in ways that further constrain equity for MLs with disabilities. When systems and policies from special education and ML education do not interface, and stakeholders do not interact, errors are inevitable—errors that can influence the learning opportunities of MLs with disabilities. Ahmed's former ESL teacher not having access to this IEP, for example, was a bureaucratic error that prevented Ahmed from receiving

Table 2.1. Snapshot of Patterned Inequities

Language-or-Disability Filter *deficit lens*	Unitary Identity *identity erasure*	Specialization Trap *siloed response*
Education problems are attributed to the language or disability of MLs with disabilities, while systemic barriers are ignored.	Education processes, systems, and policies treat MLs with disabilities as ML *or* students with disabilities—but not both.	Education stakeholders work narrowly within their professional silos for MLs with disabilities, creating a fragmented approach to support.

instructional and assessment accommodations specified in the document during ESL. Third, the specialization trap co-occurs with the second patterned inequity, unitary identity. As I will discuss throughout this book, unitary identity and the specialization trap often go hand in hand; when education stakeholders adhere to the specialization trap, focusing on a subset of MLs with disabilities, they often are replicating unitary identity, viewing and responding to MLs with disabilities as if they are only MLs *or* students with disabilities but not both.

In sum, there are three patterned inequities that are routinely experienced by MLs with disabilities: (1) language-or-disability filter, (2) unitary identity, and (3) specialization trap. Table 2.1 provides a distillation of these patterned inequities as they emerge across the levels of the education system.

To bring these patterned inequities and their interrelationship to light, I will next explore the prominent inequity of MLs' disproportionate representation in special education.

PATTERNED INEQUITIES UP CLOSE: DISPROPORTIONALITY AND SPECIAL EDUCATION EVALUATION

In Chapter 1, I argued that the inequities we have become familiar with in MLs' disproportionate representation in special education are but the tip of the iceberg. Research has shown that there are instances of both over- and underrepresentation occurring for MLs, with each presenting distinct injustices for these students. Scholars have identified a multitude of contributors to disproportionality, encompassing deficit biases toward students of color (Artiles et al., 2010; Harry & Klingner, 2022), state policies (Morgan et al., 2023; Schissel & Kangas, 2018; Umansky et al., 2017), faulty evaluation processes and data (Macswan & Rolstad, 2006; Orosco & Klingner, 2010; Ortiz et al., 2011), as well as teacher beliefs about referral itself (Park, 2020). Disproportionality is a multicausal and complex phenomenon that cannot be boiled down to simple explanations (see Artiles et al., 2010). However, research has identified several alarming practices in special education referrals that compound disproportionality. Cast in a different light, these practices take the appearance of patterned inequities, as I will explore in the sections that follow.

Overrepresentation

Traditionally, overrepresentation of MLs with disabilities is associated with misidentification. Simply put, too many MLs are wrongfully diagnosed with disabilities they do not have. Alluded to in Chapter 1, the overrepresentation of MLs in special education has been documented for some time with distinct trends. First, MLs tend to be overrepresented by disability category, particularly SLDs and SLIs, and by no small amount. National data show us that roughly 35% to 37% of students with disabilities have SLDs, but in contrast, a much higher percentage of MLs with disabilities have been identified with SLDs—anywhere between 44% to 49% (U.S. Department of Education, n.d.; U.S. Office of Special Education Programs, 2022). These same datasets also show that approximately 17% of students with disabilities have SLIs, while a range of 19% to 21% of MLs with disabilities have the same diagnosis (U.S. Department of Education, n.d.; U.S. Office of Special Education Programs, 2022). Second, overrepresentation also occurs in certain grade bands, noticeably ticking upwards in 3rd grade and sustaining elevated levels in secondary grades, especially for SLDs (Artiles et al., 2005; Hibel & Jasper, 2012; Samson & Lesaux, 2009; Umansky et al., 2017). Third, school context also seems to matter in ML overrepresentation trends, with some districts and states having disproportionate percentages of MLs with disabilities, especially in the high incidence categories of SLD and SLI (see Artiles et al., 2005; Greenberg Motamedi et al., 2016; Kangas & Schissel, 2021; Schissel & Kangas, 2018; Umansky et al. 2017). Recent data from the National Clearinghouse for English Language Acquisition (2023) indicate that in 35 states, MLs are more likely than their non-ML peers to be identified with disabilities, and the states with the largest gaps were Wyoming, Illinois, Nevada, New Mexico, and Connecticut. The same report also described an inverse pattern elsewhere in the United States; in 15 states, MLs were *less* likely to be identified with disabilities than non-ML peers, with New Hampshire, New Jersey, and Tennessee having the largest disparities in identification.

In view of these disproportionality trends and the injustices that follow an erroneous referral, special education evaluation processes have come under fire, as many students are identified as MLs first and then later undergo special education evaluation (Zehler et al., 2003). When we reexamine the criticisms levied against special education evaluations, imprints of patterned inequities are sharply visible. First, diagnostic assessments used in the evaluation process have been criticized—both the instruments themselves and how they are administered. In terms of the former, the assessments used to identify the presence of cognitive disabilities have problematic origins in their design, development, and testing. Namely, these assessments have been historically normed for monolingual children, not for the multilingual, multicultural, heterogeneous ML population (Abedi, 2009; Macswan & Rolstad, 2006; Schissel, 2019). *Norming* occurs during the design process when the parameters for a typical performance are determined. This is done by assessing a group of people to see how they normally perform (i.e., group norm). If an assessment was normed for primarily monolingual children, then the benchmarks for a typical performance are based on how monolingual—not multilingual—children perform. Viewed through the lens of patterned inequities, the norming of assessments is underlined by unitary identity, as they are designed and calibrated to measure disability; however, when administered to an ML, because of norming procedures, these assessments are unable to account for and respond to the diverse language and cultural backgrounds of MLs (Jonson et al., 2019; Liu et al., 2008; Ochoa et al., 2004; Sotelo-Dynega et al., 2013). School psychologist Sotelo-Dynega et al. (2013), for instance, examined the performance of MLs who were administered the Woodcock-Johnson Tests of Cognitive Abilities–Third Edition (WJ-III), a commonly administered intelligence assessment in K–12 schools, finding a "linear relationship between developmental language proficiency and cognitive test performance that aligns itself well in terms of the linguistic and cultural demands of the tests" (p. 794). They argue that the linguistic and cultural biases of such assessments result in poorer performance for MLs:

> In the past, such findings have been thought to reflect either a mental handicap imposed by the learning of two or more languages or an innate difference in ability between bilingual and monolingual students. Post hoc examination of the data, however, appears to support neither of those claims and instead points toward differences in English language development and acculturative experiences between the two groups as the probable basis for the differences in *measured* cognitive ability. (pp. 790–791)

Indeed, special education and school psychology processes and policies have historically struggled to account for multilingualism, often using assessments that have a monolingual and monocultural norm. In effect, these assessments position MLs as monolingual students with disabilities, whether or not they have a disability.

Second, even when district staff use assessments that have been normed for more diverse populations, schools often administer these assessments to the MLs in English (see U.S. Departments of Justice & Education, 2015), creating a murky outcome, as outward manifestations of second language acquisition can resemble some disabilities. In my studies over the years, many of the MLs with disabilities were assessed in English, even in bilingual schools, and I have encountered a number of reasons why school staff administer diagnostic assessments in English even when the ML is more dominant in an L1. These reasons range from the logistical (e.g., "We couldn't find an Urdu interpreter") to the ideological (e.g., "This assessment is 'language free'") to the very curious (e.g., "This assessment can be administered in English in secondary grades"). Yet assessing in English can result in what we call *construct irrelevant variance*, in this case a dubious score that may capture second language acquisition and not an SLD, for instance. Much like the assessments themselves, their administering showcases unitary identity; assessment administration is rigid and, many times, unresponsive, especially when MLs speak languages other than Spanish. For these children, their language learning needs are erased by processes and procedures that have a default norm: monolingual children with disabilities. This norm, however, can contribute to increasing overrepresentation and, more importantly, may shape the learning and life opportunities of MLs.

Third, the soundness of the evaluation processes overall has also come into question because of the data sources used—or more accurately, not used—and the stakeholders consulted—or also more accurately, not consulted—to make an evaluation determination. Some of the MTSS studies relating to MLs have been effective in amplifying the message that special education evaluations need to include a variety of data (i.e., assessments, classroom observations, home visits) in a variety of languages (i.e., home language, English), and from a variety of stakeholders (i.e., ESL and bilingual education teachers, parents/guardians, students themselves) (see Collier, 2011; Haas & Esparza Brown, 2019; Hoover et al., 2016; MTSS for English Learners, 2022). Yet, historically, special education evaluation data sources have been overwhelmingly monolingual, taken from just the school setting, and often fail to examine classroom ecologies and to engage key stakeholders, such as parents/guardians and ESL/bilingual teachers, who can provide critical insights into the linguistic practices and capabilities of MLs (Cioè-Peña, 2021; Klingner & Edwards, 2006; Orosco & Klingner, 2010; Ortiz et al., 2011; U.S. Departments of Justice & Education, 2015). Here, we see the specialization trap in full force; certain stakeholders are excluded from having a voice in the evaluation on the grounds of expertise. Because special education evaluation is, after all, related to disability, the specialization trap would have us assume that disability experts and data sources that directly tie to the disability should be privileged. Yet, this siloed approach leaves us with an incomplete, fragmented understanding of MLs. We also see the language-or-disability filter emerge as student assessment data (e.g., standardized content assessments, reading inventories, class grades, etc.) takes precedence over ecological data that examine the learning environment (e.g., observation of instruction, equity audits of learning opportunities). Relying heavily on student assessment data without proper investigation of the affordances of the classroom and school constitutes the language-or-disability filter at work, as internal contributors (language or disability) are assumed to be the root cause and thus are assessed.

Finally, apart from assessments and evaluation data sources, the bias of stakeholders, such as the individuals on Child Study Teams that initiate referrals in schools, has been a source of concern in ML overrepresentation (Harry & Klingner, 2022; Orosco & Klingner, 2010). Because MLs often represent several minoritized identities—often race, socioeconomic status, language, culture, immigration status, and the intersection of these—they are prone to being the subjects of bias or, in other terms, pathologizing (Kangas, 2021; Phuong & Cioè-Peña, 2022). In Harry and Klingner's (2005, 2022) ground breaking ethnographic study of race and disproportionately in special education, they characterize racial bias as layered, occurring individually and institutionally; enmeshed, difficult to disentangle from other -isms (e.g., classism, linguicism, etc.); and insidious, often not explicitly voiced but nonetheless evidenced in teacher–student interactions, physical classroom configurations, teacher expectations, and staff assumptions about families and communities. Notably, Harry and Klingner (2022) argued that while a direct link tying these biases to referral could not be established, "these biases are a built-in hegemony that creates a 'goodness of fit' between a school and some of its students, but not others" (p. 88). When we take the notions of pathologizing and "goodness of fit" together, we come to see the patterned inequity of the language-or-disability filter insofar as MLs' alleged deficiencies (e.g., language, disability) are reasoned to be the source of the problem, while the biases within the school that create a poor fit between the MLs and their education are ignored.

Underrepresentation

In the case of underrepresentation, MLs have disabilities that have not yet been identified. While MLs' overrepresentation typically receives more attention, underrepresentation creates its own injustices for MLs, occurring more often in different subgroups (e.g., MLs with autism, other health impairment, and emotional or behavior disorders), in different grades (e.g., kindergarten and 1st grade) and different states (e.g., Texas) (Artiles et al., 2005; Hibel & Jasper, 2012; Morgan et al., 2023; Ortiz et al., 2011; Samson & Lesaux, 2009). We also see some "combination effects" where MLs with certain disabilities are likely to be underrepresented at specific times in their schooling. For example, Artiles and colleagues (2005) found in several urban California schools that MLs were underrepresented for SLIs in secondary grades.

Park's (2020) ethnographic study of MLs undergoing the special education evaluation gives us some insight into underrepresentation and its embodiment of patterned inequities. In Park's study, school staff adopted either a "sooner the better" or a "wait to be sure" approach toward special education evaluation. Those who had a "wait to be sure" stance worried that prematurely referring an ML would result individually in a wrongful placement for the student and collectively in the overrepresentation of MLs in special education. Consequently, these school staff instituted arbitrary timelines by which MLs could be referred and ramped up interventions in the meantime. During professional learning opportunities with teachers, a frequent question I usually receive from a frustrated teacher is: "My district says we have to wait 4 years before referral. Is that true?" I have come to call this the *referral timeline myth*, the notion that schools must wait a given amount of time to allow ELP to develop and to gather sufficient definitive evidence that points to either language learning or a disability at work. This myth is so pervasive that the U.S. Departments of Justice and Education (2015) offered a firm clarification on the matter in their *Dear Colleague* letter:

> Other districts have a policy of delaying disability evaluations of EL [English learner] students for special education and related services for a specified period of time based on their EL status. These policies are impermissible under the IDEA and Federal civil rights laws. (p. 25)

Beyond issues of compliance with federal laws, delaying referrals for MLs is an inequity that resembles the second pattern of unitary identity. In these instances, school staff institute well-meaning policies that deprive MLs with disabilities of special education and related services. In this sense, school policies and services position them as MLs only. Delaying referrals opens space for the language-or-disability filter. Recall that in Park's (2020) study, school staff preferred to wait until they could collect data that would allow them to identify whether language learning or disability were the cause of the MLs' learning difficulties. In my work with teachers, they often inquire about iron-clad approaches that will allow them to concretely determine whether language or disability is causing learning delays. Honing in on explanations internal to the student (e.g., language or disabilities) without considering those explanations that are external to the student (e.g., learning environments) is evidence of the language-or-disability filter. Yet scholars have underscored that environmental contributors in schools, such as instruction, programming, teacher training and support, among others, must be examined and modified accordingly in MTSS and during special education referrals (Collier, 2011; Haas & Esparza Brown, 2019; Klingner & Geisler, 2008). These scholars also call on schools to assume that learning environments are contributing to MLs' difficulties and delays. As Klingner and Geisler (2008) powerfully asserted: "Another way to think about this is not that the children have disabilities, but they are in 'disabling contexts'" (p. 71).

In addition to processes and conditions in schools, state policies also contribute to the underrepresentation of MLs in special education. A well-known and controversial example occurred when the Texas Education

Agency, after identifying overrepresentation of historically marginalized groups of children in special education, instituted a cap on the percentage of children that could be identified for special education services. The law remained in effect from 2004 until 2017, after which it was rescinded due to an Office for Special Education Services investigation that found the policy noncompliant with IDEA. During that time, MLs became incrementally underrepresented in special education (Morgan et al., 2023) with the fallout being this: MLs who needed special education and related services were barred from having access to them. Their education experience in that 13-year period was an example of a policy response that inadvertently positioned MLs with disabilities as MLs only in ways that shaped their learning and life opportunities.

SUMMARY

This chapter provided an overview of the three patterned inequities common in the education of MLs with disabilities: (1) language-or-disability filter, (2) unitary identity, and (3) specialization trap. Each patterned inequity compromises the learning opportunities and life chances of dually identified students in distinct ways by promoting a deficit and bias-prone lens (language-or-disability filter), erasing students' fuller identities (unitary identity), and responding to students' needs in silos (specialization trap). In exploring these patterned inequities, several shared characteristics emerge (see Table 2.2).

First, these patterned inequities are predictable, replicating in familiar, foreseeable ways throughout education of MLs with disabilities, akin to a song on repeat. In this sense, they constitute a larger pattern. Second, even when education stakeholders encounter what seems to be a novel problem of practice in their work, if we dig below the surface, we will find one if not more patterned inequities. Take, for instance, disproportionality in special education: While it may appear to be a distinct problem of practice, if we look carefully, we will find that the same inequities resurface later in other moments in the education of MLs with disabilities. Third, patterned inequities can often co-occur, with one leading to another to another, only to circle back again. If we spot a patterned inequity, chances are there is another patterned inequity close by, extending from and reinforcing the other in what becomes a complex web. Much like when a shoot of a plant touches the soil and produces new roots, it is often difficult to decipher where one patterned inequity begins and another ends. Fourth, patterned inequities are not problems that certain types of institutions (e.g., hypersegregated schools) or certain types of people (e.g., undertrained teachers) encounter; rather, patterned inequities are pervasive, occurring across all education sites—schools, districts, state agencies, and teacher education institutions.

Table 2.2. Characteristics of Patterned Inequities

Patterned inequities for MLs with disabilities are . . .
Repeated: *replicate in similar predictable forms*
Endemic: *underlie most problems of practice*
Co-occur: *co-occur with and reinforce one another*
Pervasive: *emerge across all education sectors*
Shared: *are experienced by all education stakeholders*

Finally, patterned inequities are a shared experience, faced by education stakeholders of every type from novice teachers to seasoned building principals to policymakers. In short, patterned inequities are endemic to our work in supporting the learning and rights of MLs with disabilities.

As I argued in this chapter, patterned inequities can be detected first in special education evaluation, and then they reemerge time after time. There is a body of evidence that points to these patterns and their prevalence. In examining this evidence, however, some patterned inequities are more prominent than others in the topics explored. Because of this, readers will notice some patterned inequities surfacing in certain chapters but not in others. Collectively, the subsequent chapters of the book will bring the evidence of patterned inequities to bear in an effort to make inequities more readily apparent to, and more importantly, repairable by education stakeholders in systems, in classrooms, and in policies.

Part II

EQUITY IN SYSTEMS

CHAPTER 3

Organization of Services and Students

Systems in schools are the bedrock of equity because their influence is expansive. Systems shape pedagogical practices and, importantly, the everyday experiences students have in their schools. I encountered this almost immediately upon starting my dissertation study. Originally, I was eager to examine the instructional supports provided to MLs with disabilities. As I began to observe the ESL teachers, I found that broader service provision systems in the schools ruled out particular language supports they could implement from the very start, delimiting the learning opportunities of MLs with disabilities. There is a body of research that points to the influence of systems (e.g., academic tracks, language programming, special education inclusion models, etc.) within schools on (in)equitable learning opportunities afforded to MLs and students with disabilities alike in their classrooms (e.g., Callahan, 2005; Gándara et al., 2003; Gándara & Orfield, 2012; Kanno & Kangas, 2014; Lipsky, 2010; Stelitano et al., 2020).

Despite the centrality of systems to equity, I have found as a teacher educator that talk of the structures or systems of schools often gives way to feelings of fatalism. However, teachers and educational leaders are powerful agents of equity, able to exert influence on the conditions and structures of schools to improve the experiences and opportunities of minoritized students (for ML examples, see Athanases & de Oliveira, 2008; Cruze & López, 2020; Cruze et al., 2020; Scanlan & López, 2015). This duality is known as *structuration theory* (Giddens, 1979), the notion that institutional structures and individual agency are interdependent. In simpler terms, systems may mold our actions, but our actions can likewise mold systems. The upcoming three chapters lean heavily on this premise, addressing four systems that set the stage for the learning opportunities of MLs with disabilities: the organization of services, students, individualized plans, and teacher training. Although these systems have the markers of patterned inequities, they are within the influence of teachers, educational leaders, and policymakers, capable of being molded and improved to promote equity. Sullivan et al. (2015) offer us some heartening words to that effect:

> Although individual educators or leadership teams cannot change societal forces . . . they can ensure that detrimental organizational and institutional dynamics are not perpetuated within schools by altering the system to promote socially just policies and practice for fair resource allocation and educational decisions. (p. 5)

With the understanding that systems in schools, and in education more broadly, can be shaped by education stakeholders to promote equity, I now turn to the central focus of this chapter—the organization of services and students.

THE ORGANIZATION OF SERVICES AND STUDENTS: KEY RESEARCH FINDINGS

Perhaps no system is more influential to the learning and life opportunities of MLs with disabilities than service provision. How services are organized for dually identified students has significant implications for their academic development and the sustainment of their multilingualism. As the name of this chapter suggests, the manner in which services are organized for MLs with disabilities is inseparable from the manner in which these students are physically organized or located in their schools. Despite the relevance of service delivery to students' learning trajectories, research has just begun to examine the ways schools organize and provide services to MLs with disabilities. Much of this research, however, has focused on MLs with high incidence disabilities (i.e., SLDs, SLIs, Attention Deficit/Hyperactivity Disorder [ADHD]), while service delivery for MLs with lower incidence disabilities (i.e., emotional and behavioral disorders, visual impairment, hearing impairment) remains sorely underresearched. This emerging research has examined service provision across elementary and secondary schools and program models for both language and disability. Across these contexts, two pressing concerns emerge: first, whether MLs with disabilities have access to dual services (i.e., both language services and disability-related services[1]) and second, whether these students also experience inclusion in its fullest sense.

Access to Dual Services

When I first started researching MLs with disabilities, teachers would often retort, "special ed trumps ESL" or "disability takes precedence" as if it were a matter of fact—and as if it were a widespread mantra in their schools. However, a few years later, the U.S. Departments of Justice and Education (2015) would go on to identify the elimination of one set of services or another as a common civil rights violation for MLs with disabilities: "School districts must provide EL students with disabilities with both the language assistance and disability-related services to which they are entitled under Federal law" (p. 24). The departments further clarified that "a formal or informal policy of 'no dual services'" is prohibited. As I will explore in this chapter, I have found, however, that the practice persists in more subtle ways, especially when MLs have complex support needs (often referred to as *MLs with significant cognitive disabilities*).

If there is a clear message that providing dual services is nonnegotiable, why then is access to dual services compromised? On the surface, logistical challenges are evident (Kangas, 2014, 2017b, 2018a; Phuong et al., 2021). Perhaps the greatest logistical hurdle is time; there are only so many hours in a school day, and education leaders need to balance access to dual services with access to the general education curriculum. In Chapter 2, I shared about Ahmed, an ML with autism, whose day-to-day was a complex puzzle, fitting together the multiple services he needed. In the end, his ESL services got short shrift. In more inclusive models, another challenge involves the logistics of providing multiple services and supports through coteaching (Kangas, 2017a; Phuong et al., 2021). Although teachers are charged with coteaching in inclusive settings, special education teachers and language specialists[2] have limited experience collaborating, which can hamper their attempts to support both language and disability. Logistical challenges aside, education leaders' misconceptions—about disability, multilingualism, education laws, and dual services themselves—influence MLs with disabilities' access to dual services (see Cioè-Peña, 2021; Kangas, 2014, 2018a; Stutzman & Lowenhaupt, 2022). For example, education leaders may believe ESL and special education services are duplicative, serving similar needs and accomplishing the same end goals, rendering one service superfluous.

Experiences of Meaningful Inclusion

Existing research on inclusion for MLs with disabilities is scarce and often examines inclusion in tandem with service provision. Nevertheless, the existing evidence calls into question whether dually identified students experience inclusion in its fullest sense. A recent analysis of national data by Cooc (2023) found that MLs with disabilities less frequently participate in general education settings (62%) compared to their non-ML peers with disabilities (66%), indicating that their placements are more restrictive. While place-based understandings of inclusion (i.e., that it amounts to placement in general education settings) have historically dominated education, more contemporary conceptualizations of inclusion that are broader in nature have taken hold in research and practice. For instance, the concept of *meaningful inclusion*, understood as students' access to quality instruction, support, and interventions needed for their learning, is gaining traction (see Artiles & Kozleski, 2016; Crockett & Kauffman, 2013; Jackson et al., 2018; Stelitano et al., 2020). As researchers Stelitano and colleagues (2020) summarized, meaningful inclusion "prioritizes the quality of students' educational opportunities above placement-based definitions of inclusion" (p. 3).

With this understanding of inclusion, preliminary empirical studies suggest that even though dually identified students are placed in inclusionary settings, their meaningful inclusion is appreciably limited, as they are the recipients of (a) low teacher expectations, (b) content instruction that is far below their grade level, and (c) limited access to bilingual and English language development support (Cioè-Peña, 2017, 2021; Kangas, 2018a; Kangas & Cook, 2020). Cioè-Peña (2017) characterized this overarching phenomenon in the following manner:

> Given that the primary focus of inclusion is on the integration of students with disabilities, children who represent intersectional identities are often passed over and continually left on the margins of inclusive classrooms, schools and society. (p. 913)

The first time I encountered questions of meaningful inclusion for dually identified students occurred at a bilingual school. When identifying potential student participants for a study, I thought it curious that the elementary MLs with disabilities were all rostered with other students with disabilities into just one or two classrooms per grade. Later, I would learn these classrooms were referred to by some in the school as the "SPELL" rooms (i.e., special education + English language learner [ELL]) and were instituted so that the collective needs of the students could be better met. Comparative observations, however, allowed me to investigate the disparate learning opportunities in these "SPELL" rooms in contrast to other classrooms in the school and further revealed that the MLs were largely segregated from students who were "label-free."

This and other studies highlight a significant nexus in education—that meaningful inclusion is closely tied to service provision structures and, concomitantly, to larger issues of student segregation and integration. While organizing students based on their needs and abilities can be considered an equitable practice, as it meets students "where they are," such practices can have unintended negative consequences for certain students, ironically limiting—as opposed to expanding—learning opportunities and access to their educational rights (see Brosnan, 1983; Gamoran, 2009; Muller et al., 2010; Oakes, 2005). As the above example of the "SPELL" rooms illuminates, the physical organization of MLs with disabilities in their school buildings reflects this tension. On one hand, MLs with disabilities are placed into certain settings—whether ESL courses, special education resource rooms, or others—for the purpose of meeting their linguistic, academic, and behavioral needs and abilities. On the other hand, such placements are often accompanied by diminished meaningful inclusion as social stigma increases and access to grade-level academic content, higher academic tracks, and peers without disabilities decreases (see Cioè-Peña, 2021; Kangas, 2018a; Kangas & Cook, 2020). This tradeoff experienced by MLs with disabilities is one shared by the larger ML and student with disability populations (see Dabach, 2014; Kanno, 2021; Shifrer, 2013; Thompson, 2015; Umansky, 2016) and is reflected in what is called the "package deal" of labeling (see labeling theory; Link & Phelan, 2010, p. 575), a theory proffering that while labeling is necessary for securing services for individuals—in this case, students—it can usher in a range of negative effects.

Education policy experts Garver and Hopkins (2020) have argued that integration and segregation continue to be a primary problem of practice for district and school leaders organizing services but have cautioned against narratives that paint integration and segregation, respectively, as wholly positive or negative. In light of the package deal of labeling, MLs with disabilities can have much to gain and lose simultaneously from being labeled and receiving services. In what follows, I will reframe these complexities of organization of services and students through the contours of patterned inequities.

EVIDENCE OF PATTERNS

Language-or-Disability Filter

The language-or-disability filter crops up in a distinct way in the organization of services. In most instances, this filter is used to make sense of an existing problem, isolating language or disability as its root cause; however, in the case of services, we see a curious use of this deficit-oriented filter: Language or disability is an anticipated source of *future* difficulties even before a problem surfaces, and services are organized accordingly. Put in other words, from the very start, services are organized with the core assumption that language or disability is a limiting force and a source of struggle. This deficit frame is arguably most readily apparent in the case of MLs with disabilities' access to bilingual education programs, with educators and parents of these students adhering to what is called the *limited capacity theory of bilingualism* (Paradis et al., 2021), a belief that bilingualism and multilingualism overextend the cognitive capabilities of children, especially when they have disabilities. Believing that disability is an inhibiting force—a deficiency—in bi- and multilingual development, educators may organize services in ways that relinquish language services and dissuade parents from enrolling their children with disabilities in bilingual programming or schools. In this way, the limited capacity theory of bilingualism embodies two of the patterned inequities—a deficit lens and identity erasure. Social science research, however, serves as a compelling counterbalance to this misconception, as bilingual expert Genesee (2015) explains: "Practically speaking, there is no empirical evidence at present to justify restricting children with developmental disorders from learning two languages" (p. 12). Indeed, research studies examining the effects of bilingual exposure on children with disabilities have found that across disability categories—including SLIs, SLDs, autism, and Down syndrome—children with disabilities who were exposed to two languages achieved similar, if not higher, language and academic outcomes as children with disabilities who were exposed to just one language (see Gonzalez-Barrero & Nadig, 2018; Kay-Raining Bird et al., 2005; Simon-Cereijido & Gutiérrez-Clellen, 2013; Thomas & Collier, 2012). Beyond academics, promoting MLs' multilingualism is critical for fostering students' connection with their families and larger communities and enhancing their well-being and socioemotional development (see Cobb-Clarke et al., 2021; Han & Huang, 2010; Tannenbaum & Berkovich, 2005).

Although there is no evidence suggesting that cognitive disabilities are limiting forces in bi- and multilingualism, qualitative research has illuminated how bilingual services are nonetheless eliminated or significantly reduced to "protect" MLs with disabilities from the struggle they would invariably encounter as they receive services that allegedly magnify their cognitive burdens (e.g., Cioè-Peña, 2021; Kangas, 2017b). For instance, Cioè-Peña's (2021) study of Latina mothers of MLs with disabilities showed that educators actively discouraged the mothers from enrolling their children with disabilities in bilingual programs, anticipating the students' disability would be a source of strain on their bilingualism. As a result, Cioè-Peña argues, these students lose across multiple spheres of their lives, as their ability "to maintain healthy, supportive and loving relationships with their mothers and transnational siblings" (p. 160) suffers without access to bilingual programming.

Even when MLs with disabilities are enrolled in bilingual programs, their access to bilingual instruction can be compromised because of deficit views of their disability. Returning to the example of the "SPELL" rooms, in that study educators conveyed concerns that bilingual instruction was challenging to MLs with disabilities, and thus, in those self-contained classrooms, instruction in English supplanted the 50/50 bilingual instructional model, further underlining the intertwining of deficit orientations, services, and physical placements. In a telling moment during an interview, one teacher in that study wondered whether bilingualism for students with disabilities was too lofty a goal: "I don't know, the expectations that we have [for bilingualism] are unreasonable and they just need to be adjusted" (Kangas, 2017b, pp. 21–22). In these examples, disability is understood as the root cause of learning problems and is anticipated as a liability to both academic and bi-/multilingual development. In short, access to bilingual education services is curbed from the onset for MLs with disabilities.

Apart from access to bilingual education, in English-only school settings, the anticipated source of *future* difficulties—either language or disability—can also structure both services and placements. Perhaps the most striking example of the filter at work arose in an ethnographic study of two middle schools, in which I investigated the experiences of MLs with disabilities who had reached so-called "long-term English learner" (LTEL) status, examining their access to dual services and high-quality academic instruction (see Kangas, 2020; Kangas & Cook, 2020, 2023). Very early on in the study, I asked an ESL teacher during an interview what I should pay attention to as I began observing the students, and she gave a resounding response: "The tracks." Her reflection, as it turned out, was spot on; all the MLs with disabilities in the study were placed in the lowest academic tracks, where academic learning was remedial, behavior management persistently sidelined instruction, and students were segregated from other peers without labels. MLs with disabilities remained in these tracks even if they performed well in their classes, made the honor roll and high honor roll, and had an abundance of motivation for their learning. Camila was one such student. She was identified as an ML with SLDs in reading, mathematics, and written expression and was considered by her teachers to be high-achieving, lauded for her desire to learn, her ability to write with rich descriptive detail, and her frequent earning of honor roll. Her ESL teacher intimated that she was undermatched in the lowest track: "She does not belong in that group at all" (Kangas & Cook, 2020, p. 2438). However, in the study, his perspective was in the minority among the teachers who weighed in on students' placements. Camila, too, felt that she should progress to the next level track, believing that would be the right fit. She explained: "Because I don't like to be too challenged, but I don't want it to be too easy" (p. 2438). Despite possessing many of the markers of academic achievement, as it is traditionally understood, Camila and other similarly achieving MLs with disabilities in the study remained effectively stuck in the lowest-track courses because of the language-or-disability filter.

For students like Camila, their placements were ultimately informed by deficit framing of their perceived limited capabilities stemming from their language or, in most instances, their disabilities. The lowest tracks were the locations in which special education support was embedded through the coteaching from special education teachers, and it was the presence of this support that was used as a rationale to keep MLs with disabilities in the lowest track—even when they were otherwise high-achieving, like Camila. For instance, when inquiring with staff about the possibility of MLs with disabilities progressing into the next level track, most reported that these students should remain "right where they are" because they needed the support. Through the framing of the language-or-disability filter, disability was identified as a source of academic underperformance and, thus, in need of remediation in the lowest tracks where special educators provided support. This deficit lens was elucidated by the words of one special educator when asked whether the MLs with disabilities who earned straight As would be eligible for another placement: "Those grades you have to remember are based on accommodations, modifications. . . . We can make anyone successful. They're successful because of their IEPs and the modifications, accommodations that we've included" (Kangas & Cook, 2020, p. 2438). Her perspectives amplify how disability was deemed an internal source of academic struggle, and, on the other hand, how MLs with disabilities' successes were externalized, attributed only to the support they receive.

As these studies highlight, service provision decisions and placements were seen by teachers and education leaders as protective mechanisms, preventing MLs with disabilities from being overtaxed in certain programs (e.g., bilingual programs) or settings (e.g., higher academic tracks) because of the impacts of their disabilities. This organization of services and students is evidence of the deficit-oriented language-or-disability filter, with perceived deficits in either disability or language compromising access to services and, more broadly, to experiences of meaningful inclusion. The deficit lenses applied to MLs with disabilities are quickly followed by service provision decisions that resemble the remaining patterned inequities.

Unitary Identity

At the beginning of this chapter, I outlined the overarching research findings in service provision for dually identified students, describing one key finding nationwide: Dual services are often jeopardized for this population of students with the total relinquishment of one set of services. Compromises to dual service provision, however, continue to occur in less overt ways, often venturing into "gray areas." In such instances, schools provide dual services but do so sparingly, inconsistently, and often by teachers who lack official certifications.

Across my research, I have encountered the following murky occurrences in which dual services were technically provided but in ways that hardly rose to the level of viable support:

1. Language supports are provided by general education teachers who lack formal certification and training in ESL/bilingual education.
2. Language services are offered in limited amounts.
3. ESL teachers are relegated to the role of teachers' aides during push-in models.
4. One service is routinely canceled because it is "double-booked" with another.
5. Special education support is only provided *in English* in bilingual schools.
6. Special education or related services (e.g., speech-language) are substituted for language services.
7. Reading interventions are deemed to cover both language learning and disability-related needs.

Taken together, these practices illuminate the dubious way dual services are available to MLs with disabilities. From a compliance standpoint, these occurrences constitute cases of following the letter but not the spirit of special education and ML laws—a checking of the dual service box, so to speak, but without attention to quality of services. From the viewpoint of patterned inequities, these practices—along with the outright elimination of one service or another—are a form of erasure, annulling part of MLs with disabilities' identities, thereby rendering them as students who only have disabilities or only have language learning needs.

Indeed, the "nudging out" of certain services, I argue, is increasingly common as schools and districts wrestle with the guidance provided in the U.S. Departments of Justice and Education's *Dear Colleague* Letter (2015). Other studies point us to this alarming trend as well. For example, in their interview study of school leaders and teachers, Stutzman and Lowenhaupt (2022) found "a district-wide culture of advocating for and prioritising special education over the needs of ELs" (p. 1062). But as the authors argued, this exacerbated inequities for MLs with disabilities, as unitary identity takes hold: "This can lead to a pattern of increased funding for special education, exiting ELs only to transition them to special education, and special educators having an increased workload of ELs that they are not adequately prepared to teach" (p. 1062). In a separate qualitative study, Park (2019) found that English language support was implemented in a limited manner for 16 MLs with suspected disabilities, falling short of providing these students the quality linguistic support they needed within Tier 1 of MTSS. These studies reflect a historical trend that was first documented in the early 2000s when Zehler and colleagues (2003) conducted a national survey of hundreds of U.S. K–12 schools. The survey findings were the first to indicate that more than half (56.2%) of schools provided language services in limited "dosages"—less than 10 hours each week—or not at all (16%) to dually identified students. Some dually identified students, however, may have more or less access to language services, depending on their disability, as services are not organized uniformly for all MLs with disabilities. As a telling example of this, in a collaboration with a district, I recall examining the school records of MLs with disabilities, noticing that in contrast to MLs with SLIs and SLDs, MLs with intellectual disabilities received an additional period of special education support, leaving no room for pull-out ESL classes.

At the same time, it is not only that language services are deemed less critical than special education to MLs with disabilities; sometimes it is the reverse, and providing special education services is believed to be less urgent when stacked up against MLs' pressing language learning needs. During professional learning workshops, special educators have shared their frustrations with me when services for newcomer MLs with disabilities, those who have recently arrived in the United States, are organized in a manner that prioritizes ELP. In these cases, language learning was positioned above all else, temporarily delaying instructional support for their disabilities until their English proficiency increases. These studies collectively underscore the varied ways in which service delivery implicitly positions MLs with disabilities as if they have a unitary identity, instead of as students who have both language learning and disability needs.

In many respects, unitary identity stems from the deficit lens of the language-or-disability filter. As educators weigh which one—language or disability—creates the greater deficit for MLs with disabilities, their service provision decisions and students' physical placements follow suit. Such norms that prioritize one service over another in turn influence the educators' perception of which need, language or disability, poses the greatest challenge to the student and thus requires more attention. Take, for instance, occurrences when the linguistic needs of newcomer MLs with disabilities are believed to be more acute, resulting in deficits to their academic learning. Based on the perceived severity of these linguistic needs, MLs' special education and related services may be "put on hold" while educators provide intensive language support and attempt to sort out language learning from disability to avoid a faulty special education evaluation. This practice of temporarily delaying special education and related services, however, becomes normalized and routine in districts and schools, prompting educators to reason that newcomers' sources of difficulties are primarily linguistic.

Darell, a 3rd-grade ML from one of my studies, is another poignant example. Darell was suspected to have an SLD due to his recent academic difficulties, and in response he was placed in one of the "SPELL" rooms. Because Darell's academic performance was believed to be the result of his disability—though he had not gone through a formal evaluation—his services oriented around disability in ways that ultimately positioned him as a student with an SLD. In the end, some of his teachers were confused by his placement and believed his evaluation had taken place. In Darell's case, patterned inequities go hand in hand, each offering reinforcement to the other (see Figure 3.1).

Specialization Trap

In characterizing the organization of services and, at times, placements of MLs with disabilities, the word *silos* is commonly uttered by education stakeholders. The fact that silos have become a defining feature of—or more accurately, barrier to—service provision is unsurprising. Special education and ML education have distinct historical roots, norms and values, and responses to students' needs. Each also requires specialized training, and with this specialization comes the common sentiment that one is only qualified to support the needs that fall within one's own professional expertise. On a larger scale, schools as institutions, too, can fall into the specialization trap.

Figure 3.1. Patterned Inequities in the Organization of Services and Students

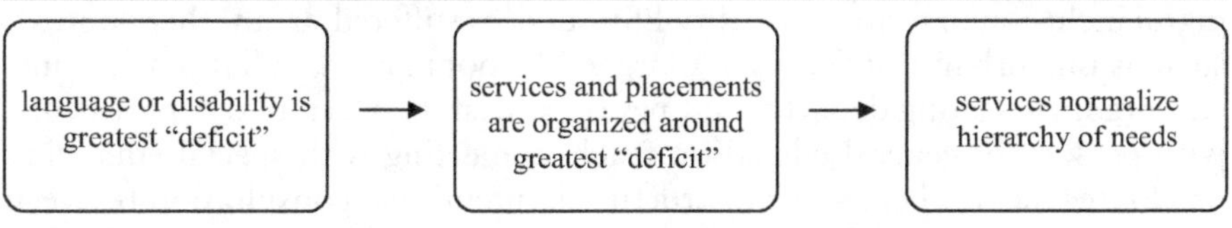

In a bilingual school with a mission to cultivate bilingualism and biliteracy, I recall an administrator shared in an interview how she felt they had to turn away MLs with autism, believing they were ill-equipped to support these students' multiple needs.

For schools that serve MLs with disabilities, the specialization trap becomes tangible in the schedules and locations of students and teachers, resulting in inequities in the quality of services. In terms of students' schedules, MLs with disabilities may receive multiple services a day, at times leaving little to no room for enriching electives. Some MLs with disabilities' daily schedules are exceedingly complex as they are shuffled from one service to the next. As I depicted in Chapter 2, services for Ahmed were the most striking example of the specialization trap. As Ahmed had autism and language learning needs, there were four specialists (ESL, speech-language therapist, occupational therapist, autism support paraprofessional) who each supported a subset of his needs, but they were unable to come together to support him overall. For instance, while supporting him in a small group setting, Mrs. Motts, his autism support specialist, focused solely on his disability, as she reported in an interview: "The reason we're being pushed into these classrooms is to take things slower . . . however, we're not in here for ESL. That's what Mrs. Franks [ESL teacher] is there for" (Kangas, 2014, p. 295).

In terms of teachers' schedules, whether and with whom they have planned collaborative time is indicative of how far they have fallen into the specialization trap, as a lack of shared planning time will result in independent, siloed efforts. After all, how can educators begin to work in concert when the structures of school close off such opportunities from the onset? In rural and suburban settings, for instance, ESL teachers may be itinerant, supporting MLs across the district and thus spending a good portion of their day driving from one school to the next. This was the case of Mrs. Franks, an ESL teacher in my study who taught across multiple elementary schools, leaving her scarce opportunity to even consult—let alone to coplan—with her multiple general and special education colleagues (see Kangas, 2014). Her antidote to this disadvantageous situation was to work independently, "pitching in" language support when and how she could in the inclusive general education classroom (Kangas, 2014, p. 296) but in ways that notably did not yield quality services. In this setting, although MLs with disabilities were integrated with other students in the general education setting, their meaningful inclusion in terms of quality ESL services suffered. In another context, such as one urban district with a larger ML population, collaborative time was organized along department lines or, at best, between two departments, with pockets of general education teachers meeting with special education or ESL teachers. There was no structured, intentional consultation between special education and ESL teachers—only opportunities for quick chats in the hall or for emails. Consequently, these specialists worked in insolation from one another, taking a piecemeal approach to meeting MLs with disabilities' needs that loses track of the whole child.

At times, siloed efforts can be the genesis of bureaucratic errors in both the services for and placements of dually identified students, as teachers work in isolation and data management systems do not interface. Imani and Mateo are two MLs with SLDs whose learning opportunities were shaped by bureaucratic errors. Mateo was erroneously enrolled in a general education English language arts class instead of an ESL class for MLs, whereas Imani had the inverse experience: Although she was formally exited from ESL, she was nonetheless still rostered for the class. Their special education case managers were unaware of these errors, as exiting records remained under the purview of the ESL department.

As previously noted, the specialization trap is often enmeshed with unitary identity. With each specialist responding to just a subset of needs, their instructional responses position MLs with disabilities in this way or that. Returning to the example of Darell, who received special education support despite having no formal diagnosis, his services were organized around what was perceived to be his greatest deficit—his alleged disability. For this reason, he was placed in a special education classroom, where he received instructional supports for his academic, not linguistic, needs. In the end, his suspected disability was reasoned to be more critical than his actual language learning needs. From this, we can see how the patterned inequities have a buoying effect on each other in the organization of his services and physical placement (Figure 3.2). Yet both patterned inequities compromise equity for MLs with disabilities by eliminating access to dual services on one hand or by providing fragmented, disjointed dual services on the other.

Figure 3.2. Patterned Inequities in the Organization of Services and Students

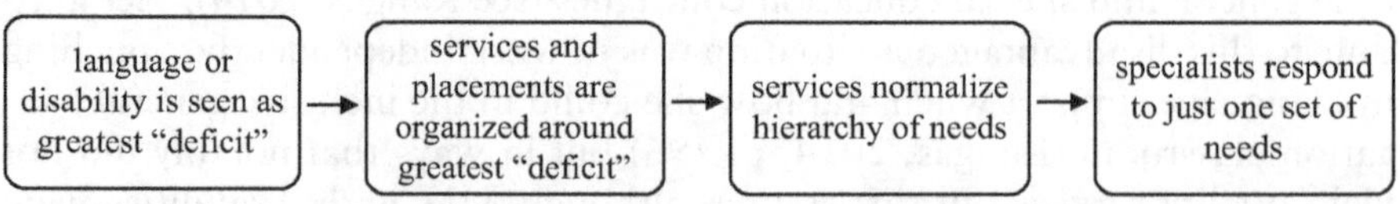

RESPONSES TO PATTERNED INEQUITIES IN THE ORGANIZING OF SERVICES AND STUDENTS

At present, the organization of services and of students is laden with inequities that affect pedagogical practices and thus the learning opportunities afforded to MLs with disabilities. Because of the expansive influence of service provision in affording—or not—students' meaningful inclusion, education leaders and teachers alike can promote equity for dually identified students by attending to the patterned inequities underlying current service delivery practices. In the remainder of the chapter, I offer concrete approaches district and school leaders as well as teachers can begin to implement to elevate equity for MLs with disabilities in their schools.

Response 1: Conduct Equity Audits

The physical placements of MLs with disabilities and their services are problems of practice that are ripe for an equity audit. In the context of schooling, an *equity audit* is "a systematic way for school leaders—principals, superintendents, curriculum directors, teacher leaders—to assess the degree of equity or inequity present in three key areas of their schools or districts: programs, teacher quality, and student outcomes" (Skrla et al., 2009, p. 3). Implementing an equity audit relating to services will enable district and school leaders to understand to what extent MLs with disabilities have access to dual services, whether these services are high in quality, and how subgroups of MLs with disabilities may have differential access (e.g., MLs with autism, newcomer MLs with disabilities, secondary MLs with disabilities, etc.). Equity audits can also be utilized to examine the placements of MLs with disabilities. In secondary schools, such equity audits could examine the extent to which MLs with disabilities are clustered within or dispersed across academic tracks. In all grade bands, equity audits can be useful for investigating whether dually identified students are rostered into de facto self-contained classrooms. Because the organization of services and students often leaves a paper trail, showing up in students' schedules and rosters, education leaders can begin their equity audits through an examination of school records, comparing MLs with disabilities' services and placements to those of their ML and student with disabilities peers. These records can be further examined by subgroups to determine whether access is equitable among MLs with disabilities as a whole. Teachers can play a vital role in equity audits, providing valuable student data (e.g., class projects, running records, portfolios, etc.) that give a more comprehensive and nuanced portrait of the current performance of MLs with disabilities. District administrators should also not shy away from surveying teachers—those who spend the most time with MLs with disabilities—regarding their perceptions of these students' learning opportunities and placements.

District and school leaders should also consider integrating classroom observations into their equity audits to evaluate the quality of the services and instruction. Observations can certainly be time consuming for education leaders. For this reason, education leaders may wish to collaborate with researchers from universities or nonprofit education organizations to conduct equity audits that incorporate multiple data sources, especially qualitative data that tend to get neglected in equity audits and program evaluations. For education leaders interested in conducting equity audits, I have provided a list of recommended resources at the conclusion of this chapter.

Response 2: Actively Debunk Long-Standing Myths

This chapter brought to the surface several myths about students' capabilities, the nature of language and disability, and dual services themselves. Apart from conducting equity audits, I argue that myth debunking is a primary job for education leaders and teachers wishing to promote equity for MLs with disabilities, often going hand-in-hand with other strategies that prompt equitable change. Below are two influential myths that circulate through schools and even local communities, and thus, may be a wise focus of education leaders' and teachers' efforts.

One myth that remains influential among educators and parents is the limited capacity theory of bilingualism. Introduced earlier in this chapter, this deficit-oriented myth remains pervasive, hindering children with disabilities from accessing bilingual programs, despite compelling research evidence that points to the benefits of bilingual learning for this population. With that evidence in mind, education leaders and teachers may wish to challenge in their schools the notion that bi- and multilingualism is out of reach for certain MLs with disabilities. When encountering parents who believe that exposure to multiple languages is harmful for their children, teachers should similarly advocate for bilingual instruction for MLs with disabilities by sharing evidence of the benefits of bilingualism for all children and allaying parents' concerns. Parents may appreciate teachers connecting them with other parents whose children with disabilities were enrolled and successful in bilingual programming. Such deficit framings are found across school contexts and communities, and thus are germane to the equity work of most educator stakeholders.

A second myth worthy of debunking is that certain services take precedence over others (see de Valenzuela et al., 2022; Kangas, 2014, 2018a). A recent guidance handbook from the New Mexico Public Education Department (2023) featured an authentic case study of two district leaders from Farmington Municipal Schools working to dismantle the barriers that existed between ML and special education departments. In the case study, the ML and special education district leaders, along with a team of other administrators, worked to debunk the common "special education trumps

ESL" myth (see Kangas, 2014) through the use of a powerful counter-mantra—"nothing trumps anything" (p. 38). By reinforcing this message across their everyday work with MLs with disabilities and interactions with one another, the district team was able to establish an ethos that emphasized the importance of addressing students' intersecting needs for the benefit of their learning. In doing so, these district leaders actively worked to dismantle the patterned inequities of unitary identity and specialization trap that previously characterized their approach to supporting MLs with disabilities.

There are several avenues through which education leaders and teachers can work to challenge these myths. First, in the case study above district leaders worked *collectively* to dismantle a myth that they felt detracted from the quality of dually identified students' education; in contrast, efforts to address myths *individually* within the confines of certain departments will not yield broader equity changes but may instead exacerbate already existing turf wars. Teachers, too, can work to challenge "special education trumps ESL" among their peers by sharing the *Dear Colleague Letter* and research studies cited in this chapter, which discuss in clear terms that no one service should eclipse another. While the *Dear Colleague Letter* is publicly available, teachers can and should request publications from researchers and academic authors, who are usually excited to share their research with those who have the greatest impact in the schooling of MLs with disabilities. Directly requesting publications that are typically behind paywalls is a useful strategy for sharing myth-busting research with colleagues.

Second, district leaders should offer joint professional learning opportunities that directly address these common myths, gathering language specialists, special educators, and even related service professionals together to learn of the empirical evidence, case studies, and federal guidance that counter misconceptions about MLs with disabilities. Professional learning opportunities in districts could also feature *refutation texts*, documents that present evidence against a common misconception with the aim to debunk it. There is promising emerging evidence on the effectiveness of refutation texts in shifting teachers' beliefs (Ferrero et al., 2020; Gill et al., 2022; Peltier et al., 2020). District and school leaders may wish to use refutation texts to anchor professional learning opportunities, providing opportunities for their teachers to encounter compelling counterevidence to misconceptions that may have guided their practice with students and collaborations with colleagues. For designing and using refutation texts, I encourage education leaders to consult the resources at the end of the chapter.

Response 3: Compose Service Schedules for MLs With Disabilities First

Patterned inequities in service provision reify in MLs with disabilities' day-to-day schedule. In interviews with teachers, schedules are routinely cited as a predominant barrier to dual service provision. Because MLs with disabilities can have some of the most complex schedules, requiring multiple services to be squeezed into the 7-to-8-hour school day, I recommend education leaders begin assembling their master schedules with MLs with disabilities as the starting point. By prioritizing dually identified students during the scheduling of services, district leaders can side-step common logistical constraints whereby services are nudged out, "double-booked" or absent altogether. As a failsafe, ML and special education leaders should also consider instituting a review of automatic master scheduling for MLs with disabilities, making manual adjustments to the students' schedules when their access to dual services has been compromised. Scheduling services for MLs with disabilities first is a practice that some districts have already put into place to improve access to dual services for students and is a worthy strategy for other education leaders to implement.

It is perhaps unsurprising that these recommendations require department district leaders to work outside of the bounds of professional silos, making collaborative master scheduling the norm. District ML and special education leaders should consider jointly examining schools' scheduling processes and procedures, looking for common issues that arise in both the daily schedules of MLs with disabilities and the teachers who commonly support them as well as instituting checks and balances that allow each department to review the ways in which services are concretely organized in the schedules of MLs with disabilities.

Response 4: Invest in Collaborative Structures

To break out of the professional silos that fragment services for MLs with disabilities, education leaders will need to implement structural changes that enhance collaboration among teachers and specialists and take an integrated approach to organizing services. As a starting point to this goal, district department leaders should consider the creation of a liaison position that bridges special and ML education. Although liaison positions in schools have typically been conceptualized as a staff member who builds connections between home and school, a special education–ML liaison would hold credentials in both specializations and would work closely with the directors of the respective departments to strengthen coordination, open pathways for two-way communication, and bring awareness to redundancies and conflicts in policies and initiatives. Districts with especially high numbers of MLs with disabilities would benefit from a full-time liaison position, while districts with lower numbers could create a position with split teaching and liaising responsibilities.

Instituting planned, intentional collaborative time between ML and special education is a structural change that education leaders will need to revisit when planning schedules of teachers. It is indeed perplexing that teachers and specialists teaching in inclusive models are expected to coteach without being provided the opportunity to plan and consult with one another (see Kangas, 2017a). While planning teachers' schedules, district leaders should examine whether ML and special education teachers are given shared, or common, planning time and then should work to reconfigure teacher schedules in ways that allow for more common planning among multidisciplinary teams of teachers. Phuong et al. (2021) asserted that inclusion for MLs with disabilities cannot be achieved without collaboration:

> In order for coteaching to be successful, it must be fully collaborative and all parties must be willing to consider scheduling needs, advocate for the students, as well as concede to other ideas. In order to do this, we need to stop having to fight for time and go from being separate unequal units of education to an integrated equal unit where all students have equal opportunities to learn while working together. (pp. 689–690)

In circumstances that make common planning time between ML and special education teachers untenable, district leaders should ensure that professional learning opportunities and in-service days foster opportunities for teachers from the departments to collaborate.

While education leaders make structural changes to promote common planning, teachers must be willing to embrace new collaborations. Phuong and colleagues' words above reflect this. In my work with ESL and special education teachers, I found they have an earnest desire to collaborate with one another, knowing that it will enhance student learning as well as their expertise, but they often do not know where to start. This is especially the case for teachers whose schools moved toward inclusion models without ample, robust training and support for coteaching. Apart from a collaborative mindset, there are defined practices, or competencies, of effective coteaching. While much has been written on coteaching practices—well beyond what can be addressed in this chapter—there are concrete actions that teachers can take to build relationships with their coteaching counterparts and to begin to work effectively together. As a starting point, ESL and special education coteachers may wish to: define their roles and responsibilities (e.g., coteaching contracts); set small, manageable goals together for improving their practices together (e.g., shared learning goals); brainstorm a list of data they can share with one another (e.g., formative assessments, ELP scores, running records); and begin reflecting on the adjustments they would like to make in their instruction for MLs with disabilities. Along with other resources, a list of recommended coteaching and coplanning tools can be found in the latter pages of the chapter.

Extending beyond coplanning and consultation, district leaders can also promote structural change in their districts through the implementation of professional learning communities (PLCs). Although a PLC can take various forms, it is commonly understood as "a group of people sharing and critically interrogating their practice in an ongoing, reflective, collaborative, inclusive, learning-oriented, growth-promoting way" (Stoll et al., 2006, p. 223). Scholarship has advocated the use of PLCs in schools to institute systemic changes, as groups of educators come together to tackle more complex initiatives and problems (see Harris & Jones, 2010; Hord, 1997; Servage, 2008; Stoll et al., 2006; Stoll & Luis, 2007). District department leaders can institute PLCs of ML and special education colleagues to reflect on and examine problems of practice that influence equity for MLs with disabilities. As these two departments come together, participating educators have the added benefit of expanding their own knowledge and skills. Take for instance, the teachers in Stutzman and Lowenhaupt's (2022) study who reported how collaboration across special education and ML education enabled them to expand their professional expertise, becoming more familiar with the other discipline's instructional practices:

> As teachers experienced more opportunities for collaboration, they were able to start to see the ways that they would benefit from the insights of another professional. This acted as a catalyst for understanding the ways that EL and special education instructional practices actually operate differently. (p. 1060)

For education leaders entertaining the possibility of PLCs dedicated to issues relating to MLs with disabilities, resources listed at the end of the chapter may be of interest.

Response 5: Move Toward Integrated Services

Systemic changes that bolster teachers' collaborations are certainly needed; however, district leaders should also consider piloting integrated services for MLs with disabilities. In schools with linguistically homogeneous ML populations, district leaders should consider offering special education support bilingually, which would allow MLs with disabilities to receive specially designed instruction for their disabilities through the linguistic support of their home language. Yet, as Cioè-Peña's (2021) study illuminated, at times, parents of MLs with disabilities may be dissuaded by educators from enrolling their children in such programs. These findings, along with the limited capacity theory of bilingualism, are a reminder for education leaders to ensure that bilingual programming and instruction are available to all MLs with disabilities, regardless of the perceived severity of their disabilities.

For district leaders with heterogeneous MLs populations, bilingual special education support may not be feasible; nevertheless, integrated models of services are still viable in these contexts. In such models, educators can implement specially designed instruction that infuses effective linguistic support for MLs' emerging English proficiency. This can be accomplished through cotaught classrooms with triads of teachers (i.e., general, ML, and special education teachers) or classrooms headed by teachers who are dually certified in ESL and special education. To move toward more integrated models, education leaders from ML and special education should begin by piloting integrated models in certain classrooms or grades and by engaging in program evaluations prior to scaling up the model in the school.

Response 6: Place Students Where They Can Thrive

A significant affordance of improving collaborative structures (Response 4) and moving toward integrated structures (Response 5) is that students' placements can be nimble—less entrenched and no longer tied to a single context. By enhancing teachers' capacities to support MLs with disabilities, education leaders can begin to detach special education or language services from specific places, especially as such locations can result in MLs with disabilities becoming "stuck" in certain academic tracks or classrooms where learning opportunities are poorer; instead, dually identified students can be placed in settings where they can thrive. In the case of academic tracking for MLs with disabilities, district leaders can revise current placement procedures to enable students like Camila to "try out" a higher track for a marking period, as opposed to ruling out their eligibility from the onset. During such trial periods, MLs with disabilities are given the opportunity to advance to or move back from higher academic tracks because of their abilities, and not due to structures that organize and cement services in lower tracks. Teachers are critical advocates for MLs with disabilities in advancing to higher tracks, whether temporarily or permanently, because their recommendation can tip the scale, so to speak, as their colleagues evaluate student data during placement decisions.

In the case of more segregated placements, while such settings are not definitively disadvantageous, as Garver and Hopkins (2020) indicate, in the case of MLs with disabilities these classrooms constitute "a dumping ground" (Sullivan et al., 2015, p. 143), where students with labels are clustered together. Reorganizing services and students to eliminate these classrooms is critical for the learning and life opportunities of MLs with disabilities. Efforts to restructure for meaningful inclusion take time, by some estimates 5 years (Horn & Carr, 2000), and thus require incremental steps (Horn & Carr, 2000; Sullivan et al., 2015). For this reason, education leaders should consider developing districtwide strategic plans that encompass equity audits, myth debunking, collaborative practices such as PLCs, and integrated services, among the other recommendations offered in this chapter, but, vitally, also address the unique needs and inequities felt by MLs with disabilities—a population that tends to get overlooked in equity initiatives. Through multiyear equity plans, districts and schools can work toward equitable structures that, as Sullivan et al. (2015) argue, are paramount for equity for students with disabilities: "This [systemic equity] entails restructuring schools to support the development of all learners so that special education does not become a means of *de facto* segregation or a dumping ground for students perceived as difficult to teach" (p. 143).

SUMMARY

This was the first of three chapters to explore equity in systems, concentrating on the organization of services and the physical placement of students as enmeshed systemic issues that influence the learning opportunities of MLs with disabilities. The chapter provided an overview of prior research on service provision and student placements and then filtered these findings through the three lenses of patterned inequities, demonstrating how anticipated sources of problems within students—that is, language or disability—guide both the services and placements they receive. Once in these services and settings, MLs with disabilities are treated as if they are language learners *or* students with disabilities, as teachers work in a highly compartmentalized manner. As a consequence of these three co-occurring patterns, the learning opportunities and education rights of MLs with disabilities are diminished. The chapter concluded with recommendations for education leaders, especially, as well as teachers to consider as remedies for the patterned inequities that may have challenged their districts' and schools' efforts to provide MLs with disabilities with access to multiple, high-quality services, while safeguarding their meaningful inclusion.

RECOMMENDED RESOURCES

On Coteaching

Beninghof, A. M. (2020). *Coteaching that works: Structures and strategies for maximizing student learning* (2nd ed.). Jossey-Bass.

Honigsfeld, A., & Dove, M. G. (2021). *Co-planning: 5 essential practices to integrate curriculum and instruction for English learners*. Corwin.

Murawski, W., & Lochner, W. W. (2017). *Beyond coteaching basics: A data-driven, no fail model for continuous improvement*. ASD.

On Equity Audits

Green, T. L. (2017). Community-based equity audits: A practical approach for educational leaders to support equitable community-school improvements. *Educational Administration Quarterly*, *53*(1), 3–39. https://doi.org/10.1177/0013161X16672513

McKenzie, K. B., & Skrla, L. E. (2011). *Using equity audits in the classroom to reach and teach all students*. Corwin.

Skrla, L. E., McKenzie, K. B., & Scheurich, J. J. (2009). *Using equity audits to create equitable and excellent schools.* Corwin.

On Professional Learning Communities

DuFour, R., Eaker, R., Many, T. W., & Mattos, M. (2016). *Learning by doing: A handbook for professional learning communities at work* (3rd ed.). Solution Tree Press.

Easton, L. B. (2009). *Protocols for professional learning.* ASCD.

Roberts, S. M., & Pruitt, E. Z. (2009). *Schools as professional learning communities: Collaborative activities and strategies for professional development* (2nd ed.). Corwin.

On Refutation Texts

Ferrero, M., Konstantinidis, E., & Vadillo, M. A. (2020). An attempt to correct erroneous ideas among teacher education students: The effectiveness of refutation texts. *Frontiers in Psychology, 11*(577738). https://doi.org/10.3389/fpsyg.2020.577738

Hale, J. (2021). *Refutation text and critical thinking.* Center for Inquiry. https://centerforinquiry.org/blog/refutation-text-and-critical-thinking/

CHAPTER 4

Individualized Plans and Teams

An astute reader will notice the title of the chapter refers to *individualized plans* and not *individualized education programs*. This wording is intentional. Although some education stakeholders may associate the term *individualized plans* with IEPs, in recent years other forms of individualized plans have arisen outside of special education in an attempt to provide K–12 students with a more tailored education. One such plan is the *Individualized Language Plan* (ILP), which has been gaining traction in ML education as a tool to promote the ELP of ML students (Kangas & Cioè-Peña, 2024). Another such plan is an *Individualized Reading Improvement Plan* (IRIP), often prompted by state-wide literacy laws that aim to increase the reading skills of students with "reading deficiencies" (see Michigan Department of Education, 2024; Nebraska Department of Education, 2019).

Regardless of their intended target student and skillset, individualized plans share many of the same structural components (e.g., current performance levels, measurable goals, etc.) and underlying aims (i.e., to support student learning on an individual basis). More significantly, however, individualized plans are *intended* to exert a systemic influence in schools, informing instruction, progress monitoring efforts, and service provision practices. IEPs, for instance, act as a lever for special education law (e.g., Education for All Handicapped Children Act, 1975; Individuals with Disabilities Education Act, 2004), aiming to offer a concrete, individualized program for student learning. ILPs, too, aspire to shape what happens in the classroom, allowing schools to move away from generic, one-size ML programming toward pedagogical practices that are tailored to the heterogeneous needs of MLs (Umansky & Avelar, 2023). With such extended reach, individualized plans, in their various forms, can be tools that move beyond matters of compliance to promote equity across multiple systems. This chapter holds on to this promise, but it also confronts how individualized plans have fallen short of their aims for MLs with disabilities, noting how these limitations link to larger patterned inequities. Believing that these existing shortcomings can be remediated and that individualized plans can realize their original intention—to promote systemic change—I conclude the chapter with recommendations and resources for educational leaders and teachers to refine not only the plans but also the practices among teams and in meetings.

THE ORGANIZATION OF INDIVIDUALIZED PLANS AND TEAMS: KEY RESEARCH FINDINGS

Compared to other individualized plans, IEPs for MLs have received more attention in education research and guidance, albeit this research remains in nascent stages. Even more underresearched are ILPs. Given these limitations, these two individualized plans are reviewed below, with more attention given to IEP documents, teams, and meetings.

IEP Documents, Teams, and Meetings

In examining IEPs for MLs with disabilities, a clear impression emerges from research: IEPs remain stubbornly and ironically resistant to individualization. Although "IDEA requires that the IEP team *consider*, among other special factors, the language needs of a child with limited English proficiency as those needs relate to the child's IEP" (U.S. Departments of Justice & Education, 2015, pp. 26–27, emphasis added), the degree to which teams "consider" language learning and the extent to which these considerations are represented in the IEP are contested in practice. Hoover et al. (2019) posited that this wide variation in how teams consider special factors in IEPs, such as language and cultural background, stems from IDEA's guidance that focuses on IEP components but not the process of IEP development. Nevertheless, they argued that the mandate to consider ELP in IEPs carries this salient implication: "that all relevant elements of an IEP must be sensitive to linguistic needs of ELs" (p. 15).

Scholars have generally advocated for a more robust representation of ELP and multilingual considerations throughout the entirety of the IEP—from Present Levels of Academic Achievement and Functional Performance (PLAAFP) to goals to specially designed instruction (Hoover et al., 2019; Hoover & Patton, 2017; Kangas, 2018b). More recently, researchers have also recommended more tailored transition planning for MLs with disabilities, specifically by better engaging with ML parents (Trainor et al., 2019; Wu et al., 2022). Taken together, this body of work rests on a critical understanding: that we cannot divorce language learning from disabilities in the context of MLs with disabilities' actual learning. Put more directly, when MLs have disabilities, their language learning is constantly present even as they are learning academic content, receiving specially designed instruction, and participating in interventions relating to their disability needs. There is no instance in which language learning disappears for MLs with disabilities just because they are receiving support for their disabilities. Yet when language learning considerations are left out of an IEP, the document—and the ML's educational program—communicates that language learning and disability do not intersect and have no influence upon one another.

Despite calls for more integrated IEPs, many of these documents fall short of incorporating ELP and multilingual considerations, so much so that it calls into question whether they are truly individualized. The lack of individualization of IEPs is not confined to just ML students, as research studies examining the content and implementation of IEPs have found these documents featuring standards-based goals (i.e., goals that regurgitate existing academic standards), generic accommodations, and underdeveloped or misaligned components (e.g., Bray & Russell, 2018; Hott et al., 2020, 2021; Landmark & Zhang, 2013; Ruble et al., 2010). As an example of these limitations, in reviewing the specially designed instruction for the MLs with disabilities in one of my studies, the most commonly listed instructional accommodations were "blanket" in nature (e.g., preferential seating, graphic organizers, access to support classrooms), applicable to almost any student, as shown in Table 4.1 below. Based on such trends, Bray and Russell (2018) attested that in their examination of IEP implementation "the IEPs were not functioning as designed or intended" and that ultimately "students were not receiving an individualized special education" (p. 262).

Putting these trends vis-à-vis IEP documents aside, IEP teams and meetings also appear to wrestle with the demands of being individualized to ML students (Cioè-Peña, 2020; Hoover et al., 2019; Hoover & Patton, 2017; Kangas, 2018a). For this reason, scholars have called for IEP teams to enhance their responsiveness to MLs and their families in and outside of IEP meetings by demystifying IEP processes and procedures; supplying IEPs in the home language well ahead of meetings; providing trained interpreters during meetings; and engaging MLs and their families as active participants in IEP development (Chang et al., 2022; Hart et al., 2012; Hoover & Patton, 2017; Jung, 2011; Rossetti et al., 2017; Zhang & Bennett, 2003).

In addition, the federal government has required language specialists to be members of MLs' IEP teams (U.S. Departments of Justice & Education,

Table 4.1. Generic Instructional Accommodations in IEPs

Access to support classroom	Access to the support classroom to take tests and quizzes and to provide student with assistance in organization, test preparation, and make-up assignments
Extended response time	Extended response time for student to process information before responding to a question or participating in a group discussion as deemed appropriate by staff and special education teacher
Graphic organizers	Graphic organizers or other organizational aids for reading and writing as deemed appropriate by staff and special education teacher
Preferential seat	Preferential seating within close proximity to instruction away from obvious visual and/or auditory distractions as deemed appropriate by staff and special education teacher
Opportunity to retake	Student will be provided opportunity to retake a failed assessment

2015), presumably to increase the likelihood that the documents, teams, and meetings will better support MLs and their families. Despite this requirement, language specialists' inclusion and engagement in teams continues to be a challenge in schools (U.S. Departments of Justice & Education, 2015). Altogether, these trends underscore the need—and the challenges—for IEPs and their related processes to respond to the individual student.

Individualized Language Plans

While research has explored IEPs for MLs with disabilities, studies are just beginning to examine ILPs, which are gaining popularity across U.S. districts and schools. While some states have required ILPs for decades, in recent years a total of 14 states have adopted the use of these documents (Kangas & Cioè-Peña, 2024), with scholarship amplifying the advantages of their implementation in ML education more broadly (Thompson & Rodriguez-Mojica, 2023; Umansky & Avelar, 2023). These documents replicate many of the components of IEPs but with a sustained focus on ELP. In some states, they are implemented for all MLs, but in others, they are required only for MLs who have a history of not making ELP gains (Kangas & Cioè-Peña, 2024), which often includes MLs with disabilities, as will be discussed in Chapter 9. One study has found that ILPs can be powerful tools for increasing collaboration and communication among educators (Thompson & Rodriguez-Mojica, 2023). In this sense, these documents expand the professional capacities of teachers. Yet just as these documents replicate the structure of IEPs, they show early signs of replicating their shortcomings as well. In our review of state-mandated or recommended ILP templates, Cioè-Peña and I discovered that many featured generic instructional accommodations or no instructional accommodations at all (Kangas & Cioè-Peña, 2024). Moreover, we discovered the documents seemed to reduce ELP goals to strictly meeting a cut score on the annual ELP assessment—a finding that also emerged from Thompson and Rodriguez-Mojica's (2023) investigation. Despite these initial inquiries, little is known about ILP development and implementation, leaving us with more questions than answers. For instance, how will ILPs be monitored, updated, and even enforced without federal backing? How can education stakeholders learn from the missteps of IEPs to improve ILPs? For dually identified students, in particular, how do ILPs interface with IEPs? And do these students have separate teams and meetings? Until empirical research catches up, these questions will likely be unresolved. However, in the interim, education leaders and teachers can take steps to ensure these plans do not replicate the patterned inequities we see in their special education counterpart, the IEP. In the upcoming pages, this chapter positions existing research findings and continued debates surrounding IEPs as evidence of two of three patterned inequities, with the hope we can take these learnings to improve individualized plans more broadly.

EVIDENCE OF PATTERNS

Unitary Identity

When we turn to extant research on IEPs, we can see unitary identity emerging prominently for MLs with disabilities in two interrelated ways: the contents of IEP documents and the occurrences of IEP meetings. In the case of IEPs, research has found the documents themselves erase the language learning needs of MLs with disabilities, positioning them unitarily as monolingual students with disabilities (Hoover et al., 2019; Kangas, 2017a, 2018a). Such erasure occurs as IEPs for MLs are commonly void of connections to students' multilingual and multicultural backgrounds. I have encountered this firsthand during my research studies and professional development sessions for inservice teachers. In thumbing through MLs' IEPs, I often see what I call the *checked box phenomenon*, whereby the IEP teams check off the box, "Is this student a multilingual learner?", but the remainder of the document shows no indication that the MLs' language and cultural backgrounds were considered in the IEP. Hoover and colleagues (2019) examined 30 IEPs from MLs with disabilities, discovering a similar pattern—that PLAAFP, annual goals, services, and accommodations were missing critical linguistic and cultural connections that would have guided teachers in better serving these students. From these findings, the researchers identified four "red flags" that indicate ML connections in IEPs are wanting (see Table 4.2).

Strikingly, all four red flags bear resemblance to unitary identity, ultimately giving the reader of the IEP no sense that the student is multilingual and has language learning needs. IEPs that contain these red flags leave teachers and staff with little to no guidance on how to support dually identified students. In this way, underdeveloped connections to language learning in

Table 4.2. IEP Red Flags for MLs

Red Flag 1	"IEPs for ELs that address only factors typically documented for non-ELs relative to cultural background, heritage, and prior experiences"
Red Flag 2	"IEPs that contain little or no equitable attention to language"
Red Flag 3	"IEPs for ELs that lack reference to research-based bilingual/ESL teaching practices"
Red Flag 4	"Upon reading an EL's completed IEP, it is unclear to another professional not involved in its development that the student is an English-as-a-second-language learner with a learning disability"

Source: Hoover, J. J., Erickson, J. R., Patton, J. R., Sacco, D. M., & Tran, L. M. (2019). Examining IEPs of English learners with learning disabilities for cultural and linguistic responsiveness. *Learning Disabilities Research and Practice, 34*(1), 14–22. https://doi.org/10.1111/ldrp.12183

IEPs can have a negative systemic influence. In a study I conducted, I observed how a lack of ML considerations in students' IEPs influenced service provision decisions. Specifically, staff justified a lack of language services because those services were not represented in the MLs' IEPs. One teacher explained the reduction and, in some cases, elimination of language services in this way:

> The IEP is a contract that the parents sign it and if we don't follow it, there could be legal troubles. And, of course, a school doesn't want to have the legal troubles, so we definitely have to prioritize one thing [special education] over another [language support], unfortunately. (Kangas, 2017a, p. 23)

The language of the IEP itself can likewise erase the language backgrounds of MLs with disabilities and, by extension, their families. As a telling example, in a qualitative study comparing the experiences of English-speaking and Spanish-speaking parents, Burke et al. (2021) reported that Spanish-speaking parents were frequently provided IEPs in English only, making a document that is already challenging to navigate in one's primary language even more incomprehensible. These findings also emerged in a qualitative interview study with Latinx immigrant parents whose children had developmental disabilities (Montoya et al., 2022). As parents divulged, untranslated IEPs were common, with some parents having to advocate for copies of their children's IEPs in Spanish. Even when documents were translated, parents reported that special education jargon in the IEPs was so dense that it obscured their understanding of what the school was doing to support their children's needs. These findings indicate that the content and language of the IEP can jointly fail to attend to the intersecting identities and needs of MLs with disabilities as well as their families.

Unitary identity also manifests in IEP meetings, as the language and cultural backgrounds of MLs and their families are rendered immaterial. Over the years, qualitative studies have reported that IEP team meetings have often lacked trained interpreters to promote MLs' and their families' engagement, denying critical information to parents and causing authentic dialogue between school and family to break down (Lo, 2008; Montoya et al., 2022; Salas, 2004; Voulgarides, 2018). The U.S. Departments of Justice and Education's letter (2015) cites a lack of interpreters at IEP meetings as a common civil rights violation. Even with interpretation services secured, IEP team meetings can remain spaces that ignore the language and cultural backgrounds of MLs and families. In her observation of IEP meetings, Voulgarides (2018) demonstrated how IEP meetings can be compliant through interpretation and yet be effectively meaningless to ML parents:

> I sat in on many special education meetings where I observed related service provider consultants reading speech, language, and/or physical therapy reports in very technical and hard to understand language to parents and our

> guardians. The reports were often delivered without contextual knowledge about a child and were very difficult to follow. The consultant would read verbatim a paragraph from the related service report in English to the district staff and then translate the paragraph, verbatim, into the parent and/or guardian's language. (p. 23)

She further observed how ML parents nodded in response, seeming to agree with the report even though its contents were largely incomprehensible. From this, she argued that although the school was compliant with IDEA mandates (e.g., IEP team held a meeting with parents, interpretation was provided, etc.), communication in the meeting was inequitable to ML parents' meaningful participation. Salas, who studied the experiences of Mexican parents in IEP meetings, found that special education jargon stifled their ability to understand and actively participate in the meetings. Salas (2004) asserted:

> Discourse patterns in the field of special education are often complex and require a certain knowledge base as to how schools work. As it is, many parents whose discourse patterns mirror the field often have trouble understanding the jargon associated with special education, which is often highly technical and reductionist in nature. (p. 185)

In the end, the author offered a sobering reminder that: "Jargon by its specific nature is designed to exclude" (p. 185). Apart from jargon, ML parents can feel excluded when they are not invited to ask questions, encouraged to share their valuable insights, or given the opportunity to make requests of IEP teams (Cioè-Peña, 2020; Lo, 2008; Salas, 2004). In sum, the evidence from the literature underscores how IEPs, teams, and meetings have struggled to account for the linguistic and cultural backgrounds and needs of MLs and their families.

Specialization Trap

When I recently held a professional learning workshop on integrating ELP and multilingual considerations into IEPs, I was somewhat surprised by the reactions I received. As I made a case for incorporating ELP and multilingual PLAAFP in IEPs, for instance, a teacher inquired at the workshop with genuine curiosity: "Why would we include ELP goals if they don't relate to the disability?" Another teacher in attendance echoed her inquiry: "What we put in the IEP should only connect to the disability, right?" These questions stuck with me because they reflect the broader challenge that IEPs face—their ironic resistance to individualization. As these questions suggest, IEPs are traditionally understood as a "special education document" developed mostly by special educators to support the students' disabilities. Likewise, there can be trepidation around IEPs given their contractual nature; naturally, teachers want to do the right thing, and the legal status of IEPs can heighten questions and concerns about the scope of IEP contents. Together, these understandings of IEPs not only challenge efforts to make the documents individualized for MLs with disabilities, but they are also emblematic of the specialization trap: Educators work in their professional silos during IEP development and as a result dually identified students receive a fragmented approach to their services and support.

Siloed approaches to IEP development are indeed a problem because they attempt to separate—and remove—language learning from disabilities, as if the two exist in isolation from each other in the minds and bodies of students. Yet language learning needs do not disappear when receiving special education support and likewise, disabilities do not up and vanish when an ML with disability enters the ESL classroom. With this understanding, IEPs that only address disability are illogical, as language learning and disability influence one another throughout learning.

In one of my studies, Lula, a 1st-grade ML who was being evaluated for an emotional and behavorial disorder, provides a helpful illustration of this point. The district where she was enrolled operated under strict disciplinary boundaries; IEPs were only for disabilities and were developed by special educators. In fact, ESL teachers historically did not even have access to the documents. If her evaluation resulted in her formal identification with emotional and behavioral disorder, Lula would receive an IEP that contained social and emotional needs and goals, as well as outlines of the emotional support services she will receive. However, having an IEP that integrated language learning considerations would have benefitted her greatly because her ELP and her disability needs intersected when interacting with her peers. I witnessed firsthand how Lula was often stigmatized by peers in her classroom because of her social and emotional needs, which limited her interactions in English. In turn, these sparse interactions with peers magnified her difficulties in forming positive relationships with her classmates. By including ML considerations throughout her IEP, however, her teachers could begin to support her needs more holistically; a special educator could attend to her pragmatic language skills in English (i.e., social, context-dependent language use), while her ESL teacher could implement behavioral supports that would promote positive relationships with peers during ESL instruction. Yet language learning and disability are often conceptualized as isolated needs for students such as Lula in ways that both defy logic and replicate the specialization trap.

The notion that IEPs are special education "territory" can explain the evidence of unitary identity we encountered in this chapter. IEPs may feature underdeveloped multilingual and multicultural considerations because they have been understood as disability-only documents. IEP meetings, too, may struggle to respond to the language and cultural backgrounds of students and families because these have traditionally been spaces with a default norm—that is, monolingual English-speaking individuals with disabilities. Another plausible explanation is that language specialists (e.g., ESL and bilingual education teachers) have not always been authentic members of IEP teams. Although there have been no studies that have directly examined language specialists' roles in IEP teams, the need for federal clarification on the composition of IEP teams would suggest that their participation is suspect (see U.S. Departments of Justice & Education, 2015). In elucidating this issue, the departments also directly linked the content of the IEP itself to the composition of the IEP team:

> To implement this requirement [inclusion of ML-related considerations in IEPs], it is essential that the IEP team include participants who have the requisite knowledge of the child's language needs. To ensure that EL children with disabilities receive services that meet their language and special education needs, it is important for members of the IEP team to include professionals with training, and preferably expertise, in second language acquisition and an understanding of how to differentiate between the student's limited English proficiency and the student's disability. (p. 27)

In my own studies on service provision, I stumbled upon the ways in which the specialization trap manifested in IEPs. When discussing their challenges in collaborating across departments to provide dual services, ESL teachers divulged, for example, that they did not have access to IEPs and were not included in IEP meetings (see Kangas, 2014, 2017a). Their exclusion from IEP development and meetings (a) communicated to the ESL teachers that IEPs were under the purview of special education and (b) positioned MLs with disabilities as solely students with disabilities. As the documents continued to reflect only the disability needs of MLs, ESL teachers' participation in IEP teams became superfluous. With ESL teachers' presence on IEP teams lacking and IEPs reflecting just special education needs, I observed how the teachers were constrained in their efforts to support the MLs with disabilities as whole children. In this respect, unitary identity and the specialization trap reinforced one another (Figure 4.1).

An example that illuminates the impact of the reinforcing nature of unitary identity and the specialization trap pertains to annual standardized ELP assessments, such as the WIDA ACCESS for ELs and ELPA21, among others. In instances where IEPs fail to address these ELP assessments, specifically the accommodations the MLs with disabilities are permitted to receive, challenges arise for language specialists during the administration of the test. For example, IEP teams may list that an ML with reading disability is permitted to have items on standardized content assessments (e.g., annual assessments

Figure 4.1. Patterned Inequities in IEP Documents and Teams

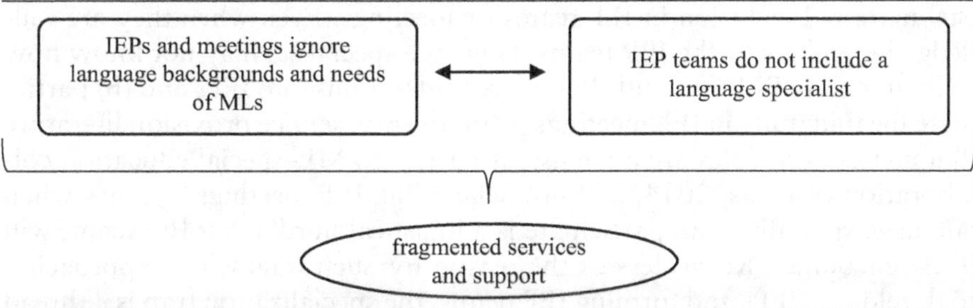

in reading and mathematics) read aloud by a teacher or paraprofessional; however, such an accommodation is typically impermissible on the reading portion of annual ELP assessments, as it would compromise the validity of the assessment. WIDA (2022) clarifies this point in its more recent assessment accommodation guide:

> Some supports that are typically available to English learners taking a content test are not acceptable supports on an ELP assessment. For example, use of a bilingual dictionary or the option to provide American Sign Language responses instead of verbal responses might be typical for a language arts or science test, but these options would not produce valid results in the context of an ELP assessment. (p. 1)

When IEPs fail to account for ELP assessments, MLs with disabilities are at risk of either taking an assessment without the accommodations their disabilities require or of opting out of portions of an assessment they need to take to meet reclassification eligibility. A district partner I collaborated with encountered this exact dilemma, and as a result, the ML Department was undertaking an initiative to revise the accommodation section of IEPs of MLs. She shared about this endeavor:

> Actually, I just sent out an email this morning that said to make sure that when they are completing IEPs . . . to mark in the IEP which WIDA ACCESS test they are taking. So, whether they're taking regular, or the Alternate, and then, with or without accommodations, and if with accommodations, which accommodations. I want to say the vast majority of the IEPs don't have it listed in there: what the accommodations are. Because they kind of skip that section. Well, that should be done in collaboration with the ESOL [English for Speakers of Other Languages] teacher.

This example highlights how the tenuous participation of language specialists on IEP teams and in IEP meetings reinforces a siloed and fragmented development of IEPs.

Such outcomes in IEPs may not always be a result of language specialists' marginal inclusion in IEP teams or meetings. Even when they are full-fledged members of the IEP teams, language specialists may not know how to (a) integrate ELP and multilingual considerations into IEPs and (b) participate meaningfully in IEP meetings. Moreover, as service provision literature illuminates, schedules are a persistent barrier to ML–special education collaboration (Kangas, 2014, 2018a). Scheduling IEP meetings at times when language specialists can participate is a logistical hurdle that IEP teams will likely encounter. Regardless of the reason for such fragmented approaches to developing IEPs and forming IEP teams, the specialization trap is a thread woven throughout, compromising access to an individualized education. With these understandings of unitary identity and the specialization trap, I now address how we can learn from the patterned inequities in IEPs to improve ILPs.

Learning From Patterned Inequities to Improve ILPs

ILPs have been gaining traction in U.S. schools (Kangas & Cioè-Peña, 2024), yet they remain underexamined in education practice. Simply put, we know very little about these documents in ML education overall, but what we do know is twofold. First, we know that these documents tend to focus on ELP and, in fact, can become preoccupied with increasing ELP, specifically boosting standardized ELP assessment scores (see Thompson & Rodriguez-Mojica, 2023). Because MLs with disabilities have a history of not making ELP gains on these assessments and thus have lower rates of being reclassified as English-proficient (Burke et al., 2016; Sahakyan & Ryan, 2018; Slama et al., 2017; Umansky et al., 2017), these documents are particularly relevant to the education of these students. In a recent research collaboration, a district partner implemented ILPs for their MLs who are not meeting standards for ELP growth and overwhelmingly, it was their MLs with disabilities who received these plans. Second, we know that patterned inequities are repeated and endemic, underlying most problems of practice, and thus are likely to resurface even in new practices in education. For this reason, it behooves teachers, school leaders, and SEA leaders to learn from the patterned inequities evidence in IEPs as a pathway to improve ILPs overall but especially for MLs with disabilities.

What lessons, then, can we learn from IEPs and apply to ILPs? In looking at the research to date on IEPs, we see that these documents are resistant to change, unable to account for the holistic needs of the students and often subject to disciplinary divides between ML and special education. Applying a patterned inequities frame to ILPs, education stakeholders should be wary of the following practices:

1. ILPs that are developed by language specialists with little collaboration among their special education or related-service[1] counterparts
2. ILPs that are void of connections to MLs' disability-related needs and goals
3. ILPs that are understood as strictly an "ML document"
4. ILPs that exist in isolation from IEPs
5. ILP teams that lack special educators and other specialists (e.g., speech pathologists, physical therapists, autism support personnel, applied behavior analysts, etc.) as members
6. ILP teams that are separate from IEP teams
7. ILP meetings that only discuss MLs' standardized ELP scores and data
8. ILP meetings that fail to engage MLs and their parent/guardians regarding their language and disability-related goals for learning

When ILPs show signs of these patterns, it is likely that MLs with disabilities will receive a fragmented education. Recognizing and responding to such practices will enable ILPs to function as powerful tools for promoting equitable systemic change in ML education. Relatedly, it is worth considering whether ILPs are necessary for MLs with disabilities or if their use for this population of students signals that siloed, disjointed efforts are already at play. After all, if IEPs were truly individualized and responsive to dually identified students, why would ILPs be needed? The content typically featured in an ILP would be duplicative if IEPs could live up to their individualized purpose by integrating linguistic and cultural considerations throughout. Thus, for MLs with disabilities, having two separate plans—one for disability and one for language learning—typifies both unitary identity and the specialization trap.

RESPONSES TO PATTERNED INEQUITIES IN INDIVIDUALIZED PLANS AND TEAMS

As the evidence presented in this chapter suggests, IEPs have struggled to live up to their individualized promise, particularly for MLs with disabilities, in ways that link to the composition of the teams and the practices that occur during IEP meetings. Although I have addressed improvements for ILPs, I hold on to the promise that IEPs, too, can promote equity for MLs with disabilities. With strategic changes by education stakeholders, IEP documents, teams, and meetings can become more individualized and responsive to MLs with disabilities. In what follows, I offer recommendations for IEPs with the understanding that they can be applied to other individualized plans emerging in educational practice.

Response 1: Systematically Review IEPs

As evidence points to IEPs possessing underdeveloped connections to MLs' language learning and cultural backgrounds, an initial step to advancing equity for this population would entail a review of current IEPs for MLs with disabilities. In preparation for such reviews, ML and special education department leaders will likely need to cultivate buy-in from their respective departments by (a) promoting the understanding that language learning and disability do not exist in isolation of one another within the minds and bodies of dually identified students and (b) debunking the myths that surround these students' capabilities and needed services. Once buy-in emerges, strategic reviews of IEPs can be initiated on a rolling basis prior to the annual IEP meetings for each student. This approach will ensure the review is systematic and yet manageable for teachers whose days are already full to the brim.

Prior to IEP meetings, language specialists can utilize a simple checklist to determine if there are components of the document that are void of linguistic connections (see Figure 4.2). For bilingual school contexts, in particular, it is critical that language specialists think beyond English to evaluate whether the IEPs include multilingual connections. As Hoover et al. (2019) remind us, IEPs for dually identified students should be meaningfully distinguishable from IEPs for monolingual students with disabilities. If IEPs fail to impart this impression, then surely their individualization is lacking. As language specialists use the checklist, they can readily identify the components of IEPs that require revision and share the results with their IEP team members. Alternatively, if district leaders desire to undertake such a review but do not wish to pile on more work for their teachers, they may want to consider partnering with researchers from higher education or with regional educational units that can conduct the review on behalf of the district. Regardless of the pathway district leaders pursue, all other critical improvements to IEPs for MLs with disabilities rest on this initial step of reviewing the contents of the documents.

Response 2: Enhance Training and Resources for Language Specialists

For language specialists, whether ESL teachers or bilingual educators, venturing into the world of IEPs—their development, meetings, and team dynamics—can be unfamiliar at best and overwhelming at worst. In many instances, language specialists may have a fervent desire to expand linguistic and cultural content in IEPs but lack the skillset to do so. As a researcher and teacher educator, I have seen this firsthand, and consequently have integrated IEP training into our current ESL certification courses. For inservice teachers, however, support for IEP development and IEP team participation is likely still needed.

Figure 4.2. IEP Checklist for ML Considerations

IEP Team, Meetings, and Communication
☐ IEP team includes a certified language specialist (ESL or bilingual education)
☐ Language specialist participates in IEP meetings
☐ Home language interpreter is present at IEP meetings
☐ IEP and all relevant communication have been translated for parents
Student Background
☐ IEP identifies the student's status as a current or former *English learner*
Current Academic and Functional Performance
☐ Current performance in English in listening, speaking, reading, and writing is detailed
☐ Current abilities in home language or additional languages are described
☐ English language and home language development needs are identified
☐ Strengths of student including bi- and multilingual abilities are emphasized
Annual Goals
☐ Measurable annual language goals are listed for listening, speaking, reading, and writing
☐ Description is included of how and when language goals will be measured
☐ Short-term objectives are provided for listening, speaking, reading, and writing
☐ Procedures are included for reviewing and sharing language progress reports
Services & Environments
☐ Language services (ESL or bilingual) the student requires are listed
☐ Frequency, duration, and location of language services are identified
☐ Languages used for instruction during language services are specified
☐ Language specialist (ESL or bilingual) is listed as the provider of language services
☐ Language, material, process modifications/adaptations in general education are detailed
☐ Languages of modifications/adaptations occurring in general education are specified
☐ Learning environments promote interaction with peers without disabilities and multilingual needs
Assessments
☐ Language and disability-related accommodations on state assessments are specified
☐ Disability-related accommodations on annual ELP assessments are specified
☐ Language and disability-related accommodations on subject assessments described
***Transition Services Planning** (if student is 16 years or older)*
☐ Language services that will support student's postsecondary plans are identified
☐ ML and academic courses will support student's postsecondary goals

Source: Adapted from Kangas, S. E. N. (2018b). Why working apart doesn't work at all: Special education and English learner teacher collaborations. *Intervention in School and Clinic, 54*(1), 31–39. https://doi.org/10.1177/1053451218762469

In the case of IEP development, language specialists and education leaders will find Hoover et al.'s (2019) book, *IEP for ELs and Other Diverse Learners*, highly useful, filled with concrete, step-by-step directions for infusing multilingual and multicultural considerations throughout each component of MLs' IEPs—from PLAAF to goals to services, and more. The book models the development of specific and measurable language-related goals, which, in my experience, can be the most challenging content to integrate for language specialists. For language specialists supporting high school MLs with disabilities, extra attention in their training should be given to forming transition goals in collaboration with the student and their family (see Trainor et al., 2019; Wu et al., 2022).

Following a systemic review of IEP content, educational leaders may wish to offer a series of hands-on workshops that draw upon above resources. Because revising IEPs can take time and there can be several components that require refining, educational leaders should plan for such IEP training to span across the school year and be more than a one-shot professional development session. Such workshops would be beneficial for the development of individualized plans overall, as the skills needed, for instance, to integrate language-related content in IEPs would also apply in the development of ILPs. Relatedly, although the book listed at the conclusion of this chapter is a recommended guide for IEP development (see Hoover & Patton, 2017), its contents generalize to ILPs as well.

In the case of IEP team participation, language specialists may need additional support to understand how they can meaningfully participate in IEP meetings. ML district leaders along with their team of teachers may wish to generate protocols to guide language specialists' engagement during meetings. These protocols should address (a) insights language specialists could share, (b) data they could bring, and (c) questions they could ask. Given the preliminary limitations of ILPs—a hyper-focus on standardized ELP assessment scores—language specialist should consider sharing perspectives and data that extend beyond such standardized data alone and that consider students' multilingual capabilities. As a starting point, I provide a list of initial suggestions for an IEP meeting protocol below (see Figure 4.3). Throughout the table, I refer to *language* broadly to reflect the ways IEP meetings can address multilingualism, and not just the ELP, of MLs with disabilities.

Response 3: Strategically Revise IEPs

Once IEPs have been systematically reviewed and language specialists have received resources and support for IEP development, the actual revising of IEPs can begin. For districts and schools with large numbers of MLs with disabilities, language-related updates to IEPs should be paced for language specialists, spread across the school year as annual meetings are held. Drafting revisions approximately one month prior to IEP meetings

Figure 4.3. Language Specialist's Protocol for IEP Meetings

Expertise to share:

1. ML's current language skills in listening, speaking, reading, and writing (L/S/R/W)
2. ML's progress in L/S/R/W over time
3. ML's progress and use in L/S/R/W in the classroom
4. ML's areas of growth in L/S/R/W
5. ML's motivation and engagement in language learning
6. ML's strengths as person and language learner

Data and Materials to bring:

1. ML's current and past annual ELP scores
2. ML's grades in ESL or bilingual classes
3. ML's classroom language assessments
4. ML's student projects and tasks
5. ML's portfolio
6. ML's writing samples
7. ML's speaking samples
8. ML's student self-reflections on language skills
9. Language-related revisions/updates to be included in IEP

Questions to ask:

IEP Team

1. How would you describe the ML's language use in your classroom?
2. What is the ML's motivation and engagement like in your classroom?
3. What questions do you have about how to best support the ML's language during learning?

Family Members

1. How do you see your child's language(s) developing?
2. What do you think are your child's needs for language learning?
3. What goals do you have for your child's language learning?
4. In the future, what is important for your child to be able to do in their languages?

Students

1. How do you see your abilities in your language(s) growing?
2. How do you think you can improve in your languages?
3. What goals do you have for your language learning?
4. In the future, what is important for you to be able to do in your languages?

will enable language specialists to work through all components of the IEP with care and to receive feedback, if needed, from other language specialist colleagues on the content they developed. As language specialists update IEPs, ML directors should identify several exemplary models that give attention to the four domains of language (i.e., listening, speaking, reading, and writing) and represent the heterogeneous learning needs and abilities found among MLs with disabilities (MLs with autism, MLs with SLDs in mathematics, MLs with complex support needs, etc.). Having a repository of anonymized IEPs will be a useful resource for current and future language specialists in the district.

Significantly, the presence of multilingual and multicultural content in IEPs is a starting point for equity for dually identified students. After all, IEPs can be replete with language-learning considerations and on paper give the impression of true individualization; however, if that content only exists on the pages of the IEP, equity is surely compromised. Voulgarides (2018) reminds us of this critical implication: IEPs can meet standards for compliance with IDEA in their content while also failing to secure students' access to their educational rights and opportunities. For this reason, updating IEPs so that their content, especially specially designed instruction, can meaningfully support general and special education teachers' pedagogical practices vis-à-vis language learning is paramount. For students with disabilities in general, the specially designed instruction component of IEPs can be alarmingly generic, for example, directing teachers to provide preferential seating for students, to allow additional time on tests and quizzes, or to utilize visual aids. For MLs with disabilities, generic language-related specially designed instruction can be similarly futile. Extra support may be needed for language specialists to move away from generic instructional accommodations to feature instead specially designed instruction that align with students' proficiency levels in English (and, if applicable, their home language) and reflect their needs across the four language domains. With more specific instructional accommodations, IEPs can exert a positive systemic impact on classroom practices and promote collective responsibility for MLs with disabilities by mitigating the specialization trap, which would have only language specialists supporting students' language learning needs.

Regardless of the revisions language specialists draft, these updates should be considered tentative until perspectives and feedback from ML families and even the students themselves are shared during IEP meetings. To ensure authentic, reciprocal engagement of families and students in meetings, I now turn to the final recommendation.

Response 4: Engage and Empower ML Families

Given the findings from research—that ML families feel overwhelmed and sidelined in IEP meetings—concerted efforts are needed to engage and empower ML families in these spaces. Several valuable resources on this very topic are readily available and can be found at the conclusion of this chapter. In working with teachers, I have found Chang and colleagues' 2022 work to be a practical resource that introduces a model—Explain, Provide, Inquire, and Coordinate (EPIC)—for IEP teams to draw upon before, during, and after IEP meetings with ML families. The purpose of the EPIC model is to ensure that IEP team members are reflecting on and adjusting their own practices to promote ML family engagement at all stages of the IEP development and revision process. In this model, at each stage, IEP team members should integrate the four core practices of explaining, providing, inquiring, and coordinating. An abbreviated summary of the EPIC model and many of its corresponding actions are captured in Table 4.3.

For individual teachers aspiring to enhance their responsiveness to and engagement with ML families, the EPIC model can be used as a checklist to evaluate one's own interactions with and responses to family members. For ML and special education leaders wishing to improve school–family engagement in IEP meetings, EPIC practices can also be used to revamp existing district and school procedures and as a tool for ongoing teacher training. Especially as rural and suburban districts and schools find themselves with increasingly linguistically diverse student populations, the need

Table 4.3. EPIC Model of Family Engagement for IEP Meetings

Before, during, and after IEP meetings, IEP team members should:	
Explain	Family and student role in IEP development IEP procedures Special education and ML-related jargon Recommendations made by IEP team Parental/family consent
Provide	Information about available programs and services Meeting agenda Names and contact information of IEP team members Translated materials and list of jargon/acronyms Draft of updated IEP content Final translated IEP
Inquire	Ask for concerns prior to and after meeting Use pauses and ask for questions often Follow up with family after meeting on phone or via text
Coordinate	Assessments and data collection prior to meeting Invitation and notification of meeting Schedules of services

Source: Chang, Y. C., Avila, M., & Rodriguez, H. (2022). Beyond the dotted line: Empowering parents from culturally and linguistically diverse families to participate. *Teaching Exceptional Children*, *55*(2), 132–140. https://doi.org/10.1177/00400599221099868

for such practices may be relatively new to IEP teams and thus requiring additional training.

SUMMARY

In this second chapter addressing equity in systems, we considered individualized plans. I began by making a case for the systemic influence of individualized plans and their transformative potential. Despite the capacity of individualized plans to be powerful tools for equity, the chapter explored evidence of IEPs' resistance to individualization, especially for MLs with disabilities, as their multilingual identities are ignored, and their language learning and disabilities are divorced from one another. These tendencies, I argue, are telltale signs of unitary identity and the specialization trap. The chapter then drew upon these patterned inequities in IEPs as a tool for improving other individualized plans, particularly ILPs, which are becoming more frequently used in K–12 schools. The chapter concluded with a series of recommended responses education leaders and teachers can enact to enhance the responsiveness of IEP documents, meetings, and team practices to dually identified students and their families.

RECOMMENDED RESOURCES

On IEP Development for MLs

Hoover, J. J., & Patton, J. R. (2017). *IEP for ELs and other diverse learners*. Corwin.

U.S. Department of Education. (2016). *Tools and resources for addressing English learners with disabilities*. https://www2.ed.gov/about/offices/list/oela/english-learner-toolkit/chap6.pdf

On Family Engagement for MLs With Disabilities

Chang, Y. C., Avila, M., & Rodriguez, H. (2022). Beyond the dotted line: Empowering parents from culturally and linguistically diverse families to participate. *Teaching Exceptional Children*, *55*(2), 132–140. https://doi.org/10.1177/00400599221099868

¡Colorín Colorado! (2023). *Special education and ELLs: Partnering with parents*. https://www.colorincolorado.org/special-education-ell/parents

Thurlow, M. L., Liu, K. K., & Mentan, C. F. T. (2022). Engaging parents or guardians in meeting the needs of English learners with disabilities. *Educational Research and Development Journal*, *25*(1), 47–64. https://files.eric.ed.gov/fulltext/EJ1361382.pdf

Urtubey, J. (2021). *4 things to know about partnering with families of English language learners.* NEAToday. https://www.nea.org/nea-today/all-news-articles/4-things-know-about-partnering-families-english-language-learners

Zhang, C., & Bennett, T. (2003). Facilitating the meaningful participation of culturally and linguistically diverse families in the IFSP and IEP process. *Focus on Autism and Other Developmental Disabilities, 18*(1), 51–59. https://doi.org/10.1177/10883576030180010

CHAPTER 5

Teacher Education Programs and Professional Certifications

As this book explores, patterned inequities possess five principal characteristics:

1. they are *repeated* and predictable,
2. they are *endemic* to most problems of practice,
3. they *co-occur* and reinforce one another,
4. they are *pervasive* across education sectors,
5. they are *shared,* experienced by all education stakeholders.

In the preceding chapters, I have highlighted the first three of these five. We saw the repeated, endemic, and co-occurring nature of patterned inequities across two key systems in schools: the organization of services and students and the organization of individualized plans and teams. As the final chapter in the series on equity in systems, it surfaces the remaining two characteristics of patterned inequities: that they are pervasive, emerging across all sectors of education, and are shared, experienced by all education stakeholders. I have been confronted with this hard truth as a faculty member who trains educators. As I take stock of *teacher education,* a term I use to encompass the many modes (degrees, professional learning, etc.) by which teachers cultivate their knowledge and skills, and teacher credentialing (licensure, certification) it is painfully evident that the patterned inequities in K–12 education have roots in higher education. The two systems, in this way, are interlocked.

I am struck by this point in each interview with teachers and administrators. Threaded across their experiences is a persistent tension in their daily work with dually identified students: Educators have a deep desire to support MLs with disabilities, but they find themselves nonplussed, lacking the tools needed to support students with intersecting language learning and disability needs. When I think about this tension, the *will and capacity framework* (McLaughlin, 1987) is top of mind. As this theory goes, educators must deal with the everyday realities of education policies, and their responses to policies are shaped by two local factors: capacity and will (McLaughlin, 1987). *Capacity* encompasses the resources and training educators have at their disposal, whereas *will* pertains to their dispositions and desires (McLaughlin, 1987). As I have discovered, educators often have the motivation and dispositions needed (the will) to support MLs with disabilities but not necessarily the skillset to do so (the capacity). If educators need capacity building to support their dually identified students, teacher education programs, SEAs, and district offices need to heed the call to better train our educators. For this reason, this chapter broadens our focus from systems in schools and districts to systems in universities, specifically teacher education programs, and in the state offices that determine the parameters for teacher certification. With this focus, this chapter underscores how patterned inequities are not just a K–12 affair but rather are crosscutting, experienced in multiple sectors by multiple education stakeholders.

While highlighting the interlocked patterned inequities in teacher education and K–12 education, this chapter highlights a disjuncture between the two: Although the number of MLs with disabilities is increasing in U.S. schools (Cooc, 2023), teacher education is not keeping pace with these demographic changes. Perhaps the most telling example of this comes in the form of bilingual special education, a K–12 programmatic approach that provides a continuum of special education services and support in the MLs' respective languages. For some time now, bilingual special education, broadly conceived, has been a well-regarded interdisciplinary approach that overcomes several problems of practice (Baca & Cervantes, 2003; Colón & Alsace, 2022; Ortiz et al., 2011). In the 1980s, bilingual special education was positioned as a solution to the historical tendency for special education to overlook the linguistic and cultural needs of MLs (Baca & Amato, 1989; Cummins, 1989; Figueroa, 1989). This message has been constant in educational research ever since. In the early 2000s, scholars advocated a bridging of special education and bilingual education, whether accomplished in- or outside of MTSS, in which teachers (a) use both languages to provide support and implement interventions, (b) examine bilingual student data, and (c) gain a fuller understanding of the student's academic and linguistic capabilities (Baca & Cervantes, 2003; Esparza Brown & Doolittle, 2008). Ortiz et al. (2011) cogently argued that through their unique insights, bilingual educators can play a pivotal role in preventing erroneous referrals of MLs for special education evaluation, as they support MLs' intersecting needs. More recently, the integration of bilingual instruction in special education services has been proposed as a solution to sidestep the tensions that emerge during service provision when language and disability, and their respective services, are pitted against one another (Cioè-Peña, 2021; Kangas, 2017b)—a critical equity issue in school systems. While the advantages of bilingual special education abound for dually identified students, teachers are not typically trained in bilingual special education nor in supporting the intersection of language learning and disability.

THE ORGANIZATION OF TEACHER EDUCATION PROGRAMS AND CERTIFICATIONS: KEY TRENDS

Usually, in this section of each chapter, I draw the reader's attention to the findings of relevant studies on MLs with disabilities, delineating what research so far has to tell us. This is a nonstarter for a chapter on teacher education because there is a woeful lack of research on teacher education for dually identified students, for reasons I will discuss later. In this section, then, I will attend to two trends in the predominant mode of teacher education, that is, in teacher preparation programs, the context that provides teachers the foundational knowledge out of which their praxis grows. These are the two trends: (a) we train teachers within the bounds of specific disciplines, in this case ML education and special education, and (b) we certify their credentials in a similar fashion.

First, although the disciplines of ML education and special education have much in common, they are specializations that have distinct histories, norms, and knowledge. I have experienced this firsthand. As an applied linguist appointed to a special education program, I often feel like an outsider. Sometimes it is the small things that serve as this reminder, such as the acronyms and jargon we use. As an example, for some time now, the two disciplines have used a plethora of different terms to refer to the same population of dually identified students: *culturally and linguistically diverse students in special education*, *English learners with disabilities*, and *emergent bilinguals labeled as dis/abled*, to name a few. Other times, the markers of our disciplinary divergence are more striking—the venues in which we read and publish; the types of research we value and prefer; and even, at times, the pathways by which we believe equity can be achieved. I will likely never forget a meeting wherein one of my beloved special education colleagues discussed a research project that examined students' "language behaviors." The turn of phrase came as a startling surprise to me; despite years of study and expertise in language education, I had never heard *language* conceptualized as a *behavior* that should be molded and changed. Though a small illustration, it punctuates how our respective disciplines shape our understandings.

Second, evolving from separate legal origins, special education and ML education are distinct areas of certification in teacher preparation programs. In its 2004 reauthorization, IDEA regulated that special education teachers across elementary and secondary public schools be "highly qualified," broadly defining what this should mean in terms of professional certifications (U.S. Department of Education, 2007). From there, states may outline more specific requirements for special education certification. ML teacher preparation stems from the Civil Rights Act of 1964 and the Equal Educational Opportunities Act of 1974 (EEOA), which collectively established that schools must ensure MLs receive support for their ELP through a viable language program. Unlike for special education, these laws do not set forth a federal general standard for "highly qualified" language specialists (see U.S. Departments of Justice & Education, 2015); establishing standards for teacher qualifications falls solely under the purview of states. Emanating from these different federal and state regulations, separate certification areas are then developed and offered by higher education institutions. In sum, certification areas are demarcated by disciplines, and each reflects a distinctive history, norms, and knowledge. The tendencies in higher education and state departments of education to divide training and certification between the disciplines set the stage for educators' constrained capacity to support students whose multiple needs fall under an array of certification areas, such as MLs with disabilities.

With highly siloed disciplinary models challenged by the increased need for teachers to work alongside one another in schools, there have been calls to reimagine and restructure teacher preparation in more interdisciplinary ways (see Carrizales et al., 2022; Coleman et al., 2023; Slanda & Pike, 2022; Stolz, 2021). By merging and blending the perspectives and skillsets of more than one professional field, interdisciplinary programs can facilitate a greater depth of knowledge for teachers, resulting in a sum-is-greater-than-the-parts phenomenon. It is no wonder why a quick internet search reveals that many colleges and schools of education espouse interdisciplinarity as a core feature of their research with and training of teachers. Despite their promise, interdisciplinary programs that bridge ML and special education remain in short supply in the United States, as will be explored next.

EVIDENCE OF PATTERNS

So far, I may have given the impression that ML education and special education are *entirely* different disciplines, and thus, what we do in the classroom as either language specialists or special educators bears no resemblance to the practices of our colleagues. This is not the case; special education and ML education have many shared pedagogical practices (e.g., explicit or direct instruction, scaffolded support). Yet they do have notable contrasts. It is these points of divergence that educators would benefit from learning through more interdisciplinary models of teacher preparation programs. Chapter 7 takes on such considerations in pedagogical practices in the classroom, but in this chapter, I attend to the main patterned inequities evident in teacher education and credentialing: Teachers need more integrated understandings of MLs with disabilities than the fields of ML or special education can afford, and yet systemically our programs and certifications are emblematic of unitary identity and the specialization trap.

Unitary Identity and the Specialization Trap

I wanted to better understand the landscape of interdisciplinary teacher education in the face of the scarcity of research on teacher preparation for MLs with disabilities. With the support of a doctoral student, I conducted two related in-depth reviews of policies and programs in the spring of 2023. We first examined the existing teacher licensure requirements in all 50 states, and then we turned our attention to schools and colleges of education to determine the existence of interdisciplinary programming at the nexus of language education and special education. In conducting this search, we collected and cataloged over 150 documents from SEA offices and universities alike. The results were startling.

Teacher Certification Requirements. Across the United States, only Illinois and Texas have a state-approved integrated bilingual special education certification area. For Texas—a state with one of the largest ML populations—this certification is relatively new, signed into state law in November 2023 (Tex. Educ. Code § 21.04891). For Illinois, the certification includes several pathways by which teachers can accrue and demonstrate knowledge of special education and bilingual education as well as proficiency in another language (Illinois State Board of Education, n.d.). Outside of bilingual special education, across the U.S., there are no state-approved certifications in (a) MLs with disabilities, (b) ESL–special education, or (c) language education–special education. For teachers, then, traditional certification programs in special education or ML education are the pathways by which they can acquire their knowledge.

These traditional programs teach teachers to be specialists, honing in on and sharpening their skills in relation to a singular social marker (e.g., disability, language), and student needs that stem from it. Boveda and Aronson (2019) argue that special education teacher preparation, on the whole, focuses on disabilities, losing sight of the many other identities that students possess. Likewise, in ML education, we see and respond to language, often overlooking other nonlinguistic identities and needs (Kanno & Kangas, 2024). For teachers, such ways of seeing and responding to students point to the patterned inequities of unitary identity and the specialization trap. By organizing teacher preparation into discipline-specific certifications, we effectively train teachers to see dually identified students through the lens of a singular need and to work in highly siloed ways to support this singular need.

With a lack of integrated credentialing, teachers' best recourse for building their interdisciplinary knowledge base is by accruing additional certifications. For instance, as of 2024, in my state of Pennsylvania, teachers can pursue a preK–12 ESL certification, an abbreviated add-on endorsement, to their initial certification in special education. Although on the surface this seems promising, I have found that layering certifications does not bypass patterned inequities because teachers with multiple certifications are confronted with two realities. First, as previously established, existing teacher preparation programs emphasize becoming a specialist. To be qualified as a specialist to teach students with disabilities in my context, for example, teachers must meet a long list of state-mandated competencies. Ensuring that teacher preparation courses meet the competencies set out by the state can feel herculean at times, leaving little room in courses for content that is valuable but not required by the state (e.g., supporting MLs with disabilities). The same applies to the ESL certification; logistically integrating disability considerations into our existing ESL certification has been daunting, despite my professional commitment to doing so. With programs adhering closely to state certification requirements, which are highly focused on discipline-specific knowledge and skills, teachers are not taught to support the intersection of language learning and disability. The default norm, therefore, is unitary identity, with a focus on supporting language or disability and yet not both. In- and preservice teachers, then, are left to put the pieces together themselves. Second, teachers work in the context of siloed departments of their districts and schools. The prior chapters in this series on equity in systems illuminated the mechanisms by which students and even their teachers are sorted by a singular label and routed this way or that for their learning and teaching, respectively. For teachers, this organization occurs along the lines of their specialization—who they were trained to be and what needs they were taught to support. Language specialists, for example, spend their days supporting MLs, meeting with ML colleagues, and engaging in professional learning opportunities germane to ML education. Thus, the conditions of their work reinforce the specialization trap: to focus on language learning with other language specialists. In this way, accruing multiple individual certifications is not a foolproof remedy for unitary identity and the specialization trap.

It is also worth noting that layering certifications can be time-consuming and cost-prohibitive for future teachers. In certain states, meeting the requirements for two separate certification areas can equate to prolonged undergraduate or graduate studies, which admittedly is unattractive to preservice teachers. Just last year, one inservice teacher I advised decided to drop the ESL certification after realizing that it would result in graduating a year later when added on to her current special education and general education certification. In short, even if students are willing to dedicate the time to earning multiple certifications, this can be financially unwise with the rising costs of higher education (see Kerr & Wood, 2023) and the low starting salaries of teachers (see Walker, 2023).

Teacher Preparation Programs. As the findings above indicated, state certification policies rarely bring together ML and special education, but what about schools and colleges of education? Do they offer multidisciplinary programs, such as full-scale master's degrees and short-term certificates? To answer these questions, in spring of 2023, we also systematically reviewed the programs offered by the *U.S. News and World Report*'s top 50 graduate schools of education, combing through their websites and manuals. The search yielded findings of a similar scale to certifications: Only one graduate school—Columbia's Teachers College—offered a degree that emphasized the intersection of language learning and disability. Apart from this review, we found only two online professional certificates, offered by Lasell University and the University of Maine, focusing on MLs with disabilities and multilingual special education, respectively. Notably, these unique programs often have a scholar specializing in the intersection of language learning and disability, whose career has been dedicated to elevating the needs of dually identified students, at the helm. One such scholar, Patricia Martínez-Álvarez (Teachers College), makes this argument for interdisciplinary programming amid its rarity:

> Most teacher preparation programs tend to focus on one branch of specialization only (i.e., special education) without connecting with other aspects that impact children's learning (i.e., bilingual education), and ideas developed in one field rarely cross over to the other field or take very long to permeate through professional boundaries. (2023, pp. 6–7)

The dearth of such programs, I argue, represents a larger cycle of scarcity. The incentive for universities to offer and for preservice teachers to enroll in interdisciplinary ML–special education programming is limited when there is a lack of corresponding state-approved certifications. Because state departments of education, too, lack integrated structures, as they are commonly organized into discipline-specific areas (the focus of Chapter 10), initiating interdisciplinary certifications is arduous.

Having incredibly few programs or certifications that center MLs with disabilities is a noticeable mismatch between teacher education and the realities of schools. While the number of dually identified students is on the rise (see Cooc, 2023), interdisciplinary teacher education programs—be they degrees, certifications, or certificates—that merge knowledge from ML and special education in some form are dismally sparse. The consequences of this lag are substantial, seeping into the structures and practices in schools for dually identified students. Put in other terms, systems in higher education and state education departments both create and sustain inequitable systems in schools that reduce MLs with disabilities into the unitary identity paradigm and that structure services into a string of isolated, specialized supports. Herein lies the pervasive, shared, and co-occurring nature of patterned inequities; all stakeholders in education experience their pull as their influence ripples through the interconnected sectors of education. But the systemic consequences for K–12 schools can be disrupted through strategic responses, as we will next consider.

RESPONSES TO PATTERNED INEQUITIES IN TEACHER EDUCATION PROGRAMS AND CERTIFICATIONS

In our recent article, Weddle et al. (2024), we offer a framework for understanding equity in ML education, arguing that *shared responsibility* is at the core. Although ML and special education publications have used this phrase liberally for decades, most conceptualizations have focused on teachers' dispositions alone. Departing from this understanding, Weddle et al. (2024) attest that shared responsibility is "embedded in the mindsets, norms, and structures" (p. 252) across *all* levels of the education system, including schools, districts, and SEAs. Shared responsibility, we also assert, is critical for MLs with disabilities, given their multiple educational needs. This is certainly the case for improving teacher education: Promoting equity for MLs with disabilities requires various sectors—districts, universities, and state education agencies—to reimagine teacher education in ways that cultivate shared responsibility instead of siloed efforts demarcated by professional specializations. Below are targeted responses that district leaders, state leaders, and university faculty can implement to achieve this aim.

Response 1: Invest in Trainings That Build Teachers' Capacities

Given the existing trends in teacher preparation programs, it is unlikely that in-service teachers have had formal educational opportunities to learn about MLs with disabilities and ways to collaboratively support student needs. Both district and state offices that offer ongoing training to inservice teachers should consider investing in professional learning opportunities that build teachers' capacities to (a) address the needs of dually identified students and (b) collaborate across disciplines. With teachers commonly working within their individual departments, opportunities to engage in dialogue and build their collaborative capacities around key problems of practice are rare and all the more exigent. Building from professional learning that directly dismantles commonly held misconceptions about the intersection of language learning and disability, districts should offer more expansive joint trainings for language specialists and special educators. This begins with the leaders of ML and special education departments making a commitment to offer shared district trainings and then identifying critical areas in which trainings are most needed. Forming a multiyear plan for professional learning that delineates measurable objectives, topics covered, resources required, and desired outcomes will be useful in consistently centering MLs with disabilities. Because the professional learning topics for supporting dually identified students and for collaboration are endless, district leaders may benefit from a flexible planning tool for their professional learning offerings, such as the one featured in Table 5.1 below. Often, ongoing professional learning hinges upon districtwide strategic

Table 5.1. Example of Multi-Year Professional Learning Plan

Overall Goals: To implement multiyear training that equips teachers with knowledge and skills to improve the quality of IEPs for culturally and linguistically diverse students.

Alignment with Strategic Plan: Supports the following goals: 3.1—to enhance services and supports for students with disabilities through evidence-based practices; 3.2—to empower students to achieve academic goals; and 3.3—to build an inclusive learning environment where all learners are given the chance to succeed.

	Central Topic	Objectives	Format	Person Responsible	Action Items	Resources Needed	Desired Outcomes
Year 1	IEP goals for MLs with disabilities	ML and special education teachers will develop language learning goals for MLs with disabilities	Workshop 1 (in-person) -importance of language learning goals in IEPs Workshop 2 (in-person) -how to write language learning goals -best practices in goal writing Attendees: all special ed and ML staff	Sofia (ML Director) Marcus (Special Ed Director) Guest speaker	Workshop 1 -Meet biweekly to develop presentation -Gather redacted examples from IEPs -Consult book "IEPs for ELs" and integrate into presentation -Reserve room and email teachers Workshop 2 -Contact guest speaker -Process speaker honorarium -Reserve room and email teachers	Workshop 1 -Presentation slides, screen -Examples and non-examples of IEP language goals Workshop 2 -TBD (based on guest speaker's requests) -Honorarium	ML and special education teachers will write sample language learning goals for MLs with disabilities IEP teams will draft language learning goals prior to all spring IEP meetings. IEP goals will be shared with ML team lead of each school for feedback
Year 2							
Year 3							
Year 4							

Adapted from best practices featured in Hanover Research. (2023). *District leaders' guide for developing a professional learning plan.* https://www.hanoverresearch.com/reports-and-briefs/k-12-education/district-leaders-guide-for-developing-k-12-professional-learning-plan plans. To increase buy-in from district administrators, the professional learning tool prompts ML and special education leaders to situate professional learning trainings for MLs with disabilities into larger district objectives. Table 5.1 is an example of how district leaders may begin to set up a professional learning plan.

Response 2: Assess the Intersectional Competence of Teachers and Teacher Educators

As districts develop a plan for training inservice teachers, schools and colleges of education need to revamp our curricula for training language specialists and special educators. To gauge how well our teacher preparation programs are supporting the needs of students with intersecting minoritized identities, faculty should assess the intersectional competence (Boveda, 2016) of their teachers. According to Boveda and Aronson (2019), *intersectional competence* captures "teachers' understanding of diversity and how students', families', and colleagues' multiple sociocultural markers intersect in nuanced and complex ways" (p. 249). As a part of this body of research, Boveda has developed the Intersectional Competence Measure (ICM), a tool that can be utilized by teacher education faculty to evaluate "the readiness of special and general education preservice teachers to (a) collaborate with diverse families and colleagues and (b) serve a complex student population, including students with dis/abilities" (Boveda & Aronson, 2019, p. 250). Although the ICM addresses intersectional student populations in general, the insights gleaned from this tool can enable faculty to understand whether greater attention is needed in the curriculum to intersectional student groups, such as MLs with disabilities, and to the systems that impact these students' learning opportunities.

How can faculty assess the intersectional competence of our teacher preparation students without first examining our own? Building from the ICM, Boveda and Weinberg (2022) advocate for the use of the Intersectionally Conscious Collaboration Protocol for Teacher Educator (ICC-TE). ICC-TE, as they describe it, is a measure that raises faculty's awareness of intersectionality and its influence in all aspects of their work as teacher educators. In naming the key uses of ICC-TE, Boveda and Weinberg also identify its relevance for MLs with disabilities:

> The tool is intended to be used as [teacher educators] prepare preservice teachers to address interconnected equity concerns, such as meeting the needs of students with disabilities who are emergent bilinguals, which cannot be fully understood or addressed when considered in isolation. (p. 9)

Using this tool, faculty can increase our awareness of the systemic conditions that shape the experiences and learning opportunities of both K–12 students and teachers who represent multiple minoritized statuses. With this greater consciousness of intersectionality, our practices, curriculum, and programming in teacher education, outlined below, can shift in directions that are more inclusive and responsive to diversity in education.

Response 3: Create New or Refine Existing Programming

Once the skills of teachers and the content of courses have been assessed, teacher preparation programs should create *new programming*, whether individual courses, certificates, or degrees, that center MLs with disabilities. Designing new programs—as opposed to embedding content into existing programs—is vital, as (a) interdisciplinary programming remains in short supply, as evidenced in this chapter, and (b) it is challenging to squeeze additional content into coursework already chock-full of state-mandated competencies and concomitant topics. While writing this chapter, I was revising the syllabi for our ESL certification in response to a slew of new competencies required by the Pennsylvania Department of Education. Examining the syllabi, I felt a sense of dread, as adding in new topics means that other topics essential to the knowledge and skill set of language specialists will get short shrift. How can we add new content in the limited confines of the existing certifications? What content can be amplified, and what can be reduced? In the end, what is best for the teachers and students? These are the questions I wrestled with, and truthfully, I felt no sense of peace with the revisions. Yet, through multiple types of programs, we can fulfill a critical need in ML and special education. For instance, teacher preparation departments can create more traditional degrees or certifications or can develop new kinds of programming, including offering continuous education credits, forming short- and long-term district–university teacher education partnerships, and applying for federal or state training grants that enhance the interdisciplinary skillsets of teachers.

Faculty should also consider how preservice teachers from across several certifications can collaborate while supporting MLs with disabilities. For instance, this could occur in field placements at schools with higher numbers of MLs with disabilities as well as in after-school and extended school year programs attended by these students. A powerful example of one such program for teacher candidates can be found in Patricia Martínez-Álvarez's 2023 book, *Teaching Emergent Bilingual Students with Dis/abilities*. Significantly, changes to the state-mandated competencies and certification areas would enable universities to break out of the disciplinary boundaries that stymie more integrated preparation for teachers. The final recommended response to patterned inequities, therefore, targets the changes that should be instituted in state departments of education.

Response 4: Institute New Teacher Education Requirements

With state-mandated competencies and certification areas having a ripple effect on the offerings of teacher preparation programs, state leaders working in ML and special education offices are vitally important in reimagining the structures that perpetuate patterned inequities in the higher education sector. Equipped with the knowledge that interdisciplinary certifications and degrees are exceedingly rare, and supporting MLs with disabilities requires particular skills, state leaders should consider three teacher education initiatives. First, following in the footsteps of states like Illinois and Texas, departments of education should offer state-approved certification areas that emphasize interdisciplinary perspectives and skills, such as bilingual special education or integrated ESL–special education. Second, if developing full-scale certification areas is not feasible, ML and special education state leaders should collaborate on instituting courses or robust competencies in teacher preparation programs that focus on MLs with disabilities. State leaders will find Boveda's ICM, as described above, as well as the topics outlined in Figure 5.1, useful as they formulate specific competencies and consider course requirements. Third, state departments of education should spearhead initiatives that incentivize and support inservice teachers in accruing additional certifications through, for example, scholarships and grants. These initiatives would support inservice special educators and language specialists in pursuing bilingual/ESL certifications and special education certifications, respectively, and would dovetail with state initiatives to remedy the special education and language specialist teacher shortage facing many districts (see Najarro, 2023; Whittaker, 2023).

SUMMARY

With a focus on teacher education programs and certifications, this chapter unearthed two characteristics of patterned inequities that had yet to be discussed in the book thus far: they are *shared*, experienced by all stakeholders in education, and they are *pervasive*, spanning across all sectors of education, from schools and districts to universities and departments of education. Through an examination of the two tendencies in teacher preparation programs—that we train teachers and certify their credentials within the parameters of specific disciplines—we see unitary identity and the specialization trap take form in the context of higher education. In Chapter 2, to describe the interconnected nature of patterned inequities, I used the illustration of a plant whose shoots stretch downward, eventually touching the ground and forming new roots. In the same way, patterned inequities in teacher preparation programs then take root in districts and schools. As

Figure 5.1. Topics for ML with Disability Teacher Preparation Competencies

Special education referral and evaluation - *Services and supports within MTSS* - *Valid assessment practices* - *Use of multiple data sources*
Access to learning opportunities - *Dual-service provision* - *Maintenance of high expectations* - *Reduction of segregated, restrictive placements*
Pedagogical skills and practices - *Instructional strategies* - *Progress monitoring and data-based decision-making* - *Formative, summative, and authentic assessments*
Asset-based, growth-oriented mindsets - *Avoidance of deficit thinking* - *Identification of students' abilities* - *Multilingualism as a strength*
Instructional collaboration - *Coplanning objectives and lessons* - *Defined roles and responsibilities* - *Implementation of varied coteaching models*
Individualized plans, teams, and meetings - *Development of plans that account for "whole child"* - *Roles and responsibilities of team members* - *Engagement with parents, families, and students*
Transition planning and reclassification - *Creation of postsecondary transition plans* - *Interpretation of student data* - *Monitoring practices*

the final chapter on equity in systems, this chapter fittingly advocates for changes not just to the ways we organize schools (and students) for learning but also revisiting the ways we structure teacher preparation programs and the state-approved certifications that hold great sway over the educational opportunities afforded to in- and preservice teachers. Through the multisector responses to patterned inequities, MLs with disabilities can have expanded access to learning opportunities and their educational rights.

Part III

EQUITY IN CLASSROOMS

CHAPTER 6

High Expectations

So far, I have discussed the expansive influence of systems in shaping the learning opportunities of MLs with disabilities. Indeed, we see the ramifications of systemic conditions crop up in K–12 schools and higher education institutions. But systems alone are not the determinants of educational equity; teachers and their actions matter—and to a significant degree. For some, perhaps, the idea of teachers acting as agents of change conjures up images of heroism when, in fact, teachers' everyday actions can spark and sustain equity in systems. This is true for all teachers, even those who are at the very beginning of their careers.

One of my favorite studies drives this point home. Investigating the practices of novice teachers, Athanases and de Oliveira (2008) found that "the core site for teachers' advocacy work" (p. 77) was none other than the classroom. I have always been drawn to this study, featuring it as a required reading in my teacher education courses, because it showcases how teachers' actions *in* the classroom promoted equity even *beyond* the classroom. The teachers in the study believed that "to address equity, a teacher must first place learning of individual students at the center of teaching" (p. 91). Painted in broader strokes with teachers, equity starts in the classroom.

This is the central premise of the chapters on equity in classrooms. Here and in the chapters ahead, I address what I see as core practices that together emphasize the individual learning of MLs with disabilities and, in the process, enact equity. These core practices are (a) holding high expectations, (b) implementing rigorous instruction, and (c) interpreting and using data soundly (Figure 6.1). These practices are inextricably linked when promoting equity in the classroom. Should one be absent, the others invariably erode. A teacher may be trained in data-based decision-making, but if they have low expectations for certain students, they will very likely view student data through this lens. Likewise, a teacher may believe all students are capable of learning academically and developing multilingually, but this belief will not compensate for a lack of training in rigorous evidence-based practices (EBPs).

These three core practices are inarguably needed for all students, but I contend even more so for dually identified students. There are two reasons for this. First, as these chapters will elucidate, enacting these core practices for MLs with disabilities is complex and riddled with ambiguity. What does rigorous

Figure 6.1. Core Practices That Promote Equity in the Classroom

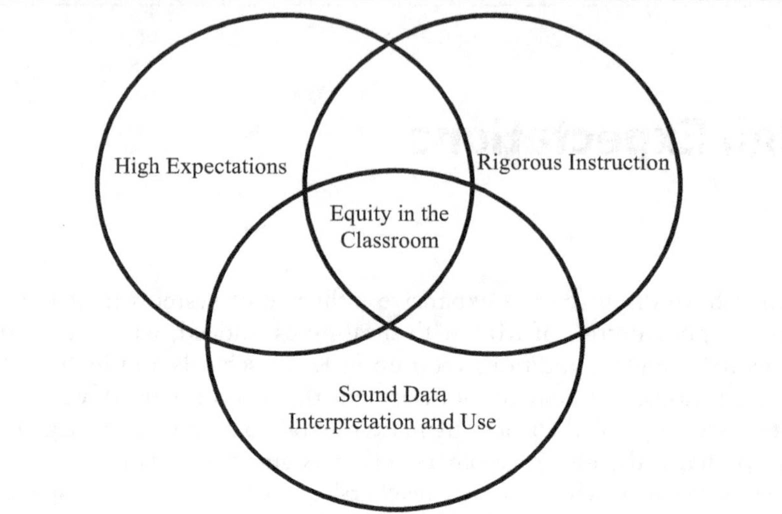

instruction look like for MLs with multiple disabilities? How can we interpret data reliably when language and disability can be so intertwined? How do we know if we have high expectations for all students? These are tough, essential questions with answers that cannot be reduced to simple typologies or checklists. Yet, we cannot shy away from these core practices because of the uncertainty that accompanies them. Second, these core practices are likely to be undermined by patterned inequities. Because of the intersection of language and disability, MLs with disabilities are more likely to be held to low expectations, receive fragmented instruction, and experience the fallout of questionable data interpretation practices (Cioè-Peña, 2020, 2021; Kangas, 2020, 2021; Martínez-Álvarez, 2023).

However, through the core practices featured in these three chapters, teachers act as change agents by elevating the learning of MLs with disabilities in ways that disrupt the influence of patterned inequities in the classroom. Smylie et al. (1999) admit that being an agent of change as a teacher is a messy endeavor:

> Expectations for teachers to promote student change, social change, and school change are long standing and firmly established. At the same time, they are ambiguous, dynamic, often contradictory, and contested. They present dilemmas that must be confronted and managed if teachers are to be effective agents of change. (p. 34)

The series of chapters on equity in classrooms address high expectations, rigorous instruction, and sound data interpretation and use, acknowledging the ambiguity and dilemmas teachers face when supporting MLs with disabilities but ultimately affirming that these core practices are indeed feasible in the everyday efforts of teachers. Underpinned by this understanding, the present chapter considers high expectations.

HIGH EXPECTATIONS: KEY RESEARCH FINDINGS

In architectural design, the keystone is the stone at the top of an arch, locking all the other pieces into place and allowing the structure to sustain its weight. Without it, the entire arch would crumble. Both as a researcher and teacher educator, I have come to see high expectations as a keystone for all other practices in the classroom. As we consider the everyday realities of K–12 teaching, it is challenging to identify a single best practice that can be enacted without high expectations; it is the practice that sustains all others.

Education research for some time has amplified the essentiality of teachers' expectations for their students. While some of this scholarship primarily conceptualizes teacher expectations as beliefs or mindsets toward students, other work emphasizes the actions and behaviors of teachers (e.g., Gentrup et al., 2020; Gershenson et al., 2016; Mayer et al., 2018; Rubie-Davies, 2007, 2014). Bridging these bodies of work, this book operates from the understanding that having high expectations is a combination of being and doing—with *being* encompassing the beliefs and mindsets teachers possess regarding their students and *doing* entailing their everyday practices. For MLs with disabilities, more specifically, *high expectations* are beliefs, practices, interactions, and decisions grounded in the understanding that they are capable and worthy of learning academically and growing linguistically.

Focusing on the *being* of high expectations, studies have examined teacher perceptions of students of color, documenting lower expectations for students who are Black or Latinx and yet higher expectations for Asian and White students (Demie, 2022; Gershenson et al., 2016; McConnochie, 2024; Wallace, 2023). Notably, one of these studies reported higher teacher expectations when there is a racial match between teachers and students of color (Gershenson et al., 2016). In terms of other identities, studies find evidence that teachers view students from lower socioeconomic backgrounds as less capable academically (Brandmiller et al., 2020; Doyle et al., 2023). Likewise, labels such as *ML* and *student with disability* often trigger lower expectations among teachers (Allday et al., 2011) even when these students performed similarly to their peers (Shifrer, 2013; Umansky & Dumont, 2021). This is of consequence because labeling and categorizing students are deeply ingrained practices in schools that shape students' sense of self, as Domina et al. (2023) describe: "Educational categories come to influence identity both by changing how students see themselves and by changing how others see them" (p. 93). For MLs with disabilities, this body of research underscores the pervasiveness and significance of low expectations coalescing around dimensions of their identities.

Focusing on the *doing* of high expectations, research has examined how expectations do not just remain a mindset but rather manifest in teachers' practices and interactions with students. Such research has probed the links, known as *teacher expectancy effects*, between teacher beliefs and pedagogical practices (Rubie-Davies, 2007), student self-concept (Friedrick et al., 2015), and student performance (Jamil et al., 2024; Kuklinski & Weinstein, 2000; van den Bergh et al., 2010). Teacher expectancy research gained traction in the mid-1960s following the well-known Pygmalion Effect experiment (Rosenthal, 2002; Rosenthal & Jacobson, 1966, 1968). In this experiment, teachers were told that certain students showed early signs of being intellectually advanced, as indicated by a nonverbal intelligence assessment, and were likely to make significant gains during the next several months (i.e., they would "bloom" or "sprout"). These students, in reality, were chosen at random and were otherwise intellectually similar to their peers. What the researchers observed was the following cycle. First, teachers formed differential expectations of their students based on whether they were identified as potentially advanced or not. Second, these expectations manifested in teachers' practice and interactions with students. Next, students believed by their teachers to be advanced internalized these expectations, and their performance on the same assessment months later shifted upwards. In short, teachers' expectations created a "self-fulfilling prophecy" (Rosenthal, 2002, p. 33).

Corroborating the Pygmalion Effect study, teacher expectancy effects have been observed in teachers' practices toward students of color, with teacher expectations explaining gaps in students' reading and mathematics performance (McKown & Weinstein, 2002, 2003; Padilla et al., 2022; van den Bergh et al., 2010). Offering plausible explanations for these gaps, contemporary research has probed the "black box" of teacher expectations, finding they translate into concrete practices, including the quality and quantity of feedback to students, management of and response to student behavior, opportunities for engagement in higher-order thinking and knowledge sharing, as well as recommendations for students to take more rigorous courses (Batruch et al., 2023; Campbell, 2012; Demie, 2022; Gentrup et al., 2020; Kanno, 2021; Rubie-Davies, 2007). In Rubie-Davies's (2007) study comparing the instructional practices of high-, average-, and low-expectation teachers, those with high expectations asked open-ended questions, readily praised students, and engaged in feedback on their learning. From these findings, Rubie-Davies argued that high-expectations teachers create academically robust and socioemotionally healthy learning environments for their students.

In all, the research underscores the being and doing of teacher expectations with two critical findings: First, low expectations are soberingly common for students with minoritized identities, and second, teachers' expectations are influential, shaping interactions and learning opportunities in the classroom. With this context, we now turn to the patterned inequity—the language-or-disability filter—that diminishes high expectations for MLs with disabilities and, by doing so, jeopardizes equity.

EVIDENCE OF PATTERNS

In one of my studies, I shadowed MLs with disabilities across all their academic classes. As these middle schoolers moved from class to class, it was striking to observe how their learning and behaviors shifted. One group of MLs with disabilities was considered unruly by most teachers, and across most of the day, learning was eclipsed by behavior management; however, in Mr. Evans's English language arts class, they were the ideal students: engaged, content, and even harmonious. When trying to make sense of this shift, I found that many likely explanations did not hold up. The class timing was not optimal; it was later in the day when students' energy levels and engagement commonly waned. The subject was not intrinsically motivating; in interviews with students, hardly anyone reported English language arts as their favorite subject, and many had SLDs in reading and writing, potentially making the class all the more undesirable. There were no differences in peer dynamics; the student composition of the class was the same. The only factor that was different was Mr. Evans. As I sat in his class, his high expectations and warmth were palpable. In one of the observations, Camila, Maria Elena, and Miguel, three focal students in the study, all worked diligently on their writing, as reflected in the fieldnotes:

> The students continue to read their warm-ups, and Mr. Evans said that he wished all of his classes wrote such great warm-ups. He said that only one or two students in his other classes write good responses, but the rest "stink." The students want to know whether they are his favorite class, and he said, "There's no doubt. You are my favorite class—by a mile." (Kangas & Cook, 2020, p. 2438)

In truth, I think about Mr. Evans quite a lot because he was a testament to the influence of high expectations. The MLs with disabilities in his class wanted to be there and were willing to work hard. Unlike in other classes where they spent little time engaging in academic learning and where teachers were observably frustrated with them, in Mr. Evans's class, learning was central and sustained throughout the class period, and his interactions with students implied they were competent and worthy of a challenge. While a "warm-up" in another class would take the entire class period, in Mr. Evans's class this was just the beginning of their learning. Aligning with what Rubie-Davies (2007) claims about high-expectation teachers, Mr. Evans created a classroom that was academically robust and socioemotionally healthy.

As we review research to date, Mr. Evans is, unfortunately, an outlier. In stark contrast, existing studies are woven together by a common thread—that high expectations for MLs with disabilities are too often hard to come by. Dually identified students are often viewed as a collection of deficits, encompassing academic aptitude, language skills and practices, and emotional and behavioral capacity, and these views reify in teachers' actions (Cioè-Peña, 2020, 2021; Kangas, 2020; Kangas & Cook, 2020; Martínez-Álvarez, 2023).

The prevalence of this deficit lens for MLs with disabilities spurred my initial conceptualization of the language-or-disability filter. In my studies, I found that when there was a perceived problem—regardless of what it might be—in the learning of an ML with a disability, educators traced the source to either language or disability and not to any shortcomings in the learning environment. In interviews with teachers, low academic assessment scores were commonly viewed through the language-or-disability filter, but so were ELP levels, class grades, reclassification rates, challenging behaviors, low engagement and motivation, chronic absenteeism, and graduation rates. As we reflect on this list, surely the genesis of all these problems cannot be language or disability alone, and yet this filter became the go-to "explanatory tool for a wide range of issues" (Kangas, 2021, p. 675). So entrenched was the understanding in schools that L2 learning and disabilities were inhibitors to learning that when MLs with disabilities succeeded, it was not recognized, highlighting the glaringly depressed expectations for these students. The case of Dimitrios, a hardworking ML with multiple disabilities, demonstrates this point. Although he earned honor roll every single marking period and was a model student in his classes, Dimitrios's teachers attributed his achievements to the accommodations provided in the classrooms, as illuminated in this exchange in an interview:

> *Mrs. Redding:* Um, he [Dimitrios] had, marking period one he actually had above a 100% because he did do some extra credit work.
> *Kangas:* That's awesome.
> *Mrs. Redding:* Um. Yes. Now, again, this is an adapted class.
> (Kangas & Cook, 2020, p. 2438)

For Dimitrios, because his language and disability were viewed as problems, low expectations for his learning abounded, even when his performance pointed to the contrary.

As another telling example, during a professional development workshop, one teacher shared that after she noticed an increase in an ML with a disability's ELP, she questioned whether the student was accurately identified with a disability. Although this issue of erroneous identification of MLs with disabilities is a real concern, her perspective illuminated the dismal expectations for students with disabilities, as disability was understood only as an inhibitor, dragging down the assessment scores of MLs.

The deficit lens of the language-or-disability filter unearths, first, the deep-seated nature of low expectations and their entanglement with linguicism, ableism, and racism in schooling, and second, their harmful impacts on MLs with disabilities. In Park's (2023) study of Luciano, a kindergarten ML with an SLI who was undergoing an evaluation for special education eligibility, she observed how, very early on, he was positioned as a problem. Luciano was often physically restrained and removed from the general education classroom. Despite having displayed similar behaviors as Luciano, White children with autism in the same school did not experience the use of physical restraint and removal. Park argued that racism and ableism together promoted the stance that Luciano, because of *his* behaviors, was incapable of being in a general education setting. Factors external to Luciano in the learning environment were not, however, examined.

Perceived deficiencies stemming from language, disability, and race, and the low expectations they conjure, also extend to the families and communities of MLs with disabilities. In Cioè-Peña's (2021) study, she documented how Latina mothers of MLs with disabilities were positioned as culpable for the perceived accumulated deficits of their children. Specifically, the language practices and cognitive abilities of these children were seen as broken in ways that connected deeply to their racial identities and disabilities, and mothers were often dissuaded from enrolling their children in bilingual programs. From Park's and Cioè-Peña's studies, we see that often, as children of color, MLs with disabilities—and their families by extension—are considered nonnormative, and consequently, expectations for these students' learning and their access to certain settings shrink. This mimics the patterned inequities explored in Chapter 3, with students' perceived greatest deficit—either language learning or disability—setting into motion their subsequent learning opportunities in terms of their services and physical placements.

These studies also point to a larger complicated reality in education for MLs with disabilities: language and disability are racialized (Annamma et al., 2013; Flores & Rosa, 2015; Phuong & Cioè-Peña, 2022; Rosa & Flores, 2017). Rosa and Flores (2017), in theorizing *raciolinguistics*, assert that language and race are "co-naturalized," so enmeshed with one another in contemporary society that they become impossible to parse. As such, even when MLs produce language that is considered standard American English, their language practices are still discredited as deficient because of their racial identities (Flores & Rosa, 2015). Making parallel arguments, Annamma et al. (2013), in their conceptualization of *disability critical race studies* (DisCrit) describe an analogous relationship between disability and race. They attest that the intellect, emotions, language, and behaviors of children of color are pathologized, seen as a deviation from the accepted norm. Race and ability are comingled in the education school system, so much so that "for students of color, race does not exist outside of ability and ability does not exist outside of race" (p. 6).

Knowing this, the deficit-based views of language and disability in the language-or-disability filter cannot be disambiguated from deficit-based views of race. Intertwined, ableism, linguicism, and racism engender expectations that MLs with disabilities cannot excel academically or grow in their multilingual proficiency. This mindset shapes the pedagogical practices and decision-making of educators. In a study of mine, MLs with disabilities enrolled in a dual language school were predominately taught in English because bilingual instruction was thought to be too taxing for them, and they were considered in many respects "languageless" (see Kangas, 2017a). In a separate study of an English-only school, the content taught in the general education classes was far below grade level. As an example, during an observation of an 8th-grade English language arts class, the MLs with disabilities were asked to identify a personal goal and then trace the hand of a classmate, writing inside each finger one sentence that described how they would achieve their goal. The fieldnotes read:

> [The teacher] explains, "List in detail the beginning steps you can take right now to begin achieving your goal." She explained the list of three steps that she would take to help her meet her goal of organizing her home. She reminded the students to not "be cheap," as the steps need to "fill the whole finger" and include details about the steps they will take. She then directed them to write a summarizing sentence on the palm. (Kangas, 2020, p. 277)

This task for soon-to-be high schoolers to write just five to six sentences about their goals was a precipitous drop from grade-level standards in English language arts to "write clear and focused text to convey a well-defined perspective and appropriate content" (Pennsylvania Department of Education, 2020, Standard Area—CC.1.4). Implicit in such tasks are low expectations for a class filled with students of color "with labels." From these collective findings, we see that when language and disability are seen as problems, low expectations and constrained learning opportunities naturally follow. Cultivating high expectations is then the keystone for promoting equity in the classroom.

RESPONSES TO PATTERNED INEQUITIES IN TEACHER EXPECTATIONS

As we seek to shift expectations upward for MLs with disabilities, I find the notion of educational dignity (Espinoza et al., 2020; Poza, 2021) a useful guide. *Educational dignity* is a framework that centers and affirms the humanity, value, and potential of each child in learning (Espinoza et al.,

2020). Through an educational dignity framework, teachers can embody both the being and doing of high expectations as they see and respond to their MLs with disabilities as whole, capable persons. The recommendations offered below are steps teachers can take to embody high expectations in their mindsets and practices as a pathway for advancing equity in their classrooms.

Response 1: Push Beyond the Labels and Stereotypes

As demonstrated in this chapter, the dual labels assigned to MLs with disabilities often give rise to deficit thinking. To push beyond limiting labels and stereotypes, scholarship calls upon teachers to know the whole child and consider the assets they bring to their learning (Herrera et al., 2023; Martínez-Álvarez, 2023). The well-known study by Moll et al. (1992) illuminated the strengths-based insights a group of teachers in Arizona gained about their Mexican students through home visits. As the teachers observed these families in their homes, they uncovered their *funds of knowledge* (FoK), the "historically accumulated and culturally developed bodies of knowledge and skills essential for household or individual functioning and well-being" (p. 133). The children had unique knowledge and skills relating to agriculture, religion, medicine, construction, and economics, among many other domains, that would not have surfaced during the school day. By learning more about the lives of their students outside of school, the teachers in the study expanded their awareness of students' assets and utilized this knowledge as a bridge to learning.

Overall, FoK rests on two interrelated premises that align with the educational dignity framework: first, that all children possess a reservoir of capabilities, skills, and knowledge that they have accumulated through their life experiences; and second, that FoK can and should be recognized and leveraged in students' learning in schools (González et al., 1995; González et al., 2005; Moll et al., 1992). Emphatically, uncovering FoK rests on first-hand personal encounters with students and their families (Moll et al., 1992). For MLs with disabilities who are commonly defined by what they lack—what they do not know and cannot do—becoming familiar with their FoK is vital. Put differently, we need to see MLs with disabilities and their families as whole and to understand more about all they know and can do. This resonates with more humanistic approaches to the education of MLs with disabilities that espouse a relational approach to supporting these students, built on personal knowledge of them and their communities (Herrera et al., 2023; Martínez-Álvarez, 2023). For instance, Herrera and colleagues (2023) propose *biography-driven instruction* for culturally and linguistically diverse learners with disabilities, which "centralizes the sociocultural, linguistic, cognitive, and academic dimensions of the learners' biography" (p. 11).

How, then, can teachers uncover the FoK of MLs with disabilities? Aside from home visits, which are often not feasible for most, teachers can utilize more sustainable, structured approaches like community walks, student and parent surveys, and class projects, essays, or presentations that inquire about and draw upon community histories, values, and practices. In some districts, there are family engagement groups geared specifically for the needs and interests of ML families, for example, multilingual parent advisory councils (e.g., MLPACs). Teachers who participate and partner with these groups, commonly comprising parents and community members, will develop a clearer understanding of the FoK their MLs bring to school. Less structured approaches, such as inviting MLs with disabilities to lunch, are equally important for forming fuller asset-based knowledge of the students. As teachers nurture deeper knowledge of MLs with disabilities as full individuals and of the resources and capabilities they bring to learning, high expectations are a natural outcome.

Response 2: Connect Deeper With ML Parents and Families

Because expectations for MLs with disabilities are interwoven with expectations of their families and communities, moving toward educational dignity entails deeper connections between schools and families. With the everyday pressures facing both teachers and families alike, fostering the home–school relationship can seem idealistic; however, some practices require a low investment yet can yield many gains.

As a foundational practice, teachers should seek to expand communication with ML families. For MLs, translating correspondence as much as possible should be a given. As a parent of a school-aged child, I often observe how district and school communications are available in English and sometimes Spanish but no other languages. Knowing that many families in the district speak Arabic, for example, I wonder how these parents can possibly stay informed and engaged. Regardless of the measures districts take to communicate with families, teachers can ensure that their communications with families are inclusive. With a multitude of translating apps, it is easier than ever for communication, whether sent digitally or physically, to be in the home language of the student.

Another critical practice is ensuring the comprehensibility of the communication of meetings with families. While securing interpreters for meetings with parents is a moral and legal imperative, being aware that the linguistic register of the meeting can be obscure is equally critical. In Chapter 4, we learned how IEP meetings are often inaccessible to ML parents because they still too often are conducted in English and are commonly so riddled with educational jargon that even when an interpreter is present, the content of the meeting is incomprehensible to parents (Salas, 2004; Voulgarides, 2018). These findings often generalize to other school-based meetings (e.g., parent–teacher conferences, information sessions). As a parent, I recall sitting in a meeting last year about my child's performance in school. Presented with a lengthy report and an endless number of acronyms (e.g., DIBELS, IXL, WISC) and assessment scale scores, even as a professor in education I found the entire process overwhelming.

To promote family members' understanding during meetings, the EPIC model—Explain, Provide, Inquire, and Coordinate—introduced in Chapter 4 offers a useful guide to teachers. This model (Chang et al., 2022), originally developed to increase ML parents' knowledge and engagement in IEP meetings, can readily be adapted for any school–family meeting. The model centers on four key practices—explaining, providing, inquiring, and coordinating—that educators should implement before, during, and following a meeting with families. For example, because some ML families may not be familiar with the U.S. school system, teachers should: *explain* the procedures of the meeting and the family's role, *provide* an agenda and relevant student data ahead of the meeting, *inquire* about concerns of the family, and *coordinate* scheduling the meeting with families. More details of the EPIC model can be found in Chapter 4.

Communication with families should not occur only when there is a concern or problem, as is often the case in schools. To forge more positive relationships with families, teachers could once every month pick a few students whose parents will receive a positive update about their children's learning, efforts, or citizenship in school. The message can be short—just a sentence or two—but should acknowledge the child by name, allowing a more personal connection to be formed. Taking it a step further, teachers should consider making a personal goal of getting to know one or two ML families each year. An informal interview or extended parent–teacher conference will allow teachers to understand more about the family, pushing beyond surface-level understandings of them and giving insight into their culture and language practices. Earlier, I offered participation in a family engagement group as a powerful opportunity to learn of the FoK among ML communities. Such groups can also provide the opportunity for teachers to deepen their appreciation of the concerns and dreams families have for their children.

Response 3: Do High Expectations

The prior recommendations have principally addressed the *being* of high expectations, but as research documents, *doing* high expectations should be evident in classrooms where educational dignity is an aim. Teachers who have high expectations for their students tend to provide ample quality feedback to students, positively manage and respond to student behavior, and build opportunities for higher-order thinking and knowledge sharing (Demie, 2022; Gentrup et al., 2020; Rubie-Davies, 2007, 2014). Notably, these high-expectation practices are also considered rigorous EBPs that support both MLs and students with disabilities alike, further underscoring the overlapping nature of the core practices needed to promote equity in the classrooms (see Figure 6.1). Chapter 7 delves into rigorous instruction for MLs with disabilities, directly addressing recommendations for managing and responding to student behavior. This chapter, then, invites teachers to consider doing high expectations in the quality and quantity of feedback they provide to MLs with disabilities as well as the opportunities they create for higher-order thinking and knowledge sharing. Both offer a two-fold benefit: expanding learning and communicating to MLs with disabilities that they are worthy and capable.

Take, for instance, teacher feedback. The feedback teachers provide their students can be understood as a powerful instructional tool, allowing students to understand how their learning is progressing. At the same time, the extent to which teachers provide students feedback communicates implicitly their dedication to and belief in students' learning. In other words, if a teacher does not think a student can utilize feedback to learn, there will be little motivation to provide such feedback. As I will share in greater detail in Chapter 7, I have too often observed MLs with disabilities receiving an abundance of feedback on their behaviors and emotions but less on their learning. While it is true that in ML and special education, feedback also encompasses other critical knowledge and skills, such as corrective feedback on language errors (see Russell Valezy & Spada, 2006) and behaviors and emotional regulation (see Aceves & Kennedy, 2024), I argue that given the prevalence of low expectations for MLs with disabilities, they need ample positive feedback on their *academic learning*, both to inform them of their progress and to communicate the expectation that they are capable of growth. Teachers wishing to enhance their feedback skills should consider the recommended resources provided at the end of the chapter.

As another higher-expectation practice, higher-order thinking and knowledge sharing fulfill the same benefits for students. In the earlier cited observation of 8th-grade MLs with disabilities tracing their hands and writing basic sentences, we can see these students are engaging in learning that emphasizes skills lower in *Bloom's Revised Taxonomy of Higher Order Thinking* (Anderson & Krathwohl, 2001), such as remembering and summarizing. In contrast, opportunities for higher-order thinking through analysis, evaluation, and creation in the classroom can have an expansive influence, promoting learning opportunities and distilling a clear sense within students that they can do challenging work. Likewise, when MLs with disabilities are positioned as generators and holders of knowledge (i.e., FoK), they can engage in deeper learning and take on a strength-based view of their own experiences, abilities, and skills. In this way, when teachers do high expectations, their MLs with disabilities reap multiple learning benefits and experience an education marked by dignity. Recommended resources on higher-order thinking and knowledge sharing can be found at the end of the chapter.

SUMMARY

This chapter explored high expectations as the first of three core practices necessary to promote equity in the classroom. Envisaging high expectations as a matter of both being and doing, I argue that it entails the belief that all MLs with disabilities are capable and worthy of learning academically and growing linguistically, as well as practices, interactions, and decisions predicated on this belief. The chapter documents that high expectations are eroded by one patterned inequity: the language-or-disability filter. Making the case that low expectations are inherent to the deficit lens, I examine how language and disability are viewed as sources of the alleged deficiencies MLs with disabilities possess in ways that are enmeshed with their racial identities. Grounded in an educational dignity approach, the chapter concludes by offering recommendations for the being and doing of high expectations. With a focus on FoK and family engagement, it invites teachers to evaluate deeply and seriously how they see MLs with disabilities and their families. At the same time, it encourages teachers to attend to their instruction and interactions, with the understanding that teachers' practices can expand or constrict learning opportunities of their dually identified students while also implicitly communicating their beliefs about these students' capabilities.

RECOMMENDED RESOURCES

On Feedback

Brookhart, S. M. (2017). *How to give effective feedback to your students* (2nd ed). ASCD.

Hattie, J., & Clarke, S. (2018). *Visible learning: Feedback*. Routledge.

Walsh, J. A. (2022). *Questioning for formative feedback: A meaningful dialogue to improving learning*. ASCD.

On Higher-Order Thinking

Rubie-Davies, C. M. (2014). *Becoming a high expectation teacher: Raising the bar*. Routledge.

Saifer, S. (2024). *Teaching higher-order thinking to young learners, K–3: Develop sharp minds for the disinformation age*. Routledge.

Stanley, T. (2020). *Promoting rigor through higher level questioning: Practical strategies for developing students' critical thinking*. Routledge.

On Knowledge Sharing

González, N., Moll., L. C., & Amanti, C. (2005). *Funds of knowledge: Theorizing practices in households, communities, and classrooms*. Routledge.

Herrera, S. G., Rodríguez, D., Cabral, R. N., & Holmes, M. A. (2023). *Equitable and inclusive teaching for diverse learners with disabilities: A biography driven approach*. Teachers College Press.

Walsh, J. A. (2021). *Empowering students as questioners: Skills, strategies, and structures to realize the potential of every learner*. Corwin.

CHAPTER 7

Rigorous Instruction

Frederick Erickson, the renowned education anthropologist, theorized that generalizable insights in education can derive from *the particular*—an idea he referred to as *concrete universals* (Erickson, 1986). For example, as we observe particular classrooms, particular students and teachers, and particular instructional practices, we can learn universal "insights that transcend the situation from which they emerge" (Merriam, 1995, p. 58). This is a comforting notion as we consider pedagogical practices that support MLs with disabilities. For this heterogenous population, there is much to account for during instruction: prior schooling experiences; multilingual skills and proficiencies; academic, behavioral, and social strengths and needs; personal histories of trauma and resilience; among many other factors. Such multifaceted differences make defining *rigorous instruction* for MLs with disabilities a complex endeavor. Effective instructional practices for an ML with a visual impairment, for instance, may yield meager results for an ML with ADHD. In writing this chapter on rigorous instruction, the prospect of summarizing the vast array of effective pedagogical approaches that can be used to support this diverse group of students admittedly had a dizzying effect on me; that would be an entire book onto itself.

However, having observed countless classrooms with dually identified students of diverse backgrounds, capabilities, and needs, I have found concrete universals in instruction take form. Irrespective of the particular ML with disability, three universals of rigorous instruction hold constant: (a) it is evidence-based, (b) it responds to the whole child, and (c) it is grounded in the belief that they are capable. This chapter contends that all teachers, regardless of their roles, can promote equity for MLs with disabilities in the classroom by ensuring their praxis embodies these universals. With this understanding, below is an overview of the key research findings of rigorous instruction.

RIGOROUS INSTRUCTION: KEY RESEARCH FINDINGS

When I was a doctoral student, I originally wanted to investigate pedagogical practices for my dissertation research. Early on in my program, I eagerly searched library databases for relevant books and articles on pedagogy for dually identified students, but I was flummoxed when my searches yielded little, with few studies turning up. With the gift of experience, now as a professor, when my doctoral students conduct similar searches that result in just a handful of publications, I reassure them such outcomes are an indicator that research for MLs with disabilities is still in its infancy. This is painfully the case for instructional practices. While scholarship has made some headway in identifying promising pedagogical practices for MLs with disabilities, its status has remained static: profoundly underresearched and scattered. At best, to form an initial understanding of "what works" for MLs with disabilities, we can look at two veins of research: one on high-leverage practices (HLPs) and the other on intervention efficacy.

For the past 20 years, professional organizations and researchers in general education and special education have developed HLPs, collective sets of practices that all teachers can—and should—implement. In special education, for example, 22 essential HLPs that all teachers should implement to support students with disabilities have been identified (Aceves & Kennedy, 2024). Developed by the Council for Exceptional Children (CEC) and Collaboration for Effective Educator Development, Accountability, and Reform (CEEDAR) Center, these HLPs are an amalgamation of foundational EBPs directly drawn from a body of empirical studies and vetted by experts in the field (Aceves & Kennedy, 2024). HLPs are grouped into broader categories of collaboration, instruction, assessment, and social/emotional/behavioral (see Table 7.1).

In ML education, organizations and researchers have yet to coalesce around a definitive set of HLPs, although, with the emergence of HLPs in both general education and then special education in the past 15 years, ML education will likely forge its own very soon. In the meantime, however, there are independent and yet largely overlapping frameworks, such as *The 6 Principles for Exemplary Teaching of English Learners* (TESOL International, 2018) and *High-Leverage Principles of Effective Instruction for English Learners* (Chang et al., 2017), each emphasizing several broad practices (e.g., build upon students' background knowledge, monitor and assess language development). *The Sheltered Immersion Observation Protocol (SIOP) Model* (Echevarría et al., 2024) outlines a more detailed list of 30 empirically based practices—what they refer to as *features*—that together support MLs. Much like HLPs, these features fall under the major categories, such as lesson preparation, instruction, and assessment, among others (see Table 7.2). While critiques of SIOP exist (see Crawford & Reyes, 2015; Daniel & Conlin, 2015), at present, this model is arguably the closest approximation to a framework of HLPs for MLs.

Critically, the aforementioned frameworks in special and ML education limitedly address the unique instructional considerations at the intersection language learning and disability. The 2024 edition of *High-Leverage*

Table 7.1. HLPs for Students with Disabilities

Collaboration	1. Collaborate with professionals to increase student success 2. Organize and facilitate effective meetings with professionals and families 3. Collaborate with families to support student learning and secure needed services
Assessment	4. Use multiple sources of information to develop a comprehensive understanding of a student's strengths and needs 5. Interpret and communicate assessment information with stakeholders to collaboratively design and implement educational programs 6. Use student assessment data, analyze instructional practices, and make necessary adjustments that improve student outcomes
Social/ emotional/ behavioral	7. Establish a consistent, organized, and respectful learning environment 8. Provide positive and constructive feedback to guide students' learning and behavior 9. Teach social behaviors 10. Conduct functional behavioral assessments to develop individual student behavior support plans
Instruction	11. Identify and prioritize long- and short-term learning goals 12. Systematically design instruction toward a specific learning goal 13. Adapt curriculum tasks and materials for specific learning goals 14. Teach cognitive and metacognitive strategies to support learning and independence 15. Provide scaffolded supports 16. Use explicit instruction 17. Use flexible grouping 18. Use strategies to promote active student engagement 19. Use assistive and instructional technologies 20. Provide intensive instruction 21. Teach students to maintain and generalize new learning across time and settings 22. Provide positive and constructive feedback to guide students' learning and behavior

Source: Aceves, T. C., & Kennedy, M. J. (Eds.) (2024). *High-leverage practices for students with disabilities* (2nd ed.) Council for Exceptional Children and CEEDAR Center.

Table 7.2. SIOP Features for MLs

Lesson Preparation	1. Clearly define, display, and review content objectives with students 2. Clearly define, display, and review language objectives with students 3. Choose content concepts appropriate for age and educational background level of students 4. Use supplementary materials to a high degree, making the lesson clear and meaningful 5. Adapt content to all levels of student proficiency 6. Plan meaningful activities that integrate lesson concepts with language practice opportunities for reading, writing, listening, and/or speaking
Building Background	7. Explicitly link concepts to students' backgrounds and experiences 8. Explicitly link past learning and new concepts 9. Emphasize key vocabulary
Comprehensible Input	10. Use speech appropriate for students' proficiency levels 11. Explain academic tasks clearly 12. Use a variety of techniques to make content concepts clear
Strategies	13. Provide ample opportunities for students to use learning strategies 14. Use scaffolding techniques consistently, assisting and supporting student understanding 15. Use a variety of questions or tasks that promote higher order thinking skills
Interaction	16. Provide frequent opportunities for interaction and discussion between teacher/student and among students, which encourage elaborated responses 17. Use group configurations that support language and content objectives of the lesson 18. Provide sufficient wait time for student responses consistently 19. Give ample opportunities for student to clarify key concepts in L1 20. Provide hands-on materials and/or manipulatives for students to practice using new content knowledge 21. Provide activities for students to apply content and language knowledge in the classroom 22. Provide activities that integrate all language skills

(continued)

Lesson Delivery	23. Support content objectives clearly 24. Support language objectives clearly 25. Engage students approximately 90–100% of the period 26. Pace the lesson appropriately to the students' ability levels
Assessment	27. Give a comprehensive review of key vocabulary 28. Give a comprehensive review of key content concepts 29. Provide feedback to students regularly on their output 30. Conduct assessments of student comprehension and learning throughout lesson on all lesson objectives

Source: Echevarría, J., Vogt, M., Short, D. J., & Toppel, K. (2024). *Making content comprehensible for multilingual learners: The SIOP model* (6th ed.). Pearson.

Practices for Students with Disabilities integrated connections to culturally inclusive pedagogies and intersectional identities, making the case that HLPs are for *all* students, not just those with disabilities (see Aceves & Kennedy, 2024). The framework argues that HLPs are compatible with culturally inclusive pedagogies, but teachers drawing upon this framework are largely left to their own devices to figure out how they can be culturally and linguistically inclusive as they implement HLPs. Likewise, the latest edition of SIOP (Echevarría et al., 2024) includes considerations for its implementation within MTSS, but the needs of neurodivergent MLs remain overlooked.

Research that squarely addresses evidence-based instruction for dually identified students examines the efficacy of discrete interventions. Such studies for MLs with identified or suspected disabilities have been increasing in recent years (e.g., Capin et al., 2024; Luevano & Collins, 2020; Powell et al., 2020; Sanford et al., 2020; Vaughn et al., 2019; Williams & Vaughn, 2020; Xin et al., 2020), as a response to the reported lower academic performance of these students. In this vein of research, studies predominately examine interventions for reading, mathematics, and vocabulary development, probing whether students make gains after the interventions' implementation. While intervention studies are needed and valuable—we need to know what works and to what degree—in my research, I have often wondered about the effects of isolated interventions when couched in the context of poor instructional practices. Put in different words, a 30-minute intervention can only be so effective if the remainder of the student's day is awash with low-quality instruction. Ensuring rigorous instruction throughout the entirety of the school day is paramount for dually identified students, and yet, patterned inequities work against two of the pedagogical universals: responding to the whole child and believing they are capable. Chapter 6 addresses high expectations in detail, while this chapter delves into teaching and supporting the whole child—a universal of rigorous instruction undercut by unitary identity and the specialization trap.

EVIDENCE OF PATTERNS

Unitary Identity

When unitary identity manifests in the classroom, it often comes in the form of pedagogy. As this patterned inequity takes hold, we will observe language specialists teaching MLs with disabilities as if they have no disability at all. Likewise, we may notice special educators and related service providers supporting MLs with disabilities just as they would for monolingual English-speaking children with disabilities. In short, instruction can often be "business-as-usual," providing support for just one set of needs.

In my school-based studies, I observed that as MLs with disabilities move from one classroom to the next, so, too, do their identities shift. The instruction they were provided in one space by one teacher would render them primarily students with disabilities, but then later, with another teacher, they would become language learners. This metamorphosis through instruction was striking. As an example, Ms. Kleinfeld, a middle school teacher in one of my studies, was a remarkable special educator by many accounts. She cotaught with general education teachers, and in their classrooms, she provided targeted support that embodied many of the HLPs for students with disabilities. I observed her adapt learning materials (HLP 13), provide one-on-one intensive instruction (HLP 20), and teach social behaviors (HLP 9), all while prioritizing IEP goals (HLP 11) for Maria Elena, Camila, and Miguel, the three MLs with disabilities in her class. When I interviewed these students, they identified Ms. Kleinfeld as one of the teachers who supported them the most by explaining ideas and helping them regulate their emotions when they were having a "bad day" (Kangas & Cook, 2023, p. 328). Attending to their language learning needs was another matter, even though the three students had significant differences in their ELP levels and skills. These needs were attended to during the students' ESL class with Mr. Salvatino, one of the school's language specialists. There, he emphasized students' skills in four language domains (SIOP Feature 22), explicitly taught and highlighted key vocabulary (SIOP Feature 9), and ensured his speech was comprehensible to the many MLs in his class (SIOP Feature 10). He was also an outlier in the study in that he was one of the few bilingual teachers who incorporated Spanish, the students' L1, into the classroom, particularly by clarifying concepts in the L1 (SIOP Feature 19). However, as our analysis of observations indicated, he did not attend to the specially designed instruction identified in the MLs with disabilities' IEPs. In sum, although many of the teachers' pedagogical practices were evidence-based, they did not address the intersecting needs of the children—a universal of rigorous instruction.

In a separate study, I discovered more entrenched instances of unitary identity. Mrs. Avery, an ESL teacher, shared that she did not support the disability-related needs of MLs during instruction because she was not privy to the contents of their IEPs. She explained: "So, when they went to special ed., they took care of their needs there. So, I didn't really know outside of like, observing myself what they might have been lacking in" (Kangas, 2017a, p. 268). Her counterparts in special education similarly asserted that they did not support language learning of MLs when they were providing push-in instruction, and relatedly, they had little understanding of ELP levels. Not possessing this fundamental knowledge of their dually identified students, teachers addressed the needs with which they were most familiar and that they felt most equipped to support. Erasure of the fuller identities of MLs with disabilities in instruction is a problem of practice that extends beyond the findings from my studies, as echoed in the numerous calls from scholars to utilize intersectional lenses that see the whole child and instructional practices that respond accordingly (Cioè-Peña, 2021; García & Tyler, 2010; Martínez-Álvarez, 2023; Ortiz et al., 2020; Spies & Cheatham, 2018; Thorius et al., 2018). Reflected in this scholarship, we see that the positioning of MLs with disabilities as if they possessed a singular identity did not occur in a vacuum but was enmeshed with service provision contexts demarcated by the specialization trap.

Specialization Trap

When pedagogical practices take up a unitary identity approach, a driving force behind it is the specialization trap. Take, for instance, the daily schedules of MLs with disabilities and their physical placements in classrooms: When they are ordered around a singular identity, it is usually for the purpose of providing specialized instruction. In Chapter 3, I shared the findings from one of my studies wherein MLs with disabilities were placed into what the school staff called "SPELL" rooms (i.e., special education + ELL). This segregated placement for nearly all students with disabilities—ML or not—allowed a specialist, in this case, a special education teacher, to provide instructional support for the students' disabilities as they learned academic content. By design, the instruction MLs with disabilities received was responsive to their disabilities, but as the chapter documented, at the cost of their language development. While MLs with disabilities were in the SPELL rooms receiving specially designed instruction, their ML counterparts without disabilities were placed in separate rooms supported by language specialists. In this example, the specialization trap promoted a fragmented approach to instruction whereby specific needs could only be addressed by a single specialist, and to accomplish this, students were physically organized into classrooms centering around a unitary identity. In this way, patterned inequities are both co-occurring, fueling the existence of the other and enmeshed with larger provision systems in schools.

In her book exploring an after-school program serving MLs with disabilities, Martínez-Álvarez (2023) discusses the entrenched specialist-driven approaches to instruction in special education: "The apparently highly specialized knowledge that has invaded the world of special education makes other teachers feel unprepared to work with children with a disability" (p. 81). In contrast to the specialization trap, Martínez-Álvarez further implores teachers to take up "humanistic approaches" (p. 81) that value and are responsive to the whole child and thus are more inclusive.

Yet such holistic approaches go against the grain of predominant models of teacher education and training, which emphasize specialization (e.g., mild to moderate disabilities, sheltered English immersion, etc.). In Chapter 5, we canvassed teacher licensure requirements across the United States, finding that only two states offered professional certifications that integrated special education and bilingual education/ESL. Moreover, we discovered a dearth of teacher preparation programs emphasizing the intersectional knowledge and skills needed to support MLs with disabilities—a lack likely stemming from state licensure requirements. The recourse for most teachers interested in the intersection of special education and ML education is to pursue separate certifications—an often time-consuming and potentially financially burdensome endeavor.

Because of these trends, teachers are trained largely along the professional boundaries corresponding to their specialization, even though this does not map onto the reality of today's classrooms or its learners. As an example, Park (2019) conducted an in-depth study of two schools' Response to Intervention (RtI) models for MLs with suspected disabilities. The findings indicated that infusing English language instruction within Tier 1 of RtI—which is necessary for ruling out English proficiency as a contributor for special education referral—proved challenging for teachers because they lacked the resources and training to do so. Through observations of classrooms and firsthand accounts from teachers, additional evidence of the specialization trap surfaces in pedagogy (e.g., Kangas, 2014; Kangas & Cook, 2023; Migliarini & Stinson, 2021). In these studies, there was a documented mismatch between the instructional practices MLs with disabilities needed and the instruction they received, often occurring along professional boundaries, with instruction responding to just one need, as if the others did not exist or were immaterial to students' learning.

RESPONSES TO PATTERNED INEQUITIES IN INSTRUCTION

In Migliarini and Stinson's (2021) study, a teacher spoke of the challenges of meeting the instructional needs of her students, powerfully sharing: "It almost takes a superhero to differentiate" (p. 82). Indeed, those reading this chapter may question the feasibility of supporting the multiple needs of dually identified students, let alone the needs of *all* their students. This chapter does not ask teachers to develop superpowers, but rather through manageable targeted recommendations for their praxis, invites them to work toward instruction that is responsive to the whole student and maintains footing in evidence—two of the three universals of rigorous instruction.

Response 1: Understand Shared EBPs

While EBPs for MLs and students with disabilities are by no means identical, some practices are certainly shared between the two—a point often overlooked in teacher education and training. Earlier I introduced HLPs (Aceves & Kennedy, 2024) and the SIOP Model (Echevarría et al., 2024), both of which offer EBPs for supporting students with disabilities and MLs, respectively. While these frameworks have been developed and fine-tuned over the past 10 to 20 years, their similarities and differences have yet to be examined. Understanding what practices converge and diverge across these frameworks is a foundational step for teachers seeking to promote rigorous instruction that supports the whole child.

In our comparison of these pedagogical frameworks, we found several critical practices common to both ML and special education, instances of *pedagogical convergence* (Figure 7.1). In contrast, we also found points of *pedagogical divergence*, practices unique to either ML or special education. Both offer pathways for teachers seeking to enhance their support of MLs with disabilities, as shared EBPs should be routine in the practices of all teachers, while practices unique to ML and special education are fodder for additional training and support for teachers.

For pedagogical convergence, there are five shared practices across these frameworks:

1. Using explicit instruction
2. Teaching cognitive and metacognitive strategies
3. Implementing scaffolds
4. Creating and leveraging student grouping
5. Promoting active student engagement

Digging beyond the surface, there are some nuances and complexities worth noting. First, though presented here as a list of separate practices, several of these practices are interrelated (Aceves & Kennedy, 2024; Archer & Hughes, 2011). For example, explicit instruction can be utilized to teach cognitive and metacognitive learning strategies (e.g., inferencing, summarizing, visualizing). Further, scaffolds are often conceptualized as a fundamental component of explicit instruction, enabling the student to move toward greater independence during learning (Archer & Hughes, 2011). Regardless of their relationship to one another, these pedagogical practices are fundamental and thus should be staples in the praxis of teachers (Aceves & Kennedy, 2024). Second, some of these shared EBPs more squarely overlap, while others display slight but critical variation. Teaching cognitive and metacognitive strategies and promoting active student engagement, for example, take on largely the same meaning and practice in the classroom. Using explicit instruction, implementing scaffolds, and creating and leveraging student grouping, however, are shared EBPs that have subtle differences that matter for implementation. Take student grouping: Teachers who thoughtfully use student grouping for MLs during learning may compose groups of MLs with the same ELP levels to facilitate differentiation or create groups with MLs who share the same L1 to foster MLs' translanguaging. Leveraging student grouping for students with disabilities may take the form of small groups that allow for more intensive explicit instruction in decoding skills in reading or for the administration of classroom-based assessments that require accommodations.

There are additional practices within the HLP framework that do not converge and yet could generalize to other student groups—a key argument made by Aceves and Kennedy (2024) in their recently updated HLP text. For example, several HLPs emphasize collaboration with professionals and families as essential practices (HLPs 1–3). Highlighted in Chapter 3, such collaborative practices are useful for all students but especially for MLs with disabilities whose needs are often compartmentalized through piecemeal approaches to service provision and instruction. These practices, however, are omitted from Figure 7.1.

Reflecting pedagogical divergence, some practices are unique to either ML or special education (Figure 7.1). For MLs, these practices generally target the creation of linguistically rich and comprehensible (i.e., understandable) classroom environments that will support their language learning, such as: (a) creating language objectives; (b) allowing sufficient wait time; (c) utilizing the L1 to clarify concepts; and (d) integrating all four language domains into instruction (i.e., listening, speaking, reading, writing), among several others (Echevarría et al., 2024; SIOP Features 2, 18, 19, 22). For students with disabilities, unique practices coalesce around supporting students' progress toward their IEP goals as well as their social, emotional, and behavioral needs. For instance, supporting students with disabilities requires that teachers: (a) provide positive feedback on students' learning and behaviors; (b) teach social behaviors; (c) design instruction and adapt materials to support individual learning goals; and (d) use assistive technologies,

Figure 7.1. Comparison of Pedagogical Frameworks

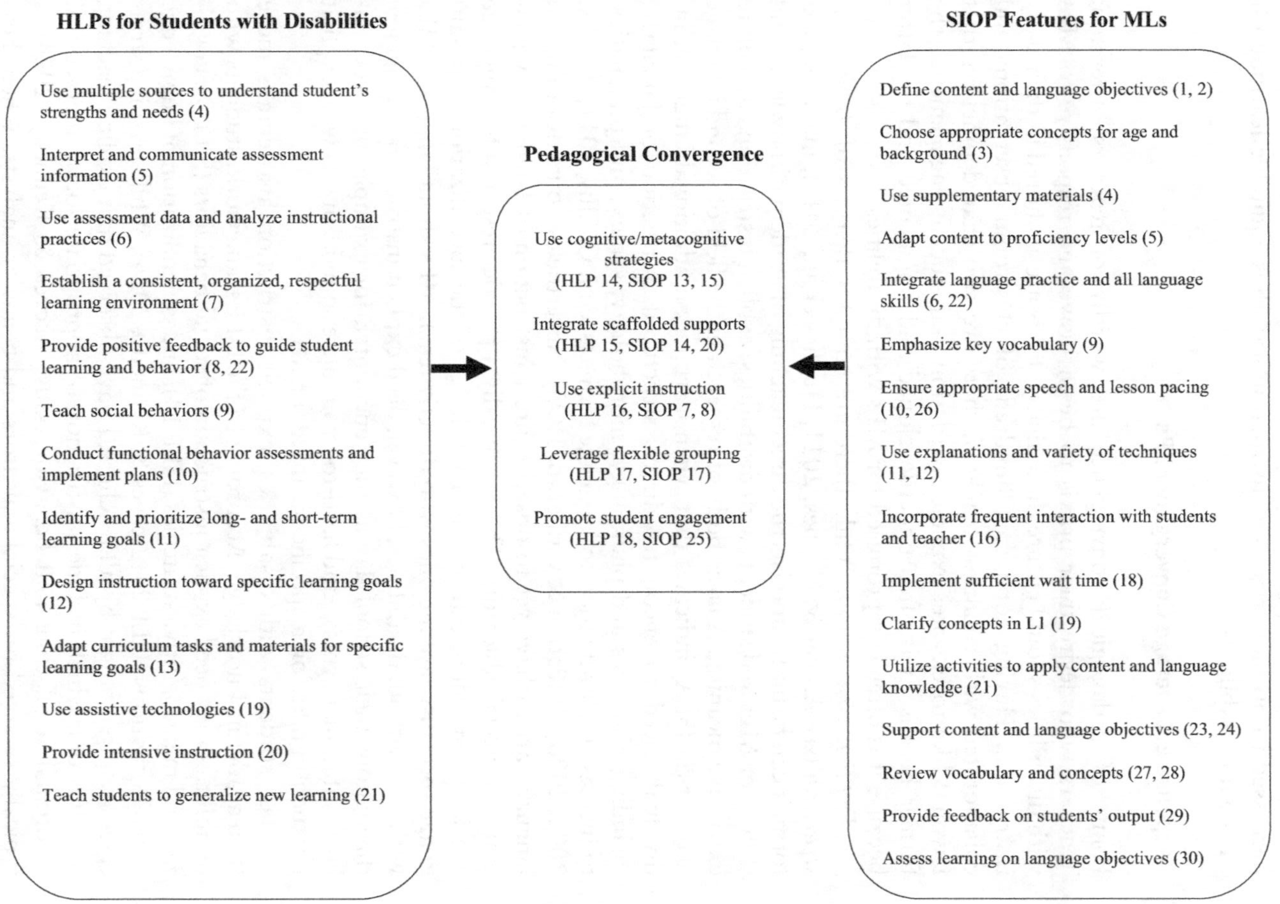

HLPs for Students with Disabilities

Use multiple sources to understand student's strengths and needs (4)

Interpret and communicate assessment information (5)

Use assessment data and analyze instructional practices (6)

Establish a consistent, organized, respectful learning environment (7)

Provide positive feedback to guide student learning and behavior (8, 22)

Teach social behaviors (9)

Conduct functional behavior assessments and implement plans (10)

Identify and prioritize long- and short-term learning goals (11)

Design instruction toward specific learning goals (12)

Adapt curriculum tasks and materials for specific learning goals (13)

Use assistive technologies (19)

Provide intensive instruction (20)

Teach students to generalize new learning (21)

Pedagogical Convergence

Use cognitive/metacognitive strategies (HLP 14, SIOP 13, 15)

Integrate scaffolded supports (HLP 15, SIOP 14, 20)

Use explicit instruction (HLP 16, SIOP 7, 8)

Leverage flexible grouping (HLP 17, SIOP 17)

Promote student engagement (HLP 18, SIOP 25)

SIOP Features for MLs

Define content and language objectives (1, 2)

Choose appropriate concepts for age and background (3)

Use supplementary materials (4)

Adapt content to proficiency levels (5)

Integrate language practice and all language skills (6, 22)

Emphasize key vocabulary (9)

Ensure appropriate speech and lesson pacing (10, 26)

Use explanations and variety of techniques (11, 12)

Incorporate frequent interaction with students and teacher (16)

Implement sufficient wait time (18)

Clarify concepts in L1 (19)

Utilize activities to apply content and language knowledge (21)

Support content and language objectives (23, 24)

Review vocabulary and concepts (27, 28)

Provide feedback on students' output (29)

Assess learning on language objectives (30)

etc. (Aceves & Kennedy, 2024; HLPs 8, 9, 12, 13, 19). In the recommendations that follow, I address how converging and diverging practices can be harnessed to promote rigorous instruction and thus equitable learning for MLs with disabilities.

Response 2: Leverage Converging EBPs

Points of pedagogical convergence are worthy of teachers' attention. Teachers who desire their praxis to be inclusive and responsive to MLs with disabilities should ensure these shared EBPs are anchored in their daily instruction. Having conducted hundreds of classroom observations and collaborated with countless teachers, there are two shared practices that I would like to elevate: explicit instruction and student engagement—the former because it is often underdeveloped and fragmented and the latter because it is often compromised for MLs with disabilities.

Explicit Instruction. While there are complex theories of *explicit instruction* (see Archer & Hughes, 2011; Hughes et al., 2017), in its simplest form, it can be understood as the direct teaching of academic knowledge and skills. For MLs and students with disabilities, explicit instruction has a more expansive meaning. A large body of research in the field of second language acquisition (SLA) indicates that when learning an additional language, individuals need to encounter direct, structured instruction of language, including phonetics and phonology, morphology, syntax, and pragmatics, to increase their attention to language forms (see N. C. Ellis, 2011; R. Ellis, 2002, 2008; VanPatten & Cadierno, 1993). Nevertheless, outside of English language arts, I have yet to observe direct instruction of language by general and special educators. This is typically a practice reserved for language specialists in schools; in the inner workings of the specialization trap, language specialists are the ones who directly teach MLs about language. MLs with and without disabilities, however, need explicit instruction of language throughout their school day as they encounter, for example, new vocabulary, unfamiliar syntax, and hard-to-pronounce sounds. In this way, explicit instruction takes on a specific meaning for MLs.

For students with disabilities, explicit instruction also entails more than academic knowledge. According to the HLP framework, students with disabilities may need explicit instruction of social behaviors (HLP 9), cognitive and metacognitive strategies (HLP 14), and generalization of knowledge to new situations (HLP 21; Aceves & Kennedy, 2024). While learning strategies are often taught by all teachers, I have observed that explicit teaching of behaviors, which includes instruction of appropriate social interactions, emotional regulation, and behavior skills (Aceves & Kennedy, 2024) is typically reserved for special educators and behavior analysts. When these individuals are not present, I observed MLs with autism and ADHD not receiving targeted instruction and support for their behaviors even though it was critical for their own and others' learning. This dynamic is emblematic of the specialization trap: a fragmented approach to support. Beyond behavior, students with disabilities may require explicit instruction to apply previously learned skills and knowledge to novel situations (HLP 21; Aceves & Kennedy, 2024). For example, in 1st grade, teachers may need to explicitly link the skill of *prediction*, previously used while reading short stories to a new science unit on light, wherein they will *predict* which objects will let in or block out light. In sum, explicit instruction encompasses a broader range of knowledge and skills that can easily be overlooked and yet, as a shared EBP in ML and special education, is foundational for MLs with disabilities.

Student Engagement. In both HLPs and SIOP frameworks, student engagement is positioned as critical for student learning of academics and language. *Student engagement* can be one of those "you know it when you see it" sort of constructs; however, in the literature student engagement is historically understood as a combination of student investment and behavior during learning (Finn & Zimmer, 2012).

In my studies to date, student engagement is among those practices that are routinely given up for MLs with disabilities. In one study, MLs with disabilities spent the majority of their class periods completing individual "make-up" work on their laptops without engagement in learning or with their peers. It was staggering how often the students sat in silence completing busywork: During 59 observations of core academic classes and pullout services (i.e., ESL, reading interventions), we observed only eight instances of active, collaborative learning (Kangas & Cook, 2020). For one group of 8th graders in the study, active engagement, especially through group tasks and projects, was not a foundational practice but deemed a privilege for classes that were "well-behaved"—a point of frustration voiced by two focal MLs with disabilities in the study.

Through a comparison of the HLPs and SIOP frameworks, I discussed five shared EBPs. By emphasizing these shared practices, this chapter by no means suggests that (a) language services and supports are interchangeable with those of special education or that (b) these practices alone will suffice for MLs with disabilities. In their well-known article, de Jong and Harper (2005) challenge the notion that "just good teaching" (JGT), universal practices that support all students, is sufficient for supporting MLs; there are distinct practices that extend beyond JGT to respond to the cultural and linguistic backgrounds of the MLs. Here, I take a similar stance: Implementing shared EPBs for MLs with disabilities is the floor—not the ceiling—for promoting equity in instruction. There are specific knowledge and skills (i.e., points of pedagogical divergence) that teachers need to cultivate in their praxis to support dually identified students as whole children. I address this knowledge and these skills in the remaining recommendations.

Response 3: Build Teachers' Capacity in Creating Linguistically Rich Classrooms

In my role as a teacher educator, I teach a foundational course in ML education. For the pre- and inservice teachers studying elementary, secondary, and special education in the course, this is their primary exposure to the fundamentals of supporting MLs. Knowing we only have one semester, I focus on the building blocks of creating linguistically rich classrooms. Indeed, in reviewing the instances of pedagogical divergence across the two frameworks, I find that many of those for MLs cannot be accomplished without (a) understanding language proficiency, (b) creating and working toward language objectives, and (c) promoting quality language input and interaction. Thus, these practices are most worthy of teachers' energies as they chart their own professional learning and continuing education.

Understanding ELP. Holistically supporting MLs with disabilities requires that each teacher—not just language specialists—understand ELP. The ELP levels of most MLs are determined by an annual standardized ELP assessment, such as the WIDA ACCESS, ELPA21 Summative, etc. For MLs with complex support needs, their ELP level may be determined by an Alternate ELP assessment. These levels or scores should be readily accessible in district and school data management systems, but if not, the school's language specialist should supply these data. Once teachers have access to their MLs' ELP levels or scores, understanding the MLs' performance in the four domains of language (i.e., listening, speaking, reading, writing) is critical; MLs may perform considerably higher or lower in certain domains, as we found in our recent study examining the ELP scores of MLs with disabilities. On the whole, dually identified students performed lowest in speaking and reading but higher in listening, with writing falling in between (see Kangas & Ruiz, in press). A single score, however, would not have conveyed such nuances. As teachers review the ELP scores of their MLs with and without disabilities, it is also important to know that these scores are only one piece of evidence; teachers should consult with their language specialist colleagues about additional ELP data from formative assessments, projects, assignments, and classroom observations, to name a few.

Once teachers know the ELP levels of their MLs, understanding what each level means is critical. I will often hear language specialists say: "He's a Level 2" or "I have a lot of Level 3s in this class." While fundamental, these levels can be opaque to their general and special education counterparts. Teachers often need more concrete knowledge of what these levels look and sound like in the classroom. ELP assessment developers have created companion resources, such as ELP standards, for teachers to utilize to deepen their understanding of each proficiency level. As an example, in WIDA states, teachers can consult the *WIDA English Language Development Standards Framework* (2020), while in ELPA21 states, there is the Council of Chief

State School Officers' *ELP Standards* (2014). Such frameworks commonly provide grade-specific descriptions of what MLs can accomplish across proficiency levels, which is useful for setting objectives and implementing instructional support for MLs in the classroom, as will be discussed next.

Creating and Working Toward Language Objectives. During their teacher preparation program, teachers become well-versed in writing learning objectives and designing their lessons to meet them. In ML education, learning objectives come in two interrelated veins: *content objectives*, aimed at content knowledge and skills, and *language objectives*, targeting the ways they will use language and the knowledge of the language system they require (see SIOP Features 2, 22–24). All teachers should have both content and language objectives identified for their MLs. For MLs with and without disabilities, language objectives can fall by the wayside in the specialization trap. Because there is no point throughout the day at which language learning ceases for MLs, working toward language objectives should be routine for all teachers.

While the practice of writing airtight prescribed learning objectives is often confined to teacher education courses, teachers should have, at a minimum, measurable language objectives or goals for their MLs that are grounded in students' ELP levels (or in bilingual schools, bilingual proficiencies) and aligned with content learning. For general and special educator teachers, your language specialist colleagues can offer helpful recommendations for areas of growth for MLs. For some MLs, specific language domains may be critical for their growth, while for others, specific grammatical knowledge may be needed. Beyond consultation with colleagues, teachers will find the ELP standards are useful resources for developing language objectives or goals, as these standards often provide descriptions of the language knowledge and skills, linking them to grade-level standards. Specifically, teachers can use the descriptions featured in these standards as the basis of their language objectives. A sixth-grade teacher, for instance, could use Standard 6–8.6 in the CCSSO's ELP Standards (2014), "An ELL can analyze and critique the arguments of others orally and in writing" (p. 24), to craft the following language objectives by ELP level:

Level 2: MLs will *identify* the author's argument by writing three to four sentences that accurately describe the argument.

Level 3: MLs will *explain* the author's argument by writing three to four sentences that accurately describe the argument in their own words.

Level 4: MLs will *explain and analyze* the validity of the author's argument by writing a paragraph that accurately describes the argument and the quality of its evidence.

By having language objectives or goals established for MLs with and without disabilities, each teacher can ensure that their praxis is responding to the child's language learning needs. A list of resources on developing well-aligned language and content objectives is provided at the conclusion of the chapter.

Promoting Quality Language Input and Interaction. In the first recommendation, I emphasized the importance of active engagement for MLs with disabilities—an EBP shared by both ML and special education. This recommendation dovetails with promoting quality language exposure (i.e., input) and interaction. Although we know from empirical evidence and even our first-hand experiences with language learning that one cannot learn a language without rich input and extended opportunities for interaction and producing language (i.e., output; Gibbons, 2014; Krashen, 1985; Swain, 1985; Walqui, 2006; Walqui et al., 2025), my studies have found that MLs with disabilities are often in linguistically poor environments (Kangas, 2017a; Kangas & Cook, 2023). In addition to working in silence, MLs with disabilities were in classrooms dominated by behavior management discourse, leaving little opportunity for robust linguistic exposure and interaction. In short, MLs with disabilities were in classrooms where language was stripped down to the bone. Not even the best language services can compensate for the deficiencies of such learning environments.

To bolster the quality of language in the learning environment, teachers should embrace *linguistic amplification* (Walqui, 1992), practices that elucidate and enrich the meaning of language in the classroom to facilitate MLs' comprehension. Examples of linguistic amplification include but are not limited to: repeating the language in alternate forms; coupling written text with oral language input; and checking on MLs' comprehension. Importantly, linguistically rich classrooms for MLs with disabilities should not shy away from the L1. An emerging line of scholarship has emphasized the importance of integrating translanguaging practices to affirm the linguistic backgrounds, support multilingual development, and deepen content knowledge of dually identified students (Cioè-Peña, 2022; Padía et al., 2024; Pryzmus & Alvarado, 2019).

Teachers wishing to ensure rigor in their pedagogy for dually identified students should consider evaluating the language practices in their classrooms through such observation and coaching tools as the SIOP Observation Protocol (Echevarría et al., 2024), Danielson's Framework for Teaching (2013), and Marzano Framework (see August & Blackburn, 2019). Using these tools, teachers can ascertain areas of strength and improvement for enriching the language in the classroom. A list of observation tools can be found at the end of the chapter.

Response 4: Build Teachers' Capacity to Support Students' Goals and Social, Emotional, and Behavioral Needs

Countering the fragmented approach by which special educators and other related service providers support disability, all educators need an expanded capacity to respond to disability and thus move toward the universals of rigorous instruction: using EBPs and responding to the whole child. Based on my classroom observations, the following are worthy starting points for expanding their praxis for MLs with disabilities: (a) understanding and working toward individualized goals and (b) supporting the social, emotional, and behavioral needs of students.

Understanding and Working Toward Goals. Just as understanding the ELP of MLs with disabilities is a building block for responsive pedagogy, so is understanding the goals enumerated in their IEPs. While this may appear rudimentary, language specialists have a history of limited participation in IEP teams, despite the federal mandate to do so (U.S. Departments of Justice & Education, 2015). In even more baffling circumstances, language specialists may not even have access to their MLs' IEPs, as recalled in the earlier example from my study. Any efforts by these teachers to support the disability-related needs of MLs are incidental at best. Despite this gap in practice, knowing and working toward MLs' individualized goals throughout the day is critical for MLs with disabilities' overall success.

Paralleling my earlier argument, as the ELP needs of MLs with disabilities do not fade in and out across the day (i.e., unitary identity), likewise, the individualized goals of these students should not go on the proverbial back burner whenever the special education teacher or other specialist leaves the room. To take a step toward responsive instruction, general educators and language specialists should consult with their special education colleagues and the remainder of the IEP team regarding the goals that can be addressed through their instruction. Given that many MLs have identified SLDs in reading, they likely have goals that can be naturally incorporated into and emphasized during language services. Such an example includes the following goal of an ML with an SLD in reading, mathematics, and written expression: "When given a writing prompt or writing assignment, the student will use correct grammar and sentence formation while maintaining focus on the prompt . . ." Some goals, however, may need to be targeted by specific individuals during designated times (e.g., content-area instruction, social skills, intensive reading intervention). An ML with an SLD in mathematics may have goals that can primarily be addressed during mathematics and possibly science (e.g., "When given curriculum-based assessments, the student will demonstrate her understanding of computation, estimation, and problem solving . . ."). Understanding which goals can be shared among teachers and other specialists requires that IEP teams discuss goals and their interface with each service and content area. As districts make improvements in the authentic inclusion of language specialists in IEP teams, keeping MLs' individualized goals at the fore during language instruction can be more easily accomplished. A list of recommended resources on IEPs for MLs with disabilities is provided at the end of Chapter 4.

Improving Support for Social, Emotional, and Behavioral Needs. Across my observations of classrooms, one critical pedagogical finding stands out: In classrooms where the social, emotional, and behavioral (SEB) needs of students are unmet, learning suffers. In interviews with language specialists and general education teachers, they shared how they felt ill-equipped to support the SEB needs of their students with disabilities. This is no surprise, given that many teachers do not receive this training outside the context of specialized programs (i.e., special education, behavior analysis, social-emotional wellness).

Now more than ever, however, teachers need a solid foundation of skills in social–emotional learning. In the wake of COVID, recent estimates indicate that 75% of high school students in the United States have had one or more *adverse childhood experiences* (ACEs; Anderson et al., 2022), traumatic events or experiences that occur in childhood and adolescence (U.S. Centers for Disease Control and Prevention, 2024). ACEs among school-aged children are correlated with lower academic performance, increased problem behavior, and poorer mental health (Blodgett & Lanigan, 2018; Crouch et al., 2019; Myat Zaw et al., 2022). In the ML population, ACEs are common among refugees and recent arrivals who are fleeing crises in their home countries (Ertanir et al., 2023). In my most recent study, ESL teachers reported that ACEs, especially among their secondary MLs with disabilities, were prevalent and increasingly challenging for them to support. They relayed the difficulty of focusing on academic and language learning when MLs with disabilities had such pressing SEB needs. With ACEs on the rise, language specialists and general education teachers, in particular, should consider focusing their future continuing education on social–emotional learning.

Closely tied to SEB, it is vital that teachers gain in-depth knowledge of providing positive, constructive feedback to all students regarding their behaviors (HLP 8, 22). Having an individualized or schoolwide positive behavior support system in place is insufficient if teachers are inadequately supported in its fundamentals. As I previously discussed, many of the MLs with disabilities in my studies were in learning environments heavily reliant on punishment. Consider the earlier example from my study where I found MLs with disabilities sitting most of their school day in silence. The 8th-grade MLs with disabilities, in particular, were barred from interactive learning opportunities, such as group work, in many of their classes. Although seen as a preventative measure to preserve learning, this ironically had the inverse effect, decreasing students' engagement and opportunities to interact in the language. This practice was implemented in contravention of the schools' larger positive behavior support systems. Moreover, in my ethnographic studies, supporting behavior was a practice reserved for special educators, and consequently, instruction would often grind to a halt when they were not present.

When they possess the essential knowledge of positive behavior support, teachers can more effectively enact the supports identified in students' individualized behavior plans as well as implement classwide plans that foster a welcoming, well-functioning learning environment. Gaining practice in the fundamentals of positive behavior support, such as introducing positive reinforcement, emphasizing structure and organization in the classroom, and teaching SEB norms and skills, can be transformative for teachers (Center on Positive Behavior Support and Interventions, 2024). Through increased capacity to support and respond to student behavior, opportunities to learn for MLs with disabilities can expand as academic content and student engagement take center stage.

SUMMARY

In this second chapter on addressing equity in classrooms, we turned our attention to rigorous instruction. I began the chapter by describing the three universals of rigorous instruction for all MLs with disabilities: it is evidence-based, responds to the whole child, and is grounded in the belief that they are capable. Countering the first two universals, unitary identity and the specialization trap work in tandem in pedagogical practices, resulting in fragmented instruction for MLs with disabilities. After documenting these patterned inequities, the chapter introduces two frameworks of EBPs—HLPs (Aceves & Kennedy, 2024) and SIOP (Echevarría et al., 2024)—used in special education and ML education. By comparing these two frameworks, the chapter offers teachers points of pedagogical convergence and divergence, proffering that converging EBPs are foundational and thus should be implemented in the praxis of all teachers, while diverging EBPs should be the basis for teachers' ongoing professional learning both in and outside their districts and schools. To support teachers in making such equitable changes, the chapter supplies readers with recommended resources for expanding their pedagogical capacities.

RECOMMENDED RESOURCES

On Language Objectives and Language-Rich Classrooms

Ellevation. (n.d.). Crafting language objectives for English language learners (ELLs). *Ellevation Blog*. https://ellevationeducation.com/blog/crafting-language-objectives-support-english-language-learners-ells

Gibbons, P. (2014). *Scaffolding language, scaffolding learning: Teaching English language learners in the mainstream classroom* (2nd ed.). Heinemann.

Himmel, J. (2012). *Language objectives: The key to effective content area instruction for English learners.* ¡Colorín Colorado! https://www.colorincolorado.org/article/language-objectives-key-effective-content-area-instruction-english-learners

Walqui, A., Bunch, G., & Mueller, P. (Eds.) (2025). *Amplifying the curriculum: Designing quality learning opportunities for English learners* (2nd ed.). Teachers College Press.

On ML Observation Frameworks

Danielson, C. (2013). *The Framework.* The Danielson Group. https://www.danielsongroup.org/framework/

Echevarría, J., Vogt, M., Short, D. J., & Toppel, K. (2024). *Making content comprehensible for multilingual learners: The SIOP model* (6th ed.). Pearson.

On Social-Emotional Learning and Positive Behavior Support

Center on PBIS. (2024). *Supporting and responding to students' social, emotional, and behavioral needs: Evidence-based practices for educators.* Center on PBIS, University of Oregon. https://www.pbis.org/resource/supporting-and-responding-to-behavior-evidence-based-classroom-strategies-for-teachers

Fenner, D. S., & Teich, M. (2024). *Social emotional learning for multilingual learners.* Corwin.

Frey, N., Douglas, F., & Smith, D. (2022). *The social-emotional learning playbook: A guide to student and teacher well-being.* Corwin.

Simonsen, B., & Meyers, D. (2015). *Classwide positive behavior interventions and supports: A guide to proactive classroom management.* The Guilford Press.

CHAPTER 8

Sound Data Interpretation and Use

In K–12 education, teachers are charged with making data-based decisions that not only guide their instructional practices in the classroom but also determine future learning opportunities for students. For instance, teachers review reading benchmarks and use those scores to provide differentiated phonics instruction. Consulting course grades and standardized content assessment scores, teachers also make recommendations for students' placements into academic tracks. Given a portfolio of evaluation evidence, teams of teachers and specialists determine whether students need special education and related services. In the everyday practice of teachers, there are many decisions to make and even more data to review.

Despite its prominence in praxis, data-based decision-making comes with two layered and unsettling realities that education research and practice are just beginning to confront meaningfully. First, few teachers are adequately trained to read and understand student performance data. This gap in knowledge connects intimately to teacher education programs, which, especially for ML education, tend to give limited attention to assessment, and to inservice professional learning that rarely provide further robust training in this regard. Second, data for MLs with disabilities are complex, at best, and inconclusive and unactionable, at worst. We know that in education, it is possible to be data-rich but information-poor. If there was one population for which this was true, it would be MLs with disabilities. Many factors render this so, as this chapter will explore. Nevertheless, decisions still need to be made in the education of dually identified students, and they do need to have a firm grounding in data.

This final chapter on equity in the classroom addresses the core equitable practice of sound data interpretation and use for MLs with disabilities, taking on the complexity and murkiness that accompanies student performance data at the intersection of multilingualism and disability. I entitled this chapter *Sound Data Interpretation and Use*, as opposed to *Evidence-Based Decision-Making,* to foreground both the complicated nature of data at the nexus of language learning and disability and teachers' critical role in making sense of it. More simply, for MLs with disabilities, making decisions based on evidence is more complex than just looking at the evidence. The chapter offers a pathway through the mire, arguing for the possibility of seeing and

Figure 8.1. Elements of Sound Data Interpretation and Use

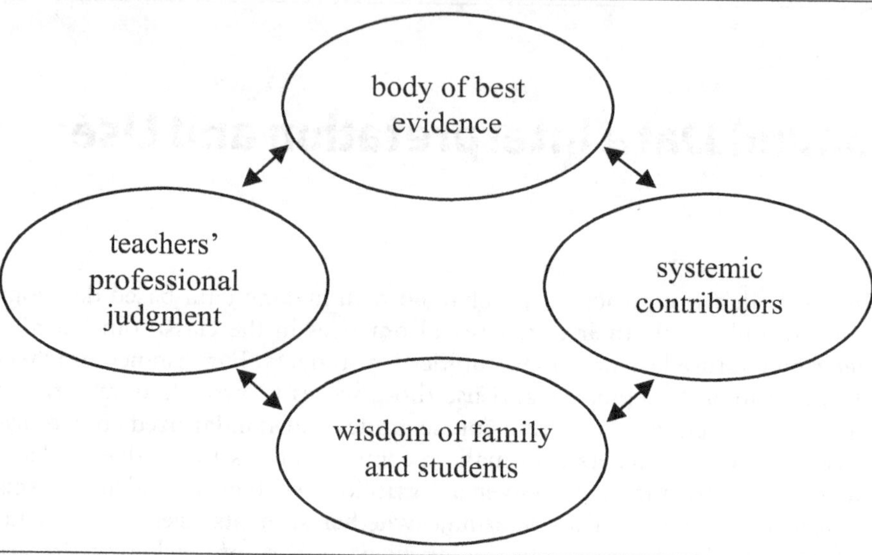

using data soundly—meaning logically and validly. To do so, I build on the National Center for Systemic Improvement's (2018) framework for evidence-based intervention selection and implementation, positing that viewing and acting upon data with soundness for MLs with disabilities requires considering (a) the best possible body of evidence, (b) systemic contributors, (c) wisdom and goals of students and their families, and (d) professional judgment of teachers (Figure 8.1), each of which is addressed in the prior research reviewed below.

SOUND INTERPRETATION AND USE OF DATA: KEY RESEARCH FINDINGS

Much of what we know about the use of evidence in making decisions regarding dually identified students is derived from MTSS, specifically RtI, scholarship. Collectively, this research has pointed to the importance of three of the four elements to guide interventions, instructional decisions, and high-stakes decisions for MLs, such as referral to special education.

Regarding the first element, the *best possible evidence*, RtI scholarship resoundingly echoes the same message: A body of complementary data is needed to understand how dually identified students are performing academically and linguistically (Collier, 2011; Esparza Brown & Ault, 2015; Haas & Esparza Brown, 2019). This body of data can include assessments (standardized, summative, or formative), class projects and grades, running records, writing samples, and teacher observation, among many other sources. This research also emphasizes three critical biases that can undercut the validity of data for MLs with identified and suspected disabilities. First, if used, standardized assessments and other psychological measures must be validated for the ML population—a perennial issue that continues to compromise the accuracy of data (see Project ELITE, Project ESTRE²LLA, & Project REME, 2015). Second, English-only academic performance data can introduce confounds during progress monitoring (Hoover, 2008) because these data may capture MLs' skills in English—and not their academic knowledge. Thus, in many instances, bi- and multilingual data are necessary to develop a complete portrait of the MLs' academic performance (Esparza Brown & Ault, 2015; Swanson et al., 2020). Even these data, at times, do not yield surefire answers, as some commercially developed assessments in MLs' home language can also underestimate their abilities compared to more authentic language assessments (Macswan & Rolstad, 2006). Finally, some data, such as classroom observations or teacher reports, may be collected nonsystematically and thus be tainted with bias (Estrada & Wang, 2018; Hill et al., 2014).

Addressing the second element, *systemic contributors*, RtI research also calls attention to the importance of examining the quality of the learning environment surrounding the child (Collier, 2011; Esparza Brown & Ault, 2015; Haas & Esparza Brown, 2019; Klingner & Geisler, 2008). Underscoring this point, Hoover (2008) asserts that inequitable opportunity to learn can be a central barrier to fair and nonbiased progress monitoring. As we consider the systemic barriers MLs with disabilities experience in accessing learning opportunities as well as the poor-quality instruction they often receive, as documented in prior chapters, Hoover's assertion rings true. Without examining the learning opportunities afforded to MLs with disabilities, whether in terms of instructional quality, efficacy of interventions, or access to services, teachers cannot rule out whether these opportunities are resulting in the performance trends they observe in the data of MLs with disabilities.

RtI research acknowledges the importance of the third element, *families*, although to a lesser extent. In this literature, parents are seen as serving a dual role: They are partners in high-stakes decision-making and experts on their own children, offering valuable insights and data (Project LEE, Project ELLIPSES, & Project ELITE, 2021; Roseberry-McKibbin, 2021). In terms of the latter, parents and other family members can offer unique perspectives into their children's educational history as well as capabilities in the home language. In terms of the former, parents are vital stakeholders in any RtI system implemented in schools and thus, individually, should be informed and engaged about their children's progress and, collectively, should have a voice in how RtI is conceptualized and enacted (Learning Disabilities Association of America, n.d.; National Center for Learning Disabilities, 2011).

As a critical limitation, however, RtI research has not centered the perspectives of students themselves as a valuable data point, particularly for decisions that influence their subsequent educational trajectories (e.g., special education referral). For MLs in secondary grades, in particular, this is a significant oversight that contravenes larger advocacy in ML scholarship for students to have a voice in their own education, specifically regarding the services and interventions they receive (Brooks, 2022, 2023; Kangas & Cioè-Peña, 2024). The absence of student voice, I argue, is illustrative of ableist decision-making that devalues the perspectives of students with disabilities as subjective and ill-informed.

While three elements—the best possible body of evidence, consideration of systemic contributors, and wisdom and goals of students and their families—are addressed in RtI research, acknowledgment of the importance of the fourth element, professional judgment, in data-based decision-making is alarmingly scant. In education, *professional judgment* is akin to the construct of *clinical judgment* often used in the medical and psychological fields to capture the interpretive decision-making of trained professionals. Teachers can be trained to systemically collect, review, and analyze data, but when so much of our performance data in schools is muddied for MLs with disabilities, professional judgment becomes paramount. Schalock and Luckasson (2005) argue that clinical judgment, or in this case professional judgment, is always needed but becomes all the more crucial under any of the following circumstances:

1. When formal assessments have significant limitations
2. When individuals have complex conditions and needs
3. When legal requirements influence the assessment of the individual
4. When cultural and linguistic factors impact the information required to make a decision

Applied to education, we can see that these circumstances are common in the education of MLs with disabilities and thus require a high level of professional judgment while making sense of their performance data.

Reflected in the literature above, four elements of sound data interpretation and use are critical to teachers' efforts to teach and assess MLs with disabilities. Yet these elements are eroded through the patterned inequity of the language-or-disability filter.

EVIDENCE OF PATTERNS

As discussed in this chapter, so much of our knowledge base regarding best practices in data use at the intersection of language learning and disability is derived from RtI. Significantly, RtI as a framework also emphasizes the exigence of accurately parsing out ELP from disability so students can receive the support they need and also be appropriately referred for special education evaluation (Collier, 2011; Klingner & Geisler, 2008; Ortiz et al., 2011). Teachers and administrators, then, are tasked with disentangling the two as they collect and interpret student performance data. Distinguishing between disability and L2 learning is a matter of equity: If educators fail to make correct distinctions, MLs could be misidentified with a disability, or MLs with an undiagnosed disability that is assumed to be a manifestation of language learning could fall through the cracks. The emphasis on disentangling L2 learning from a disability, however, has led to an unintended consequence in understanding student performance data: the language-or-disability filter.

My studies on reclassification reinforced to me the ubiquity of the filter in teachers' sensemaking of data. In my first reclassification study on MLs with disabilities—who by the time of the study had become LTELs—I bore witness to the language-or-disability filter used frequently in reclassification decision-making. Throughout this study, teachers commonly attempted to parse out L2 and disability to understand what was holding back the MLs with disabilities from achieving higher ELP scores needed for reclassification. When teachers believed disability was the culprit for low ELP assessment scores, they recommended reclassification, reasoning that disabilities would never allow MLs to make sufficient progress and thus language services were superfluous. Seldom did the educators in the study consider whether the learning environment was a contributor to the students' reclassification ineligibility, even though students were placed in low-track courses where exposure to grade-level curriculum, linguistically rich instruction, and support for their ELP were all scant (Kangas & Cook, 2020).

Years later, I conducted a related qualitative study in a different district, finding that teachers made similar determinations about the influences of disability.[1] In this district, ESL teachers who were the primary decision-makers in reclassification took an idiosyncratic and nonsystematic approach to what data they reviewed and how they reviewed it, often relying on their gut instincts to determine whether disability explained the lack of ELP and academic growth they observed among their MLs with disabilities. Maribel, for example, shared how she used her "gut" to help her determine whether the ML with a disability was still learning English and thus should remain in language services:

> Because once you get to know a student, you can tell what it is, you know—if language is truly, if our instruction here is truly helping them, you know. Or would they benefit more from special ed? Which I think a lot of times they do, you know? But I think it's really going with your gut. (Kangas & Ruiz, in press, n.p.)

Rubi, another ESL teacher in the district, reported eschewing ELP assessment data for her instincts in reclassification decisions: "There's a lot that

I don't buy into here. So, I'm hesitant to use some of the stuff that—so I think here it would be more like, it would be more of a feeling." She described further: "But there have definitely been times that I've looked at a kid and been like, 'I don't really think this student should reclassify'" (Kangas & Ruiz, in press, n.p.). Like many of her colleagues, Rubi turned to her instincts, especially as she felt that standardized ELP data were highly flawed, as MLs especially in the secondary grades grew tired and unmotivated to take the ELP assessment year after year.

In the same study, we also found evidence of the filter in reclassification reports completed by ESL teachers, as anecdotal judgments regarding the delimiting nature of disability were commonly used as "data." In one section of the report, IEP teams were required to provide the data used to inform reclassification recommendations. Teachers would list disability as a root cause of academic and linguistic "problems" and would thus recommend that MLs no longer receive language services. One report listed, for example, the following so-called data for an ML with an intellectual disability: "Limited language in both English and Spanish—no identifiable language needs related to English. Does not have acquisition needs. Speech and disability are his concerns—not language." Another report indicated the following for an ML with a disability: "Mental needs along with his education diagnosis supersede all his English language needs." Similarly, another report indicated for an ML with an SLD in reading: "His issues are more related to his IEP rather than his second language abilities. She [ESL teacher] reports him exiting."

In this study, the complicated, troubling layers of the language-or-disability filter are glaring in decision-making. First, teachers' instincts, divorced from data, became a driver for decision-making. In this way, the use of the best possible evidence fell apart. Second and related, in these studies, teachers' instincts were grounded in the deficit assumption that disability was the cause for the challenges MLs with disabilities experienced. But instincts and professional judgment are not the same; in this study, professional judgment was ultimately supplanted by biases and hunches. Third, explanations external to the students were overlooked by most in their decision-making. In the entire ESL Department of nearly 20 teachers, only two discussed inadequacies in the learning environment, even though many MLs with disabilities, particularly those with more complex support needs, were on a so-called "consult model." In this dubiously named model, ESL teachers checked in with students and offered perspectives to their special education colleagues but did not provide language services. In the end, the delimiting effects of disability were zeroed in on as the explanation for students' ELP scores, while systemic contributors, particularly a lack of services, were ignored. Overall, many of the elements of sound data use and decision-making were compromised by the language-or-disability filter.

More recent studies illuminate how the language-or-disability filter can supplant data for MLs with disabilities and cause educators to overlook systemic contributors, resulting in diminished learning opportunities for the students. Investigating a schoolwide positive behavior support system, Stinson et al. (2025) found that when MLs with disabilities did not conform to the expected behavioral outcomes of the interventions, they—and not any shortcomings in positive behavior support implementation—were seen as a problem, unruly and undeserving of a general education placement. Consequently, MLs with disabilities, who were children of color, were "labeled as deficient or disabled and relegated to 'services' rather than increased opportunities for affirmation, learning, or belonging at school" (p. 14). Park (2023), too, unearthed a strikingly similar finding on the role of bias in the language-or-disability filter and its connection to limited opportunity to learn. Recall, from Chapter 6, Park's study examining the learning experiences of Luciano, a young Latinx ML with an SLI who was being evaluated for special education services. During classroom observations, he was subjected to physical restraint and removal from the classroom, as well as constant one-on-one adult supervision because his yet-to-be-identified disability was believed to make him a danger to himself and others. For this reason, he was seen as someone who could not learn in the general education environment. As Park points out, however, the learning environment went unexamined: "Instead of wondering if there was something in the environment that was creating distress for Luciano, however, the staff decided that these behaviors meant he needed to have adult supervision" (p. 15). In these examples, as biases of the language-or-disability filter overtook data-based decision-making, the quality of the learning environment was seen as immaterial to the behaviors MLs with disabilities exhibited because the disabilities of these students were believed to be the source of the problem.

RESPONSES TO PATTERNED INEQUITIES IN DATA USE AND INTERPRETATION

To shift away from the language-or-disability filter toward valid and logical data interpretation and use, teachers should consider how each of the four elements—the best possible body of evidence, consideration of systemic contributors, wisdom and goals of students and their families, and professional judgment of teachers—can be incorporated and brought into parity with one another (Figure 8.1). In what follows are recommendations to that effect.

Response 1: Collect and Use the Best Possible Evidence

Whether in or outside of MTSS, the best possible evidence to guide pedagogical practices and other decision-making is a plurality of evidence. Yet in the everyday realities of teaching, certain data, particularly standardized and other commercially developed assessments, become privileged. I saw this in one of my studies wherein teams of teachers invested considerable time amassing multiple kinds of data for academic tracking placement decisions; however, when the time came, the state standardized academic assessment scores in reading and mathematics determined students' placements. The MLs with disabilities in the study, in particular, were disadvantaged by this practice, winding up in the lowest tracks. As reviewed in this chapter, using data from such assessments tends to obscure our understanding of what MLs with disabilities can do. Thus, the best possible evidence is drawn from a variety of sources, including authentic assessments, course projects and tasks, running records, writing samples, and student observation, among many others (see MTSS for ELs, 2022). Data in and about the L1 are also critical for developing a fuller portrait of the academic and linguistic capabilities of MLs with identified or suspected disabilities.

Even with a plurality of evidence, there are unavoidable limitations to the data frequently used in schools. When so much of our student performance data is in and about English, making data-based decisions can be far from cut-and-dried. This brings to the surface two implications for teachers' use of data. First, it is practically impossible to differentiate between language learning and disability using English-only data. Second and related, even if disambiguating language learning and disability were a tidy endeavor, it is unlikely that a binary either/or—language *or* disability—could explain trends in data. It could be both, and it could be neither. Take, for instance, teachers examining ELP assessment data of an ML with an SLI. If the data show a plateauing effect in the ML's ELP scores, this trend could be a consequence of both language and disability or neither language or disability but other factors altogether, such as interruptions to services due to COVID, potential bias in the ELP assessment, or ML's strong dislike of the assessment itself. Yet trying to parse out language and disability in such circumstances makes two faulty assumptions: (a) that language learning and disability exist independently of one another within MLs with disabilities and (b) that external factors are not contributing. In light of this dilemma, we must seek out data and perspectives from ML families and data that probe the quality of the learning environment, both of which are discussed further below.

Response 2: Value Data and Perspectives From the Family

It was enshrined as a legal protection under IDEA (1975) that parents of students with disabilities are to be partners in major decision-making regarding their children. Compliance perspectives aside, ML parents provide valuable insights and much-needed data that can both drive pedagogical and intervention decisions and augment the English-only data often emphasized in school settings. Teachers can systematically seek out data and perspectives from parents and other family members through a myriad of sources, including interviews, surveys, inventories, child-made artifacts, and home visits. Through these data sources, family members can provide critical information regarding their children's educational history, developmental milestones, oral language and literacy skills, and academic abilities, as well as social, emotional, and behavioral strengths and needs. Building from the recommendations offered in Chapter 6, "High Expectations," families often contribute a strength-based perspective that is important and yet can get lost in student performance data.

Data from the family should not just be collected; these data must also be valued during decision-making. When compared to standardized school-based data, however, family perspectives and the data they share can be trivialized and discredited as subjective. I grappled with this personally when asked to complete a parent report for an evaluation of my child, only to see that it was not authentically incorporated into the decision-making of the team of educators. It struck me as a facade—of technical compliance—to collect family data and then ignore it. Throughout this book, I advocate for a model for authentic family engagement that values the perspectives and voices of parents. Teachers can utilize these practices offered in the model to authentically inform their decisions for instruction and the other critical decisions they make.

Response 3: Collect Ecological Data

In their ground-breaking book *English Language Learners: Differentiating Between Language Acquisition and Learning Disabilities*, Klingner and Eppolito (2014) call for an ecological framework when interpreting student performance data in RtI. In this ecological framework, teachers consider factors external and internal to the student as they make sense of a body of data. Klingner (n.d.) further advocates that teachers begin with the presupposition that "there is nothing wrong with the individual and that systemic, ecological, or environmental factors are the primary reason for learning problems. Maintain this hypothesis until data suggest otherwise, and all plausible external factors have been ruled out" (p. 1). Teachers should take a three-pronged approach to rule out external factors in the learning environment.

First, teachers should advocate for their school and district leaders to implement equity audits. In Chapter 3 I introduced readers to equity audits, recommending their use to understand MLs with disabilities' access to dual services, bilingual programs, and the least restrictive learning environments. Because systemic inequities in districts and schools have an expansive influence, shaping pedagogical practices and teacher–student interactions, interrogating opportunity to learn through equity audits is critical.

Second, the quality of instruction provided to MLs with disabilities needs to be examined. In prior chapters, I offered recommendations for enacting pedagogical practices that are rigorous and grounded in high expectations, including EBPs such as:

1. using explicit instruction,
2. teaching cognitive and metacognitive strategies,
3. promoting active student engagement,
4. creating linguistically rich classrooms,
5. leveraging student grouping,
6. supporting students' social, emotional, and behavioral needs,
7. implementing scaffolds,
8. understanding students' goals,
9. expanding opportunities for higher-order thinking and knowledge-sharing, and
10. engaging in positive feedback on student learning.

Teachers should consider evaluating the extent to which these practices are evident for all students, and especially MLs with disabilities. Ruling out a lack of access to rigorous, strength-based instruction is essential for understanding student performance data. More detailed information on implementing and examining these practices can be found on pages 93–97 and 107–117.

Third, an ecological framework also takes a hard look at the interventions used to support MLs with disabilities. Because interventions can embody the patterned inequity of a unitary identity, ignoring the language backgrounds of MLs, teachers should evaluate the appropriateness of interventions. Hoover (2008) developed a guide for identifying interventions that are culturally and linguistically responsive (Figure 8.2). Teachers, school-based teams, and educational leaders should consider utilizing this guide to rule out inappropriate interventions as a contributor to concerning patterns in student performance data.

Response 4: Differentiate Between Professional Judgment and Bias

When teaching MLs with disabilities, professional judgment is indispensable. Professional judgment cannot exist apart from data; when it does, it morphs into bias. Schalock and Luckasson (2005) draw similar distinctions between clinical judgment and bias, asserting that clinical judgment "should not be thought of as a justification for abbreviated evaluations, a vehicle for stereotypes or prejudices, a substitute for insufficiently explored questions, an excuse for incomplete or missing data, or way to solve political problems" (p. 6). As we reflect on their words, we see a parallel between professional judgment and the language-or-disability filter's embodiment of these faulty practices; the filter (a) operates as a shortcut when data are ambiguous and incomplete, (b) is highly influenced by personal beliefs, assumptions, and prejudices, and (c) enables insufficient questioning of systemic contributors. For these reasons, differentiating between professional judgment and bias is necessary for all teachers of dually identified students.

Figure 8.2. Guide for Identifying and Using Appropriate Interventions

_____ Student's most proficient language for instruction is identified

_____ Student's level of acculturation and adjustment to school environment is determined

_____ Discrepancies between teaching and learning style differences are identified

_____ Culturally and linguistically relevant instructional interventions are attempted and results documented

_____ ESL and/or bilingual education instruction is implemented

_____ Sufficient time and opportunity for student to make satisfactory progress are provided relative to acculturation and English proficiency levels

_____ Authentic or other criterion-referenced tests are used to assess student progress and socio-emotional development

_____ One or more classroom observations are made to observe student interactions in the academic environment and ensure fidelity of implementation of interventions

Source: Hoover, J. J. (2008). Data-driven decision making in a multi-tiered model. In J. K. Klingner, J. J. Hoover, & L. M. Baca (Eds.), *Why do English language learners struggle with reading? Distinguishing language acquisition from learning disabilities* (pp. 75–92). Corwin.

To help distinguish between the two, Table 8.1 includes reflective questions for teachers to ask themselves about the data they collect and use.

SUMMARY

This was the final of three chapters to focus on equity in classrooms, addressing sound data interpretation and use. I demonstrated how the language-or-disability filter tarnishes valid and reliable decision-making by replacing data with bias and overlooking systemic contributors. Recommending a model of decision-making that encompasses the (a) best possible body of evidence, (b) consideration of systemic contributors, (c) wisdom and goals of students and their families, and (d) professional judgment of teachers (Figure 8.1), the chapter offers teachers a way to navigate the complexities and challenges that accompany student performance data for MLs with disabilities. Through this model, teachers can have more confidence that the decisions they make are valid, sensible, and equitable. But how teachers view data and make decisions is just part of the picture. This series of chapters amplifies this point, arguing that equity in classrooms cannot be achieved without three core practices: high expectations, rigorous instruction, and sound data interpretation and use (Figure 6.1). These practices are

Table 8.1. Reflective Questions to Detect Bias in Data Use and Interpretation

Data Sources

1. What data sources am I using?
2. Am I relying on multiple data sources?
3. Am I over-relying on standardized, commercially developed assessments?
4. To what extent do data sources include authentic, classroom-based assessments and tasks?
5. Are there data that have already been collected that I can use?
6. Have I collected or accessed data from students' L1?
7. What data or information from families have I considered?
8. If data include teacher reports or observations, were these conducted systematically?
9. What data have I collected, or do I have, about the quality of instruction students receive?
10. Have equity audits about students' learning opportunities been conducted?

Data Interpretation and Use

11. Before making instructional decisions, have I reviewed all pertinent data?
12. How has my review of data been systematic?
13. As I review data, do I view them in parity, seeing each source as equally important?
14. Is a singular data source driving my decision-making?
15. To what extent do I value the data and information I have received from families?
16. Have I compared English-only data to L1 data?
17. Have I solicited insights on the data from my colleagues?
18. To what extent am I relying on hunches, intuition, or instincts to make decisions?
19. Am I trying to distinguish language learning from disability in English-only data?
20. How have I considered systemic contributors as I view data?

inextricably linked, with one unable to exist in praxis without the others. Operating as powerful agents of change, teachers can center these core practices in their classrooms and, by doing so, advance equity and expand learning opportunities for their MLs with disabilities.

Part IV

EQUITY IN POLICIES

CHAPTER 9

Academic Standard Policies

Renowned political scientist Harold Lasswell (1951, 1956) argued that policy—and the study of policy—should ultimately strive for human dignity. Indeed, many policies in education aim for that laudable goal by safeguarding the rights of children and a promising future for their lives. Entire frameworks of laws and policies, in fact, have arisen to protect the human dignity of our most vulnerable school-age children. Under two frameworks of laws and policies (i.e., special education, ML education), one would reason that dually identified students stand to be doubly protected. Legal scholar Perry Zirkel (2021) asserts, however, that MLs with disabilities "are at a particularly difficult intersection between two very different legal frameworks" (p. 60). Without careful attention from education stakeholders, this "difficult intersection" of laws and policies can have the paradoxical effect of compromising equity through eroding, rather than building up, the protections and rights of MLs with disabilities. Afforded such tenuous protections, the "full potential" of ML and special laws have yet to be realized for dually identified students (González et al., 2024, p. 1).

In the preceding chapters, we have encountered the role of patterned inequities in on-the-ground policymaking—how educators grapple with the complexities of supporting dually identified students and the ways in which their responses to these complexities effectively create policy in classrooms, schools, and districts. These chapters have emphasized the dual role of educators as *agents of policymaking* and critically as *agents of change.* This final section of chapters on equity in policies shifts our attention from on-the-ground policies to macro policies and the contexts in which they are developed. The chapters ahead envisage SEA leaders, those working in departments of education across the United States, as, like educators, agents of policymaking and change, able to influence the learning opportunities of MLs with disabilities. To highlight this perspective, I decided to use the term *state leaders*—not the commonly used *state policymakers*, *state directors*, or *state coordinators.* As we consider their roles in advocating and enacting change at both the state and local levels (Hopkins et al., 2022; Weddle, 2023) and with uncertainties arising with the second Trump presidency, state leaders, I contend, are some of the most consequential stakeholders in the education of MLs with disabilities.

With this stance, Chapter 10 explores the conditions in which SEA leaders develop and refine policies, while this chapter examines state policies themselves, specifically *academic standard policies*, which encompass the state policies that establish thresholds for student performance and growth. Such policies often specify achievement standards for academic content (i.e., English language arts, mathematics), reading, graduation, and ELP, among others. Because state academic achievement policies are so numerous, this chapter will use reclassification policies as an example from which insights are transferable to achievement policies writ large. Through a focus on both the policies themselves and the contexts that mold them, Chapters 9 and 10 will evidence the pervasive and shared nature of patterned inequities, with inequities manifesting in achievement standards policies and challenging the work of SEA leaders. These chapters embrace Lasswell's understanding of policy—that despite the presence of patterned inequities in policy and the work of SEAs, it can ultimately work toward greater human dignity for MLs with disabilities.

RECLASSIFICATION POLICIES: KEY RESEARCH FINDINGS

Unlike most other labels assigned to students in K–12 schools, the *English learner* label is intended to be temporary (for discussion of terminology, see Notes). Ideally, a student will receive language services, progress in their English proficiency, and eventually be reclassified from *English learner* to *former English learner* status. This reclassification is predicated on students meeting grade-level standards for fluent English proficient (FEP), which, as ESSA (2015) mandated, must be defined by states through a specific set of criteria. A growing body of research indicates that for some students, the *EL* label is far from temporary. Dually identified students are one such population, as they are disproportionately less likely to be reclassified as FEP (Burke et al., 2016; Slama et al., 2017; Umansky et al., 2017). Federal data from 2018 provided a snapshot of this disturbing trend; MLs with disabilities comprised only 0.8% of the 14.2% of MLs reclassified as FEP and just 3.6% of the 27.4% making progress in their English proficiency (National Clearinghouse for English Language Acquisition, 2021). These national data corroborated earlier findings from Kieffer and Parker's (2016) examination of reclassification patterns in New York City Public Schools. Their findings demonstrated that compared to their ML peers, MLs with disabilities take as many as four additional years to meet the threshold for ELP required for reclassification. Disaggregated by disability category, MLs with SLIs met reclassification criteria after 6 years of language support, while MLs with SLDs required 8 years to be reclassified. As a consequence, a large proportion of MLs with disabilities reach LTEL status, spending upwards of 5 years receiving language services without being exited (Burke et al.,

2016; Kieffer & Parker, 2016; Shin, 2020). Although percentages vary across the nation, in some states, nearly half of dually identified students become LTELs (Sahakyan & Ryan, 2018). Notably, reclassification is also linked to another disproportionality trend: the overrepresentation of MLs in special education in secondary grades (Schissel & Kangas, 2018; Umansky et al., 2017). As MLs with disabilities have lower chances of reclassification than their ML peers without disabilities, they become "left behind" in language services, a phenomenon referred to as the *reclassification bottleneck* (Umansky et al., 2017). With the number of MLs with disabilities building over time, by secondary grades, they become overrepresented in special education—a disproportionality trend that has been documented for some time (see Artiles et al., 2005).

In 2016, I first made the connection between reclassification and overrepresentation when I was observing a science class at a local high school. My colleagues invited me to join their ongoing study, and they thought some preliminary observations would help me become better acquainted with the school staff and students. Following the observation, I asked the teacher some additional questions about the students, and her one answer had a haunting effect on me: "Most of the kids here are dual identified." It struck me as peculiar—wrong, even—that in a class of 20 MLs, far more than half were dually identified as *English learners* and *students with disabilities*. She would be the first of many teachers and administrators who would share that many of their middle school and high school MLs who had identified disabilities were "stuck"—forever labeled an EL and never able to exit. Certainly, this is not the case in all secondary schools, but in my local context, the disproportionality trend of MLs with disabilities was startling. It gnawed at me as a researcher, setting me on the path to examine reclassification.

Beyond revealing disproportionately low exiting rates, research also indicates that for all MLs, not just those with disabilities, reclassification can become a critical equity problem of practice. While receipt of language services is a civil right guaranteed for all identified MLs, studies have found that remaining in language services for a lengthy period is associated with unequal and exclusionary learning opportunities, such as limited access to peers, rigorous content-area instruction, and college preparatory courses, as well as social stigma (Callahan & Shifrer, 2016; Dabach, 2014; Menken et al., 2012; Thompson, 2015)—many of the very same issues illuminated in Chapter 3, "Organization of Students and Services." While it is true that holding MLs back from exiting compromises equitable learning opportunities, on the other hand, prematurely reclassifying MLs with disabilities can deprive them of language services, which are vital for accessing the general education curriculum and disability-related services (Kangas, 2024). Reclassification, in sum, is a high-stakes decision that carries significant consequences for the learning and life opportunities of all MLs, but given the differential reclassification rates, especially those with disabilities.

With the abysmally low reclassification rate among MLs with disabilities, the question then becomes *Why*? Research is just beginning to take up this empirical question, but a canvassing of scholarship suggests there are three predominant perspectives on the matter. The first perspective I will call *disability barrier,* which offers that disability itself is an inherent barrier to ELP growth and, by extension, reclassification. In this perspective, disabilities are seen as a delaying force in the acquisition of English (see de Valenzuela et al., 2022; Kangas, 2021; Kangas & Schissel, 2021). Thus, when MLs with disabilities do not meet the state-established criteria for exiting, it reflects the constraining influence of their disabilities. This deficit perspective adheres to the *limited capacity theory of bilingualism* (Paradis et al., 2021), a myth that contends bilingualism is beyond the reach of children with disabilities, exceeding their cognitive capabilities. As we recall from Chapter 3, there is robust evidence that indicates that multilingual children with disabilities attain higher linguistic and academic achievement as well as experience greater socioemotional benefits when they have rich exposure to two languages and those languages are nurtured (see Cioè-Peña, 2021; Gonzalez-Barrero & Nadig, 2018; Martínez-Álvarez, 2023; Simon-Cereijido & Gutiérrez-Clellen, 2013; Thomas & Collier, 2012). This is true of multilingual children with complex support needs (Kay-Raining Bird et al., 2005)—those for whom the limited capacity theory of bilingualism is perhaps the most entrenched (Shenoy et al., 2022). Weighing this evidence, the limited capacity theory is the least plausible explanation for the disproportionately low number of MLs with disabilities meeting reclassification criteria, and yet, as I will detail later in this chapter, it is pervasive in schools and implicitly codified in some state policies.

The second perspective, *conflation barrier*, maintains that measuring ELP skills and growth of dually identified students through standardized ELP assessments is impossibly challenging because many disabilities, such as SLDs in reading, SLIs, and intellectual disabilities, among others, often have a language basis (de Valenzuela et al., 2022; Shenoy et al., 2022; Umansky et al., 2017). As mandated by ESSA (2015), scores from standardized ELP assessments are the anchoring reclassification criterion for every state. From there, states can require additional criteria that demonstrate ELP, but by and large, standardized ELP scores alone are the sole measure of ELP in the United States, regardless of whether MLs have disabilities or not (Kangas, 2024). Most MLs with disabilities take the general ELP assessment, of which there are several used in the United States (e.g., WIDA ACCESS, ELPAC, ELPA, TELPAS); however, a very small percentage of MLs—those with complex support needs—take the alternate ELP assessment (Alt ELP) used in their state (National Center for Educational Outcomes [NCEO], n.d.), such as the Alternate ACCESS, Alt ELPA, or Alternate ELPAC.

In the conflation barrier stance, it is not the bi- and multilingual capabilities of children with disabilities that are called into question, but rather the instrumentation (i.e., general and alternate ELP assessments) used to measure ELP growth. In a lecture I recently gave, after discussing reclassification for MLs with disabilities, an attendee astutely asked: How can we parse out language from disability when there is "so much language wrapped up in disability?" The question hit me hard; in some respects, we can never disentangle the two, and the data we have at our disposal are not silver bullets in these efforts. Shenoy et al. (2022) best captured the challenge of relying on Alt ELP assessments in measuring language growth for MLs with complex support needs: "By explicitly linking students' level of language proficiency to their communication development, which is highly influenced by their disability, English language proficiency is thus conflated with disability" (p. 178). This conflation, in my view, is a more likely explanation for the limited reclassification rates of dually identified students.

The third and final perspective takes a *systemic barrier* stance—that there are both *school-based barriers* and *policy-based barriers* that inhibit reclassification for MLs with disabilities (Kangas, 2021; Schissel & Kangas, 2018). The earlier chapters of this book took a deep dive into school-based barriers to MLs with disabilities' reclassification eligibility; sparse language services, linguistically unresponsive IEPs, poor-quality instruction, and low expectations, for example, all would work against MLs with disabilities in accelerating their ELP. With the existence of such systemic barriers, in their guidance to SEAs, Park and Chou (2019) emphasize that reclassification should occur within the context of access to services: "Before any considerations for exiting EL status are made, the schools will have ensured that the EL with disabilities receives both special education and related services as well as EL services" (p. 5).

Policy-based barriers include but also extend beyond the conflation barrier perspective, as ELP assessment scores are just one systemic factor—albeit a foundational one—that may influence MLs with disabilities' reclassification eligibility. These reclassification policy barriers are at the heart of this chapter, and as I contend, they boil down to the patterned inequities we have seen so far in the other sectors of K–12 education and generalize to other academic standard policies. While all three patterned inequities manifest in reclassification policies, this chapter will address just two: unitary identity and language-or-disability filter. The final patterned inequity, the specialization trap, will be explored in Chapter 10, as I argue that the siloed nature of SEA offices operates as the context in which academic standard policies are created.

EVIDENCE OF PATTERNS

While research has found differential and frankly alarming reclassification rates among MLs and MLs with disabilities, there is a lack of studies examining reclassification policies for dually identified students. In my work supporting ML SEA leaders, they are eager to know more about the reclassification policies across the United States, wishing to ensure their state policies and LEAs' practices can be responsive to these students' needs during reclassification. In reaction to this need among SEA leaders and the paucity of research, in 2023–2024, with the support of the Spencer Foundation,[1] I conducted an analysis of state reclassification policies for MLs with disabilities from all 50 states and the District of Columbia. To elucidate the patterned inequities in reclassification policies, in what follows, I draw from and synthesize the findings from this analysis along with the few reclassification studies centered on MLs with disabilities.

Unitary Identity

Among the patterned inequities, unitary identity is the most prominent in reclassification; by its very nature, reclassification centers MLs and their ELP, but in the process, disability is erased. It should be no surprise that accounting for disability in the reclassification of state policies and their local implementation has been arduous; not only do individual criteria required for reclassification need to account for the intersection of disability and language but so do the procedures that schools and districts follow. Notwithstanding, some state policies have attempted to address the intersecting and enmeshed language and disability-related needs of dually identified students during reclassification. However, given the mandate from ESSA (2015) for statewide standardized exit criteria, most reclassification policies tend to treat MLs as a monolith, eliding considerations of disability and its heterogeneity. With reclassification carrying high-stakes implications for learning opportunities, this elision is particularly damaging for MLs with disabilities.

In examining policies and policy research, we first see that reclassification policies promote this erasure through the criteria that are required for FEP. In my research policy analysis, I found that a score from a standardized ELP assessment was the sole criterion used to exit MLs in 42 states, whether they have or do not have disabilities (Kangas, 2024). Likewise, for MLs with complex support needs, more than half of the states strictly use a score from an alternate ELP assessment. Researchers, organizations, and testing consortia alike have cautioned against the use of a single measure, like an ELP assessment, to make high-stakes decisions like reclassification (see AERA/APA/NCME, 2014; Linquanti et al., 2016; WIDA, 2025), especially for those who are dually identified students (Kangas, 2024; Park & Chou, 2019). For MLs with disabilities, scholars—myself included—have questioned the construct validity of language assessments (de Valenzuela et al., 2022; Schissel & Kangas, 2018; Shenoy et al., 2022), that is, the extent to which the assessments actually measure what they purport to measure, in this case, ELP. Reflecting a conflation barrier stance, these same scholars argue that ELP assessments, to some extent, cannot address the influence of disabilities that have a language basis, and thus, may be inadvertently measuring disability and not ELP. Highlighting this tension, Randez and Cornell (2023) use the example of adult language learners with autism, who very often experience anxiety especially when confronted by situations and events outside of their usual routine. Taking a high-stakes language assessment may exacerbate their anxiety and thus negatively influence their performance. In the end, the authors argue that language assessments fail to consider autism among language learners and thus inadvertently may be measuring its influence:

> Few would say that a single assessment is inherently equitable for all test takers, but one of the underpinning arguments of standardized assessments is that they are equitable for most. However, *who* is included in that *most* needs further clarification. Fundamentally, if the assessment creation process never considered a test taker with ASD [autism], no accommodation can retroactively make it applicable to that test taker. (p. 996)

While this argument was made in the context of standardized language assessments used in higher education, the same challenges are true in K–12 ELP assessments. The conflation of language learning and disability in the testing of children, as Schissel (2019) attests, has been a pervasive issue throughout U.S. history, with direct impacts to children's access to citizenship and appropriate school-based services.

With this issue at hand, accommodations have been positioned as the solution, leveling the playing field for MLs with disabilities when they take ELP assessments. But, literature suggests that accommodations, too, ironically present their own form of erasure, often overlooking—instead of directly supporting—MLs' disabilities (Abedi, 2009; Randez & Cornell, 2023; Schissel & Kangas, 2018). As an example, during professional development workshops and webinars, repeatedly teachers ask me what they should do when the accommodation specified in an ML's IEP is prohibited on an ELP assessment. An oft-cited issue they provided was a restriction of the use of read-alouds on the reading portion of the ELP assessment. In this instance, educators were faced with two unsatisfactory, if not ethical, options: First, the ML with disability can skip that portion of the assessment, but this would leave them without a reading domain score and as a result without an overall composite score. Second, the ML with disability could take that portion of the assessment without the accommodations in their IEP, thus violating the ML's plan and compromising further the validity of assessment data. As progress, some states and testing consortia have developed procedures for computing proficiency scores in the absence of a missing domain score (i.e., domain exemptions), which has been a promising step toward addressing disability during ELP assessment.

Despite such progress, the assessment accommodations commonly allowed during ELP and academic assessments have an unclear evidentiary basis for MLs and students with disabilities alike (Abedi, 2009; Abedi & Ewers, 2013; Liu et al., 2020; Rios et al., 2020). Further, research examining assessment accommodations for dually identified students, in particular, has been altogether scant (see Abedi, 2009; Christensen et al., 2013; Minnema et al., 2006). In Abedi's (2009) review of assessment and accommodation practices, he discussed how commonly used assessment accommodations were empirically validated with MLs *or* students with disabilities, but not for students with both needs. Moreover, Abedi raised concerns about the differential impact of some accommodations—that they may benefit some MLs with disabilities and not others. For instance, a common assessment accommodation outlined in the IEPs of MLs with disabilities is testing in an alternate room with minimal distractions. To what extent, however, does this accommodation have a differential impact, allowing MLs with SLDs, ADHD, and autism to perform better on the assessment, but not MLs with SLIs? Without close examination of differential impact, a commonly used accommodation provided often to MLs with disabilities may not be effective for *all* MLs with disabilities. In the end, Abedi (2009) reasons: "Due to an extremely complex situation in the assessment of ELLWD [MLs with disabilities] students, these accommodations are often ineffective and may even provide invalid assessment outcomes" (pp. 23–24). He argues that while some accommodations fail to level the playing field for MLs with disabilities, others, when implemented, could fundamentally impact the construct being measured by the assessment.

Third, we see glaring erasure of disability, particularly cognitive disabilities, in the historic lack of Alt ELP assessments. Similar to general ELP assessments, Alt ELP assessments measure the four domains of language (i.e., listening, speaking, reading, writing), yet they align with alternate achievement standards for ELP. There are several Alt ELP assessments; common differences between these assessments and general ELP assessments are that they may be (a) untimed or shorter in duration, (b) administered one-on-one, (c) administered on paper, and (d) nonadaptive (i.e., does not adapt to student's performance on prior question items) (see California Department of Education, 2024; WIDA, 2024). Of significance, a very small percentage of all MLs with disabilities are permitted to take these assessments (NCEO, n.d.), as ESSA (2015) set a cap for the percentage of students able to participate in alternate achievement standards and therefore take alternate assessments: just 1%. While this cap was not specifically set for Alt ELP assessments (NCEO, n.d.), because only MLs with complex support needs who have alternate achievement standards should be given the assessment, this 1% cap has become the de facto guide for participation in Alt ELP assessments.

In 2018, de Valenzuela and colleagues (2022) conducted an analysis of Alt ELP policies, finding that many states did not have an Alt ELP assessment in place (n=14) or had yet to determine a cut score on these assessments needed for reclassification eligibility (n=12). Much, however, has shifted and continues to shift in the ELP assessment landscape. As a part of the policy analysis referenced above, I wanted to examine what I call *alternate reclassification policies*, which encapsulates policies addressing the exiting of MLs with complex support needs who participate in Alt ELP assessments. Examining the availability of Alt ELP assessments as well as the establishment of Alt ELP criteria needed for reclassification, I noted several subtle changes, but much had remained stubbornly the same. Despite 5 years passing between de Valenzuela et al.'s (2022) analysis and my own, 12 states had yet to identify or were in the process of identifying alternate ELP reclassification criteria. Without designated assessments or established exit criteria, MLs with complex support needs have no viable pathway for reclassification. Apart from these policy trends, Alt ELP assessments insufficiently account for the diverse communicative repertoires of MLs with complex support needs, including those who use symbolic communication such as signed language, Braille, and augmentative and alternative communication (Shenoy et al., 2022).

In the midst of these erasures, notably, states have taken steps to account for the intersection of language and disability. These efforts have been met with challenges, however. Returning to my 2024 reclassification analysis, some states developed what I call *exemption policies* that enable individual or entire subgroups of MLs to reclassify under separate reclassification criteria. These exemption policies came in two forms. Some states have instituted *individual exemptions*, a more case-by-case approach in which LEAs can set individualized reclassification criteria, often in connection with the goals established in an IEP by members of the IEP team. Another approach enabled LEAs within the state to submit a waiver to the SEA for individual MLs, often those with disabilities, to be exited. Other states enacted *population-wide exemptions*, allowing all MLs with disabilities to exit under separate criteria. At the time of the analysis, only one state—my home state of Pennsylvania—had a population-wide exemption policy in place. Importantly, other states, for example, Rhode Island, once had a similar population-wide exemption in place but only briefly, after which the policy was replaced. In my work with ML SEA leaders and K–12 teachers, they have expressed their desire for reclassification policies to account for disability, with state leaders inquiring if exemption policies, whether in the form of different criteria or different ELP scores, were permissible for these students. At present, no external-facing guidance has been issued from the U.S. Department of Education on the permissibility of exemption policies in their varied form, although the rescinding of and general uncertainty about such policies among SEA leaders together indicate that these policies are likely deemed incongruent with ESSA's mandate for standardized reclassification criteria. As a researcher and policy consultant, I see an urgent need for the U.S. Department of Education to offer external, formal guidance on the issue of exemption policies, as SEA and local educational agency leaders alike continue earnestly to seek solutions to the limited reclassification of MLs with disabilities. Yet in the current federal landscape, this guidance may not come for some time. In the meantime, the uncertainty around exemption policies will continue, further amplifying the challenges of accounting for disability in a policy that is and has been all about language. In this way, the unitary identity patterned inequity remains entrenched in reclassification.

Language-or-Disability Filter

As discussed above, de Valenzuela et al.'s (2022) analysis of Alt ELP assessment policies found that many states had yet to adopt an alternate ELP assessment or a required score for reclassification, illuminating the unitary identity patterned inequity. Reflecting the language-or-disability filter, however, were state policies that effectively barred reclassification for MLs with complex support needs, specifying that no score on the assessment was sufficient to meet grade-level standards of ELP (n=2). Put in starker terms, these policies conveyed that *any* ELP skills of MLs with complex support needs are unilaterally subpar. Moreover, de Valenzuela et al.'s analysis also uncovered that three states' reclassification criteria for the alternate ELP assessment stipulated achieving the same score for 3 years (i.e., a plateauing score), which they assert is evidence of deficit-based understandings of the bilingual potential of MLs with disabilities. The authors postulate:

> This reveals the assumption that lack of progress is due to level of disabilities, rather than lack of ELP. However, if EL services are provided to ELs with complex support needs only in English, it may be that they fail to make sufficient progress because this instruction is inaccessible. (p. 10)

In my recent analysis of the alternate policies, two new states had ruled out the possibility of exiting through an alternate ELP score of any kind, again on the grounds that that these scores and the Alt ELP standards they reflect were not on par with grade-level expectations for ELP (Kangas, 2024). The prevalence of requiring consecutive ELP scores, however, increased since de Valenzuela et al.'s (2022) analysis, with now six WIDA states requiring either 2 or 3 years of the same ELP score.

Implementation, too, of reclassification policies can emulate the language-or-disability filter. In Chapter 8, I documented how teachers' decision-making relied on the filter to understand why MLs with disabilities were not reaching the required ELP scores, presupposing that disability operated as an inhibitor to language growth and reclassification. These findings, along with those from the policy analyses, signal deficit-based understandings of disability that underpin both state reclassification policies and the implementation of these policies in LEAs where exiting determinations are made. At the same time, such policies may also indicate an earnest desire among SEAs and LEAs to not unnecessarily retain MLs with complex support needs in language services given the negative consequences that can accompany delayed reclassification.

In review, reclassification policies and their implementation in LEAs tend to embody the language-or-disability filter, assuming that disability operates as an inhibitor to bi- and multilingual proficiency, despite ample empirical evidence that points to the contrary. Reclassification policies also surface unitary identity, attending to language alone and not its intersection with disability. This unitary identity response transpires through the policies' (a) reliance on standardized ELP assessments—that cannot fully disambiguate language and disability—as the sole indicator of FEP and thus the only datum used to reclassify; (b) use of assessment accommodations that have limited empirical basis for levelling the playing field for MLs with disabilities; and (c) lack of considerations for MLs with complex support needs who take alternate ELP assessments. Equipped with these lessons, we now turn our attention to the ways to remedy patterned inequities in state policies.

RESPONSES TO PATTERNED INEQUITIES IN ACADEMIC STANDARD POLICIES

At the beginning of this chapter, I proffered that reclassification policies are just one type of academic standard policy in which we can see patterned inequities materialize for MLs with disabilities. In fact, the lessons we learn from reclassification policies for dually identified students are transferable to many other academic standard policies, such as those that specify performance benchmarks for content learning, reading, and graduation, to name a few. A handful of states, such as New York and Massachusetts, have assessment-based graduation requirements. Citing similar concerns as those raised in this chapter, New York State announced a forthcoming shift away from requiring state assessments, the Regents exams, to graduate high school, favoring instead other data sources that would showcase students' performance (Closson, 2023).

Standardized assessments have played an outsized role in defining and measuring student performance ever since the passing of No Child Left Behind, a reauthorization of the Elementary and Secondary Education Act, in the early aughts (see Au, 2023; Groen, 2012; Menken, 2008; Perlstein, 2007; Schissel, 2019). While views of standardized assessments vary vastly across education—from useful tools that provide common understanding of student performance to instruments of oppression—their presence in state policies will likely remain into the foreseeable future, and thus my stance is that to ignore this reality will leave MLs with disabilities all the more vulnerable. SEA leaders can work toward improving academic performance policies, I argue, by attending to the: (a) disproportionate weight standardized assessments carry in high-stakes decisions; (b) limitations of these assessments in capturing diverse abilities, skills, and language practices; and (c) complications they may introduce for learning opportunities and trajectories of MLs with disabilities.

How can SEA leaders know whether their state policies show signs of patterned inequities? There are several characteristics that cut across many of the academic standard policies and the standardized assessments they require. State policies are likely to compromise equity for MLs with disabilities when they have the following characteristics:

1. Reliance on a score from a single standardized assessment
2. Dependence on assessments or measures that conflate language learning and disabilities
3. Use of assessment accommodations that have limited empirical support
4. Discrepancy between allowable assessment accommodations and the students' needs
5. Lack of procedures for not participating in parts of assessments
6. Absence of or constrained availability of alternate assessments
7. Prohibition on individualized considerations or exemptions
8. Benchmarks with low standards for certain subgroups
9. Assumption of students' perceived deficits as cause of not meeting benchmarks
10. Evidence of disproportionate policy impact for certain subgroups

Policies that possess some or many of these characteristics are likely in need of change. In what follows, I offer SEA leaders recommendations for improving reclassification policies, while also making connections to standard policies overall for dually identified students.

Response 1: Broaden the Range of Data Used

While ESSA requires states to use a standardized ELP assessment in reclassification, SEA leaders should consider broadening the range of data used to determine FEP status. Given the diverse abilities and skills as well as complex needs of MLs with disabilities, multiple data types will provide a more comprehensive understanding of their ELP. Park and Chou (2019) describe the approach as drawing from a "body of evidence" (p. 11), mirroring this book's broader calls for sound data use and interpretation for dually identified students. Requiring additional evidence or criteria to exit is a balancing act, however. For example, studies have found that when used as a criterion to exit, achieving a certain score or level on standardized academic assessments can be an impediment to MLs' reclassification (Linquanti, 2001; Robinson-Cimpian & Thompson, 2016). For the reasons reviewed, tacking on more standardized assessment requirements will likely further diminish the reclassification eligibility of MLs with disabilities. Conversely, removing all other criteria except an ELP assessment score is unlikely to measurably boost reclassification for dually identified students. Consequently, states may want to include local data that demonstrates ELP as a requirement for reclassification; for example, student portfolios, classroom-based assessments, performance in grade-level academic courses, student observation, and parent input.

When local data are considered as evidence in reclassification, states will need to clarify appropriate versus inappropriate evidence. Studies have found that for MLs with and without disabilities alike, anecdotes and personal biases can creep into reclassification when teacher input is a criterion to exit (Estrada & Wang, 2018; Hill et al., 2014; Kangas & Schissel, 2021; Mavrogordato & White, 2017). In conversations with state leaders, they conveyed serious concerns to me that teacher input and decision-making during reclassification can constrain exiting for certain MLs who teachers believe are more—or less—academically capable. This valid concern, I argue, should not cause the elimination of the role of teachers in reclassification but further amplifies the importance of supporting educators' use of data in decision-making—a topic I addressed in Chapter 8. To avoid the inequities that come with bias and anecdotal evidence, states would do well to provide a list of data sources in which educators can ground their input and reclassification recommendations and to offer professional learning opportunities for LEAs on data-based decision-making. At the end of this chapter, I provide a list of reflective questions for SEA leaders to use as a tool for better understanding their state's reclassification criteria (see Figure 9.1).

Applied to other standards of academic performance, policies should avoid the use of a single score to drive understanding of students' skills and growth. As no one piece of evidence can tell a full story, no single piece of evidence should drive policies that often have high-stakes ramifications (e.g., grade retention, high school graduation, etc.). Evidence that spans from standardized to local enables complementary, holistic understanding of MLs with disabilities' current performance as well as areas of strength and growth.

Response 2: Attend to Heterogeneity Among MLs With Disabilities

Reclassification policies for MLs with disabilities can better attend to the heterogeneity of this population by, in part, revisiting policies pertaining to MLs with complex support needs. In some states, this means identifying an

Figure 9.1. Reclassification Polices: Reflective Questions for SEA Leaders

The questions below aim to support (a) ML and special education SEA leaders' understanding of their state's reclassification policies and (b) subsequent revision of reclassification policies and procedures.

1. In your state, what does the landscape look like for MLs with disabilities?
    a. How many are there?
    b. Do you see disproportionate representation of MLs in special education, especially in secondary grades?
2. What are your reclassification criteria for MLs with disabilities? Are they different from the criteria for MLs without disabilities?
3. What are your exit criteria for MLs who take alternate ELP assessments (i.e., MLs with complex support needs)?
4. Based on what has been discussed in this chapter, what do you think about your state's reclassification policy?
5. How would you modify your state's reclassification criteria (i.e., requirements to be reclassified)?
6. What forms of evidence is your state requiring for ELP?
7. To what extent does your state's policy rely on a single ELP score for reclassification?
8. In an ideal world, what evidence would you like to see required in the policy?
9. What would it take to require LEAs to use the data identified in item 8?
10. What local data do LEAs have available that they are not currently using?
11. Does your state have an exemption policy? Has your state sought guidance from the U.S. Department of Education on this policy?
12. What additional evidence would you like LEAs to collect and use?
13. How would you modify your state's reclassification procedures (i.e., process LEAs follow during reclassification)?
14. In LEAs, who commonly makes reclassification decisions?
15. To what extent is reclassification a multistakeholder decision that includes teams?
16. Who would you like to see involved in reclassification decisions?
17. Does your state's policy empower families and older MLs with disabilities to be involved in their own reclassification decisions? How?
18. Who at the SEA level can best contribute to your state's reclassification policy for MLs with disabilities?
19. What expertise at the SEA level is needed to refine your state's reclassification policy?
20. How do you envision collaborating with your SEA colleagues on reclassification?

Alt ELP assessment, while in other states it involves establishing an Alt ELP assessment score—along with other ELP evidence—as needed for reclassification eligibility. Without either an established assessment or reclassification criteria, MLs with complex support needs will be unable to exit. Further, ML SEA leaders in states that have a prohibition on reclassification with an Alt ELP assessment score should urgently revoke these policies. Allowing a prohibition to remain, first, communicates that MLs with complex support needs can never be proficient in English—a misconception that lacks evidentiary support—and second, creates a direct policy-based systemic barrier to reclassification for these students. See reflective questions on Alt ELP assessments in Figure 9.1.

Some states have reclassification criteria that specify an ML with complex support needs can exit after 2 or 3 consecutive years of the same score as a mechanism to expand reclassification eligibility. Such policies were likely instituted to expand reclassification for these dually identified students. However, SEA leaders should know that multiyear score comparisons are relatively new in their use, and in response to their increasing prevalence, during a meeting with state leaders that I attended in 2024, U.S. Department of Education staff provided technical guidance to SEA leaders, clarifying that such criteria are noncompliant with federal mandates. Aside from compliance, multiple documented complications can arise from requiring multiple years of scores. First, ELP assessments change. Any policy that requires consecutive scores across 2 or 3 years will likely encounter issues with assessment revisions and therefore the comparability of scores (see Kangas & Schissel, 2021). Second, as COVID-19 has taught us, mass interruptions to learning can occur, which further complicates MLs' performance on standardized ELP assessments and teachers' efforts to understand these scores. Finally, these policies can implicitly convey the message that MLs with complex support needs cannot reach FEP status. In their communication with and guidance to LEAs, SEA leaders may need to reaffirm the multilingual capabilities of *all* MLs with disabilities.

Extending these recommendations further, SEA leaders should work across offices to revisit academic standard policies for students with complex support needs. This should include efforts to eliminate academic standard policies that bar students with complex support needs—whether MLs or not—who take alternate assessments from achieving a milestone, such as grade promotion and graduation. Similarly, states that have policies requiring multiple years of standardized assessment scores as a prerequisite for reaching achievement standards and milestones will first need to seek guidance from the U.S. Department of Education, leading professional organizations, or policy experts on the viability of these policies and then to revisit them continually in light of changes to the assessments as well as large-scale disruptions (natural disasters, pandemics, etc.) to learning that may occur for students.

Response 3: Advance the Roles of Teams in LEAs

During a webinar for SEA leaders on reclassification for MLs with disabilities, attendees were asked to offer the words that came to mind when they thought of this topic. Words like *complicated* and *complex* were routinely offered. With such complications and complexities associated with accounting for disability in reclassification, team—and not individual—decision-making should be mandated in policies that require teacher input of some form. While some states require multidisciplinary teams to oversee reclassification processes and to provide input, other states have yet to specify the educators who should be involved. For MLs with disabilities, team-based approaches are advisable (Kangas, 2024; Park & Chou, 2019), allowing individuals to bring together their collective expertise and ameliorating potential issues of individual bias. In my reclassification study, I often thought it was a missed opportunity when special educators immediately deferred to language specialists in all matters relating to ELP, including reclassification; while many language specialists command a depth of knowledge about English language acquisition and proficiency, due to constraints of teacher licensure and training, their knowledge of disabilities and their influence on language can be underdeveloped. They would benefit from the knowledge and experiences of their special education counterparts in reclassification.

Fortunately, the structures for team-based decision-making are already in place for MLs with disabilities, with the presence of IEP teams. These teams are multidisciplinary in nature, as for MLs with disabilities, a language specialist or another professional with expertise in second language learning is a required member (U.S. Departments of Justice & Education, 2015). Reviewing ELP data and making reclassification decision-making may then be folded into the annual IEP meetings (Burho & Thompson, 2021), depending on the time of year these meetings are held. Future policies for reclassification—and other academic standards—will need to elucidate the role of IEP teams in forming ELP goals, monitoring ELP progress, reviewing ELP data, and ultimately making reclassification decisions. Such clarifications are needed as educators' perceptions about the suitability of including language learning in IEPs vary considerably (Kangas, 2018a), and IEP teams' consideration of language learning and culture show similar disparities. As discussed in Chapter 4, some SEAs and LEAs are instituting individualized language plans and teams to oversee ELP progress monitoring and reclassification decisions, and yet for MLs with disabilities, such additional plans and teams can perpetuate silos and create additional disjunctures between the services and supports MLs with disabilities are provided.

Response 4: Engage Parents as Decision-Makers

To date, only two states require parent consultation as a criterion for exiting; in California, parent consultation is a listed requirement for all MLs, and in Minnesota, parent consultation is an additional reclassification criterion for those taking an Alt ELP assessment (Kangas, 2024). Outside of these contexts, parent notification of reclassification (e.g., a letter) is the norm. As a parent of a school-age child, I have become increasingly disturbed by this approach to reclassification for several reasons. First, IDEA (2004) codifies parent engagement as a legal protection for parents of students with disabilities; this, of course, includes dually identified students. Second, parents have unique insights into their children—their language capabilities, needs, and goals. As Burho and Thompson (2021) assert, parents should have a voice in whether language services are discontinued. Third, parent engagement has been considered a critical practice for best supporting MLs and students with disabilities alike. Why reclassification should be exempt from this is bewildering.

For these reasons, SEA leaders should incorporate parent input as a requirement for reclassification. Parent consultation during reclassification can take varied forms—from meetings to phone calls to written feedback. As states consider integrating parent consultation, there will certainly be a need to clarify what is—and is not—meaningful parent engagement. For instance, holding reclassification meetings in which there are no interpreters available would hardly constitute authentic parent consultation. Similarly, telling parents what reclassification decision *should* be made, instead of engaging in a two-way discussion of what decisions *can* be made, would not rise to the level of authentic engagement (Burho & Thompson, 2021).

Here, much can be learned from prior research on parent engagement in IEPs, specifically the importance of engaging parents before, during, and after IEP meetings in ways that are culturally and linguistically responsive and that treat them as collaborative decision-makers. Such engagement and the inclusion of parental input should be a fixed feature of any academic standard policy, given their importance in the learning and life opportunities of dually identified students.

Response 5: Incorporate and Empower Students

As IDEA (2004) affords parents a voice in their children's schooling, it also requires that, when appropriate, students with disabilities attend their own IEP meetings and contribute to their own transition planning. In stark contrast, however, ML education has no such provisions for reclassification; MLs' perspectives as students are often neglected, as demonstrated by their varying levels of awareness of their own status as *English learners* (Brooks, 2022) and their frustrations with the limited learning opportunities and stigma associated with language services (Brooks, 2023). Without student voice, Brooks (2023) attests, we cannot ascertain whether language services are supporting MLs: "adult-driven, test-based decision-making misses youths' experience of schooling, which is fundamental to assessing equity, and thus overall effectiveness, of an instructional program" (p. 8).

Reclassification shapes learning opportunities and further, is a process that is particularly relevant for older MLs with disabilities in secondary grades. Thus, SEA leaders may wish to update reclassification policies to stipulate student input, particularly of secondary MLs with disabilities, as part of exit procedures. Possibilities include the inclusion of MLs with disabilities, along with their parents, in reclassification meetings or integrating discussions about reclassification into IEP meetings and into transition planning. To guide the development of such procedures in reclassification and other academic standard policies, SEA leaders should consult student-centered approaches widely recommended in special education during IEP and transition planning, such as focusing on the overall—not just academic—well-being of the student, prioritizing the goals and dreams of the student and their family, and ultimately, allowing the student and family to take the lead in their education and postsecondary planning (Exceptional Children's Assistance Center, n.d.; IRIS Center, n.d.; National Parent Center on Transition and Employment, 2023).

SUMMARY

Examining state reclassification policies, this chapter chronicled how such academic standard policies typically hinge on standardized assessment scores. For dually identified students, this overdependence on standardized assessments, namely ELP assessments in reclassification, illuminates two of the three patterned inequities: language-or-disability filter and unitary identity. Through both reclassification policy development and implementation, the disabilities of MLs are both blamed and ignored in contradictory fashion. In terms of blame, resembling the language-or-disability filter, disability is assumed to be an inhibitor to multilingual development of MLs with disabilities, while systemic barriers to ELP growth remain unacknowledged and unattended. In terms of ignoring, disability is not—or, at best, is limitedly—accounted for in the criteria required for reclassification, demonstrating unitary identity at work. As I have argued throughout this book, patterned inequities go hand-in-hand. Where there is unitary identity, for example, close behind, there is often the specialization trap and vice versa. Conspicuously missing from this chapter is the influence of professional silos on the formation of state policies. In the next chapter on policies, I attend to the specialization trap in SEAs, establishing the structures and conditions found within the SEA level to the patterned inequities reified in state policies.

CHAPTER 10

State Policy Contexts

As I relayed in the very beginning of this book, the notion of *patterned inequities* developed after I began collaborating with SEA ML leaders. Working as a researcher and teacher educator, I had become familiar with the problems of practice teachers encountered when supporting dually identified students, and as time went on, I began to see these problems of practice conforming to three endemic and often co-occurring patterns. I had not yet realized that these patterned inequities teachers experienced were shared with another key education stakeholder: SEA leaders. This insight came to me in late 2020 when I was invited to join a group of ML SEA leaders and K–12 researchers who convened frequently in the midst of the challenges that arose during the pandemic. When the SEA leaders in this group discussed MLs with disabilities, I heard familiar beliefs, responses, and conditions resurface, but this time in the context of state departments of education. Through these conversations, I came to a new understanding of the ubiquity of patterned inequities: They are repeated and predictable as well as pervasive and shared, spanning all education sectors and challenging the efforts of all education stakeholders. In sum, patterned inequities in the education of dually identified students have five primary characteristics:

1. they are *repeated* and predictable,
2. they are *endemic* to most problems of practice,
3. they *co-occur* and reinforce one another,
4. they are *pervasive* across education sectors,
5. they are *shared,* experienced by all education stakeholders.

In this second and final chapter on equity in policies, I bring patterned inequities in state-level policy efforts more fully and clearly into view. In Chapter 9, I illuminated how state achievement standard policies replicate patterned inequities by commonly engaging in unitary identity responses, erasing the disabilities of MLs. When this erasure does not occur, these state policies can implicitly take up the language-or-disability filter by assuming disabilities are injurious to language learning. Here, I will detail how these patterned inequities intersect with state-level structures that operate according to the specialization trap. More simply put, the patterned inequities evidenced in policies connect intimately to the context in which they are developed—the siloed, specialist-driven organization of SEA departments and offices.

SEAS: KEY RESEARCH FINDINGS

SEAs and the professional staff working within them are understudied, and yet most agree that these contexts and their leaders wield significant influence in the education system (Brown et al., 2011; Garcia, 2021; Hopkins et al., 2022; Smarick & Squire, 2014). The role of state leaders has expanded exponentially over the past several decades, as SEAs are charged with the administration of federal and state laws, allocation of funding and resources, provision of technical assistance to LEAs, and management of professional licensure and training of educators, among many other responsibilities (Brown et al., 2011; Hodge et al., 2024; Smarick & Squire, 2014; Umansky et al., 2018). Despite their significance in shaping and implementing policies across these and other key responsibilities, research that examines state leaders' work is still in nascent stages.

What little we do know about state-level work in education indicates that state leaders contend with heavy workloads and bureaucratic hurdles that together stymie their efforts in realizing reform (Brown et al., 2011; Smarick & Squire, 2014). Referencing the demands placed on SEAs, Finn and Petrilli (2014) state: "Observers have lamented the fact that state education agencies lack the capacity to play the reform-leadership roles that they've been asked to take on" (p. 1). Apart from the general conditions experienced by many in SEAs, as I will discuss in the upcoming pages, state leaders work within the confines of siloed offices and departments, often demarcated by federal funding streams and professional disciplines. Within their distinct departments ML and special education leaders, as emerging scholarship documents, negotiate unique roles and responsibilities.

A more in-depth, nuanced understanding of ML SEA leaders' work comes from a recent examination of a research-practice partnership (RPP)—between SEA leaders and researchers who collaborate on problems of practice in promoting equity for MLs (see Hopkins et al., 2022; Weddle, 2023; Weddle et al., 2024)—in which I am a participant. The RPP study unearthed the multifaceted roles state leaders constantly perform, attending to the improvement of ML education both at the SEA and LEA levels (Hopkins et al., 2022; Weddle, 2023). At the SEA level, ML state leaders in the RPP shared how they championed the needs of MLs in broader state initiatives, worked across SEA offices on state ML frameworks, and navigated the changing political landscapes of their state governments. At the LEA level, ML state leaders also ensured districts and schools upheld federal and state laws, developed resources for education leaders to use, and collaborated with LEAs in ways that extended beyond compliance monitoring. The insights gleaned from this larger RPP study showcase the role of SEA leaders in promoting equity for MLs with their states through multiple channels and at multiple levels.

While no similar in-depth inquiries into the experiences of special education SEA leaders exist, there is indication that special education state directors and administrators have formidable responsibilities in arguably an even more litigious context (Massanari, 2001; Mayes & Zirkel, 2000; National Association of State Directors of Special Education [NASDSE], n.d.). While they too seek to elevate the needs of a distinct student group across other state offices and initiatives (NASDSE, n.d.), special education state leaders' work includes monitoring LEA compliance with federal laws, in this case IDEA; developing their states' laws and policies for educating students with disabilities; and taking corrective action when LEAs fail to uphold the legal rights of students with disabilities (Mayes & Zirkel, 2000). Many of these responsibilities parallel those in ML education, with the notable exception of corrective action. In contrast with their special education counterparts, ML state leaders felt that they could offer guidance—not prescription—to LEAs given the nature of local control (see Hopkins et al., 2022). As another distinction, special education SEAs are also at times directly responsible for providing services to students with disabilities (Mayes & Zirkel, 2000), further demonstrating the expansive scope and reach of these leaders' roles. Adding to these complexities, ML and special education state leaders engage in this work in the siloed structure of their state offices, which, as I will explicate below, are animated by the specialization trap.

EVIDENCE OF PATTERNS

In the specialization trap, education stakeholders operate narrowly and independently within the realm of their expertise, addressing only needs that fall under their specialization. With an eye on just a subset of MLs with disabilities' needs, reductionism of these students occurs; they become a fragment of needs, and efforts to support them holistically collapse. In the end, this siloed tendency traps state leaders, preventing them from effectively supporting MLs with disabilities. At the state level, the specialization trap is multilayered, evidenced in the (a) structure of SEA offices and departments, (b) expertise of SEA leaders, and (c) professional organizations supporting these leaders.

First, just as the separate legal origins of ML and special education structure teacher preparation in those two fields, they also influence the organization of SEA offices and departments. Given the expansive role of special education state leaders, each state has an office dedicated to special education, although the naming of these offices can vary (e.g., Department of Special Education, Exceptional Student Services, Office of Enhancing Student

Opportunities, etc.). In states with higher concentrations of MLs, such as California and Texas, it is also common to have an entire office dedicated to ML education or Title III of ESSA (e.g., Multilingual Support Division, Division of Emergent Bilingual Support). Contexts with smaller ML populations, for instance, New Hampshire and Vermont, may have an individual SEA leader overseeing ML education for the entire state. Regardless of the size of their staffing, ML and special education are distinctly separate state offices.

Amid demanding responsibilities and separate departmental structures, opportunities for cross-office coordination and collaboration become challenging for state leaders to realize. Reflecting on these conditions, the ML state leaders in Hopkins et al.'s (2022) aforementioned RPP study reported working in silos and often alone as "singletons" (p. 607). When I hear state leaders relay the challenges of collaborating across offices, I am reminded of a teacher, Mrs. Franks, in one of my studies. Recall, from Chapter 3, that Mrs. Franks was an itinerant ESL teacher who was tasked with coteaching with numerous teachers across multiple schools. Her days consisted of driving from one building to the next, with her schedule not allowing for consultation and coplanning with her colleagues. Try as she might to collaborate with colleagues, the structures of the ESL programming tied her hands from the start. Doing the best she could, she was forced to settle when supporting MLs with disabilities, working in isolation, focusing only on language, and often "pitching in" where she could in the cotaught classroom. In similar fashion, ML and special education SEA leaders must coordinate their efforts and collaborate with multiple colleagues to support the education of dually identified students, yet the structures and supports of state departments of education can render such efforts unfeasible, with ML and special education SEA leaders "pitching in" where they can. During a presentation I gave to state leaders, one special education leader in attendance voiced her frustration, describing how she had the desire to collaborate with her ML counterparts to advocate for MLs with disabilities, but the conditions of their work, such as the priorities of their superiors and pressing emergencies in LEAs, got in the way.

With separate ML and special education offices and SEA leaders working in silos, state policies, guidance, and initiatives are prone to inadequately address the intersection of language and disability. As an example, in their analysis of state guidance manuals, Baker et al. (2024) found that less than half of states had publicly available resources for their LEAs relating to dually identified students. They further found significant variation in the depth of these resources—from comprehensive guidance manuals to webpages with a series of links to resources created by the U.S. Department of Education and other organizations. The authors viewed these findings through the lens of *institutional habitus* (Bourdieu, 1977, 1990; Byrd, 2019), arguing that the paucity of resources reflects an institution's beliefs and values, in this case the beliefs and values of states. From working with state leaders, however, I see these findings in a different light—an artifact of the siloed offices of SEAs. As another example, we witnessed evidence of the specialization trap in Chapter 9 in reclassification policies, which have been slow to account for disabilities, often positioning MLs as language learners only. When we consider the structure of state offices, however, it is no wonder reclassification policies "treat" MLs with disabilities through the lens of language. Afterall, the requirement by ESSA (2015) for states to develop standardized reclassification policies comes under the responsibility of ML state offices and their leaders.

Second, corresponding to offices in which they are employed, state leaders' expertise further reinforces the specialization trap within SEAs. Garcia (2021) characterizes state leaders as essentially specialists, who have been trained by institutions of higher education, earned degrees in an education or policy field, and are members of professional disciplines. Special education state leaders, thus, tend to be specialists in special education and similarly, ML state leaders are specialists in multilingual education. On the surface, it may seem unremarkable that special education directors and coordinators hold degrees in special education and have a wealth of professional experience working as special education teachers and district leaders. Likewise, it is no great surprise that ML state leaders often hold degrees in TESOL or bilingual education, have served MLs in LEAs in the role of teachers and administrators, and have their own personal histories learning languages. The professional origins of state leaders are consequential to the specialization trap. Chapter 5 examined teacher education programs as a site in which the specialization trap is firmly rooted; the training and credentialing of ML and special educators are siloed, specialist-driven enterprises, with very few programs offering the robust interdisciplinary knowledge and training needed to support MLs with disabilities. In this way, state leaders trained in teacher education programs are likely to be specialists in ML education or special education—but not both—and to respond accordingly in their state-level work. Complicating matters further, state leaders can be responsible for establishing teacher certification credentials in their states, which directly influence the siloed, specialist-driven nature of teacher education programs.

Third, the specialization trap within SEAs surfaces also in the professional organizations supporting and providing technical assistance to state leaders, as they too are structured around disciplines. For ML state leaders, for instance, there is the National Association of English Learner Program Administrators (NAELPA), while for special education state leaders, there is the National Association of State Directors of Special Education (NASDSE), among others. Larger organizations, such the Council of Chief State School Officers (CCSSO), serve all SEA leaders, but given the specialist nature of state-level work, it is divided into "Collaboratives," with one focused on English Learners (ELs) and another on Assessing, Standards, and Education for Students with Disabilities (ASES). These organizations provide valuable opportunities for state leaders to deepen their expertise; however, when we take a step back and consider the professional worlds of state leaders, we can see they are ordered by specializations.

For this reason, I was excited about the opportunity to partner with the National Center for Systemic Improvement (NCSI), an organization that supports special education state leaders, on a webinar addressing reclassification of MLs with disabilities. For the webinar, we sought to bring ML and special education state leaders together and to position reclassification policies as a cross-office issue. This idea—I am sheepish to admit—did not immediately occur to me because reclassification is a process that falls under the expertise of ML state leaders. But, as I gained more knowledge of reclassification of dually identified students, I realized it cannot be a matter for *only* ML SEA leaders to address; reclassification must be a shared responsibility. In fact, the recommendations I offered in Chapter 9 for ameliorating the elision of disability in reclassification policies require the valuable expertise of special education state leaders. In Weddle et al. (2024), we argued that *shared responsibility*—a notion that has been associated historically with teacher mindsets—pertains to each level of the education system, including state offices and their leaders, and encompasses more than a mindset; it also includes norms and structures. Through this lens, I believed a webinar that brought ML and special education SEA leaders together and gave them resources and tools for future collaborations on reclassification was an inroad to cultivate shared responsibility in the mindsets, norms, and structures around reclassification. This was just a one-time initiative; more sustained cross-state collaborations are needed. For sustaining longer-term and continued shared responsibility in SEA offices, there are several recommendations for state leaders to consider.

RESPONSES TO PATTERNED INEQUITIES IN SEAS

Even when facing hard-to-budge silos, state leaders can act as agents of change, developing consequential policies and guiding LEAs in critical matters of access and equity for historically underserved children. But, as this and the prior chapter have showcased, promoting equity in the education of MLs with disabilities across multiple levels of the school system requires state leaders from ML and special education working together. Even though siloed structures of SEA offices can have a wearying effect on state leaders and a stifling impact on their collaborations, the price of state leaders operating within the confines of their respective offices is too costly for dually identified students. Through collaboration, ML and special education SEA leaders can challenge the specialization trap within their states and LEAs and in the process, achieve what NCSI (2021) calls *systems coherence*—"a consistency of beliefs, policies and procedures, and practices" (p. 1)—in state departments and offices of education. With the dually identified student population undoubtedly on the rise across most states (see Cooc, 2023), systems coherence in SEAs is paramount. Below are foundational recommendations to support state leaders as they attempt to expand the collaborative capacity of their SEA offices, working toward greater systems coherence in high-priority areas at the interface of special education and ML education.

Response 1: Build Collaborative Structures

In my very first study on services for MLs with disabilities, I found that collaboration and the conditions that support them are a chicken-and-egg phenomenon (see Kangas, 2017a). Teachers could not collaborate because their schedules did not afford coplanning and consultation time; yet their schedules were unlikely to change if "collaborations" consisted of teachers working in isolation even when sharing the same physical space. In this way, collaborations and working conditions are cyclical, having a reciprocal effect on one another. The same holds true for state leaders; SEA structures and processes have no need to foster collaboration if the specialization trap pervades state leaders' efforts.

As an initial step to nudge SEA processes out of their specialist-driven silos, state leaders can regularize collaborative meetings between ML and special education offices. Standing meetings afford several benefits. They convey that collaboration is a norm in the education of MLs with disabilities, while modeling for LEAs the possibilities of working across ML and special education. Also, standing meetings between offices can last beyond the tenure of any one state leader, which is critical given the turnover within some departments of education. Finally, carving out collaborative time now—and not later—can lead to more consistent and productive collaborations. ML state leaders often report being invited to meetings with their colleagues from other offices to provide an "ML perspective." While initially promising, these invitations and the opportunities to impart valuable insights about the needs of MLs often came too late into an initiative to be meaningful or productive.

As they establish standing meetings, state leaders should consider the following guiding preparatory questions:

1. Who from our departments should be invited?
2. How often should we meet?
3. What is the most productive format for the meeting (in-person or remote)?
4. Who will be responsible for scheduling meetings?
5. When will we create and share an agenda?

6. Who will build the agenda?
7. How can we set goals or objectives for each meeting?
8. Who will lead the meeting or take ownerships of the agenda?
9. Where will we store materials and resources related to our meeting?
10. When will we set aside time to work between meetings?

After instituting standing meetings, SEAs should consider the creation of a liaison position that bridges special and ML education to strengthen systems coherence within states. This liaison would work across departments to elevate the specific needs of MLs with disabilities and to lead collaborative efforts among SEA colleagues, thereby opening pathways for two-way communication and bringing awareness to potential oversights and misalignments in state policies and initiatives. With the increasing prevalence and heterogeneity of MLs with disabilities, I argue such liaisons are needed at both state and local levels. In Chapter 3, in fact, I recommended that LEAs create similar positions within their districts as a strategic response against fragmented responses and even competition among services and supports for dually identified students. Likewise in SEAs, such a position is a structural move toward systems coherence.

In states with higher numbers of MLs with disabilities, hiring a new cross-department staff member would be both reasonable and warranted. In states with fewer dually identified students, appointing an existing member to spearhead interdepartmental initiatives and coordination for MLs with disabilities may be the most prudent pathway to take. For this state leader, the departments should consider formally adjusting their roles and responsibilities, allocating a certain percentage of their time to cross-department work to avoid piling more work on already taxed state leaders. If budgetary constraints preclude the hiring of new staff and reallocation of staff time proves untenable, a third option states may consider is hiring a part-time consultant or forming a mutually beneficial partnership with education organizations or researchers. Such external partnerships can help expand the collaborative capacities of SEA offices to benefit MLs with disabilities even within the confines of limited resources and time.

Response 2: Establish Shared Expectations and Processes for Collaboration

With the responsibilities state leaders bear, they have no time to waste. In states where collaborations across ML and special education are new or underdeveloped, the next critical step state leaders can take is establishing shared expectations and processes for their work together. I underestimated the significance of these actions until only recently. As one of the researchers participating in the earlier referenced RPP study, we would work for months at a time on a specific problem of practice. Forging productive collaborations across state-level offices was such a significant problem of practice for ML state leaders that we dedicated 8 months of meetings and resource development to it. In these discussions, SEA leaders envisioned productive state-level collaborations in stark contrast to perfunctory interactions with colleagues that seemed to focus on checking a box (i.e., "yes," the input of ML or special education colleagues was provided). The state leaders and researchers in the group worked together to develop a framework that state leaders could use to identify and sustain collaborations. Entitled the SASSY Framework, the group defined effective cross-office collaborations as Systemic, Accountable, Sustainable, Strategic, and Yields Results (see Table 10.1). By defining effective state-level collaborations, SEA leaders could have some assurance that they were approaching their collaboration with shared expectations.

This framework also serves as a useful tool for cultivating processes for collaborations. State leaders could begin collaborations by setting defined goals and outcomes as well as identifying the roles and responsibilities for each party. Identifying a plan for communicating with one another will be imperative. These tasks are foundational to virtually any collaboration. So, too, is the creation of a shared cross-office online space in which initiatives and resources can be shared, viewed, and updated in live time. Throughout my research with LEAs, I have discovered that the specialization trap often results in inefficiencies and even errors; with each department having their own databases or online repositories of resources, ML and special education leaders in districts and schools can often be working with incomplete and outdated information. Such divisions are liabilities for state leaders as well.

These fundamentals aside, collaborative processes will vary depending on the scope of the task at hand. State leaders, for instance, will need to establish processes for creating manuals, guidance, and frequently asked questions (FAQs) documents; responding to technical assistance requests;

Table 10.1. SASSY Framework for Effective SEA Cross-Office Collaborations

Systematic	The collaboration has clearly defined and shared common goals and outcomes, as well as defined processes for collaboration.
Accountable	Each collaborator contributes to the project and brings something specific to the table with clearly defined roles and accountability for participation.
Sustainable	Ideally, collaborations once established live on beyond the efforts of any one person.
Strategic	The collaboration leverages strategic opportunities and brings resources together to support MLs.
Yields Results	The collaboration achieves documented results that support educational improvement for MLs.

and designing professional learning opportunities for LEA, among others. Moreover, as departments undertake new initiatives that are high priority, processes for coordination are paramount. For instance, an ML office may be in the process of revising its state reclassification criteria, while a special education or assessment office is also reissuing guidance on alternate academic achievement standards. These initiatives must be coordinated and aligned, otherwise LEAs may be presented with unclear, or worse, discrepant guidance on Alt ELP assessments.

As a final step, state leaders should also consider forming a communications plan for LEAs regarding matters involving MLs with disabilities. At times, communication with LEAs can fall along disciplinary lines, with ML state leaders disseminating information to district ML directors and similarly, special education leaders contacting district special education directors. State departments may wish to develop joint communication shared with ML and special education LEA leaders to foster shared understandings of the needs of MLs with disabilities at the local level.

Response 3: Advocate and Manage Up

The more I become familiar with SEAs, the more apparent it is to me that working toward equity for MLs with disabilities requires state leaders advocating and managing up. In addition to their siloed structures, state offices are hierarchical, with at times multiple levels of state leaders working under cabinet members who all support the head of the education department for an entire state, whether a commissioner, superintendent, or deputy of education. In contrast to state professional staff, such as state leaders, Garcia (2021) characterizes the commissioners of education at the top of the hierarchy as politicians. Commissioners may be elected or appointed into office (Scudella, 2013) and at times, do not share the same professional knowledge and experiences as state leaders (Garcia, 2021). These key differences can result in ML and special education state leaders becoming critical advocates for MLs and students with disabilities, respectively, within their states. Hopkins et al.'s (2022) study reported, for instance, state leaders needing to advocate up the SEA hierarchy, gaining the support of superiors who could then, in turn, advance ML concerns in the state.

Promoting equity for MLs with disabilities within states will require similar championing efforts. There are two avenues through which advocacy efforts can be targeted. First, the unique needs of MLs with disabilities deserve attention. While MLs with disabilities present some of the most pressing challenges in education, because of the small size of the population compared to other student groups, policies and initiatives most germane to their education tend to be put off for later. ML and special education departments can work together to continually elevate this population, bringing awareness of their unique needs to upper-level state leaders and politicians.

Second, structures and resources that would facilitate cross-office coordination also require advocacy. Those in the top of the state hierarchy may be unaware of the temporal, fiscal, and human resources it requires to work across state offices on policies and initiatives that would best serve these students. Through their relationships and rich knowledge base, the professional staff of SEAs, as Garcia (2021) attests, are powerful intermediaries in enacting policy change.

Shifting From Collaborative Processes to Collaborative Products

So far I have attended to processes, that is, the "how" of cross-office SEA collaboration. The products derived from SEA collaborations—or the "what"—are equally critical to address. Unquestionably, there are countless initiatives that could serve as the focus of ML and special education leaders' collaborations. Initiatives that are a shared priority among the offices are a cogent starting point, as there is likely to be buy-in among colleagues as well as momentum that state leaders can leverage. With research and policies for MLs with disabilities still in nascent stages, identifying only a few shared priorities can feel overwhelming. Where should state leaders begin?

As reflected in Baker et al.'s (2024) review of state resources for dually identified students, many states have focused on generating guidance and other resources pertaining to referral and evaluation of MLs for special education for LEAs to follow. Referral and evaluation are wise choices because linguistically and culturally responsive identification of disabilities functions as a nucleus, influencing all subsequent schooling experiences and opportunities for students. But other critical problems of practice in the education of MLs with disabilities, like those centered in this book, remain profoundly overlooked and deserving of much more attention. While each is pressing, there are three that I would like to elevate—because of their wide-ranging influence—as most deserving of state leaders' joint attention: (a) teacher certifications and competencies, (b) IEP documents and teams, and (c) reclassification policies. Because Chapter 9 was dedicated to reclassification, here I will address the first two priorities in the remaining recommendations.

Response 4: Revisit Teacher Certification Credentials

Existing teacher education programs and professional certifications are oriented around siloed disciplines of ML education and special education. This siloing of knowledge and skills in teacher education sustains fragmented responses to the needs of dually identified students in LEAs; we see vestiges of silos in MLs with disabilities' services, physical placements in schools, individualized plans, and instructional supports, as documented in previous chapters. Thus, SEAs revising their state-mandated competencies and certification areas for teachers would have an expansive influence on the education of MLs with disabilities, rippling through multiple sectors and impacting multiple stakeholders (see Table 10.2).

State leaders can consider three pathways for their revisions to teacher education credentials and competencies. First, ML and special education SEA offices should introduce state-approved certification areas that emphasize interdisciplinary perspectives and skills, such as bilingual special education or integrated ESL–special education (as we see in, e.g., Illinois and Texas). Second, within existing certification areas, SEA offices should institute required courses and/or robust competencies that address the needs of MLs with disabilities. A list of potential competencies that state leaders can consider adopting can be found in Figure 5.1. Third, state leaders can institute incentives and supports for in-service teachers to pursue additional certifications. Through state scholarships, grants, and loan forgiveness programs, these initiatives can support inservice special educators and language specialists in accruing bilingual/ESL certifications and special education certifications, respectively.

Response 5: Amplify Guidance and Training for IEP Documents, Teams, and Meetings

IEPs are a second area in urgent need of SEA leaders' joint attention. While IDEA (2004) requires IEPs to "consider" the language and cultural backgrounds of MLs, interpretation of this mandate in LEAs varies significantly and often with dismal results. Chapter 4 delves into initial research on the IEP contents, indicating that IEPs often are written as if MLs with disabilities are monolingual children with disabilities—void of connection of language learning and culture (Hoover et al., 2019; Hoover & Patton, 2017). Furthermore, multiple studies report that IEP meetings are conducted in a manner that is virtually inaccessible to ML parents; held in English and at times without an interpreter, loaded with jargon, and predicated on knowledge of special education processes, IEP meetings can be overwhelming and alienating to multilingual parents who deserve authentic engagement as key decision-makers in their children's education (Burke et al., 2021; Montoya et al., 2022; Salas, 2004; Voulgarides, 2018). The existing shortcomings of IEP documents and meetings require urgent action from states. IEPs are intended to guide the education of students with disabilities, providing a plan for services, instruction, and accommodations. In this way, improving IEPs for MLs can and should introduce systemic changes that expand the everyday learning opportunities of these students.

In prioritizing IEPs as the focus of state collaborations, state leaders can take the following course of action. First, SEA leaders should carefully consider the proposition that IEPs, by definition, are supposed to be individualized, and these documents cannot be individualized for MLs if connections to language learning are absent. Anchored in this understanding,

Table 10.2. High Priorities for State Cross-Office Collaborations

	Problem of Practice	Call for SEA Leaders	Rationale for High Priority Choice
Teacher education competencies and certifications	Teachers need unique knowledge and skills to support the learning of MLs with disabilities. Teacher education programs and certification areas are highly siloed, often further fragmenting knowledge and skills of teachers.	Revise teacher education competencies and certification-areas to account for the knowledge and skills needed to support and expand learning opportunities for MLs with disabilities.	Revisions to competencies and certification areas can influence knowledge and practices of teachers, education leaders, state leaders, and teacher educators.
IEPs	IDEA requires IEPs to "consider" MLs' language and culture as well as requires that IEP meetings be accessible to ML parents. IEP documents and meetings often fail to be responsive to the linguistic needs of MLs and their families.	Develop guidance that offers robust interpretations of IDEA's mandate and supports LEAs in instituting linguistically responsive IEPs, teams, and meetings.	Guidance can influence goals, instruction, services, and instructional supports for MLs with disabilities and improve ML parents' experiences with LEAs.
Reclassification (see Chapter 9)	MLs with disabilities are disproportionately less likely to be reclassified as English proficient. State-defined criteria for *English proficient* are likely contributing to low reclassification rates.	Refine reclassification criteria to draw upon a wider body of evidence and to involve multidisciplinary teams.	Modified reclassification criteria can expand reclassification eligibility for MLs with disabilities, influencing their subsequent learning opportunities.

Table 10.3. Additional Priorities for Cross-Office Initiatives

Asset-based lens	Access to advanced courses Challenging ableism, racism, and linguicism Inclusion in bilingual education programs Seal of biliteracy Twice exceptional MLs/gifted education
Coteaching and collaboration	Coteaching models Consultation meetings Data sharing Integration of services Progress monitoring Shared responsibility
General and Alt ELP assessments	Accessibility and accommodations Alt ELP screeners Domain exemptions Eligibility ELP benchmarks Progress monitoring
ILPs	Composition of ILP teams Connection to IEPs Multiple ELP data sources Parent/family engagement Student input Team-based decision-making
Services	Access to bilingual education Dual service access Language services for MLs with complex support needs MTSS Myth of "disability trumps language" Waiving language services

ML and special education state leaders can develop clear guidance to LEAs on the robust integration of language learning into IEP goals, services, and specially designed instruction. Second, state leaders from ML and special education can offer guidance and training that (a) emphasize the importance of language specialists on IEP teams and (b) foster their authentic participation in IEP development and meetings. Finally, state leaders need to amplify guidance and training for teams around engaging and empowering

ML families before, during, and after IEP meetings. Additional details for enhancing contributions from language specialists in IEPs as well as promoting ML families' engagement during IEP meetings can be found in Chapter 4.

Outside of teacher education competencies, IEPs, and reclassification, in Table 10.3 are additional high priorities worthy of ML and special education leaders' collaborations.

With high priorities at the fore, I urge state leaders to consider collaborating on the development of externally facing resources. With the turnover of K–12 teachers and administrators as well as the shortages of special education and language specialists (Blad, 2024; Najarro, 2023; Whittaker, 2023), publicly available resources for LEAs, such as manuals and policy guides, can serve as much-needed guides for teachers and school leaders who are new in their roles. In short, such externally facing resources can have a longer shelf life and more expansive influence if they are extended to multistakeholder groups (e.g., teacher educators, researchers, and parents). Some states have already embarked on publicly available guidance manuals relating to dually identified students, but for state leaders wishing to develop such resources, a list of exemplary models and supporting readings are listed at the conclusion of the chapter.

In state contexts in which resources for LEAs are firmly in place, SEA leaders should consider offering cross-department professional learning opportunities for LEAs. With many teacher education programs remaining entrenched in disciplinary silos, educators are in need of professional learning that strives for integrated, interdisciplinary understandings of issues most central to MLs with disabilities' learning. What's more, professional learning opportunities themselves can adhere to the specialization trap, further bifurcating the knowledge and skills of educators into special education or ML "camps." The topics delineated in Table 10.3 dovetail as list of avenues for future professional learning webinars and workshops of joint interest and need for any educator supporting MLs with disabilities.

SUMMARY

With a focus on SEA departments and offices, this chapter foregrounded the multilayered nature of the specialization trap with states, evidenced in the structure of state offices, disciplinary expertise of state leaders, and professional organizations supporting them. The specialization trap in SEAs encourages ML and special education leaders to work in their respective silos, thus creating fertile ground for the remaining patterned inequities to take root in state policies and initiatives. Addressing this latter point, Chapter 9 centered reclassification policies as an example of how patterned inequities undergird academic achievement standard policies of states. Reclassification policies tend to overlook disability or to render it—and not the quality of instruction, services, and learning opportunities—as a stunting force in ELP and multilingual growth. Collectively, these two chapters on policies showcase the co-occurring and reinforcing nature of patterned inequities; where one takes hold, another shortly follows, operating together as a buttress. Through improved collaborations at the state level, ML and special education state leaders can together jointly advance policies and initiatives that account for the whole child—not just disability or just language. In these two chapters, state leaders are encouraged to take on teacher education, IEPs, and reclassification, as priorities for their collaborations. Addressing these three high priorities in future cross-office collaborations can appreciably expand the learning and life opportunities of dually identified students.

RECOMMENDED RESOURCES

State Policy Guides

California Department of Education. (2019). *California practitioners' guide for educating English learners with disabilities.* https://www.cde.ca.gov/sp/se/ac/documents/ab2785guide.pdf

Massachusetts Department of Elementary and Secondary Education. (2019). *Guidance for supporting English learners with disabilities.* https://www.doe.mass.edu/ele/disability.html

New Mexico Public Education Department. (2023). *English learner students with disabilities guidance manual.* https://webnew.ped.state.nm.us/wp-content/uploads/2023/10/Identifying_Serving_ELs_Disabilities_Guidance_FINAL.pdf

Virginia Department of Education. (2019). *Handbook for educators of English learners with suspected disabilities.* https://www.doe.virginia.gov/home/showpublisheddocument/32709/638047251265570000

Resources for Developing Policy Guides

Burr, E. (2019). *Guidance manuals for educators of English learners with disabilities: Ideas and lessons from the field* (NCEO Report 410). National Center on Educational Outcomes. https://nceo.umn.edu/docs/OnlinePubs/NCEOReport410.pdf

Park, S., Martinez, M., & Chou, F. (2017). *CCSSO English learners with disabilities guide.* Council of Chief State School Officers. https://ccsso.org/topics/supporting-english-learners

U.S. Department of Education. (2016). *Tools and resources for addressing English learners with disabilities.* https://www2.ed.gov/about/offices/list/oela/english-learner-toolkit/chap6.pdf

U.S. Department of Justice & U.S. Department of Education. (2015, January 5). *Dear colleague letter: English learner students and limited English proficient parents.* https://www2.ed.gov/about/offices/list/ocr/letters/colleague-el-201501.pdf

Part V

CONCLUSION

CHAPTER 11

Pathways Forward

An equitable education for dually identified students is marked by access to opportunities—for learning and exercising their educational rights. When equity is safeguarded, as we compare the schooling of MLs with disabilities to that of all their peers, we should see no discrepancy in their opportunities to grow academically and multilingually in inclusive, supportive, and rigorous settings. As this book underscores, working toward this aim requires something from each of us as education stakeholders: our awareness and response.

OUR AWARENESS

Awareness of patterned inequities is paramount. Without this knowledge, education stakeholders cannot intervene in the practices in systems, practices in classrooms, and policies that diminish the promise of free and appropriate public education (FAPE) for MLs with disabilities. Throughout this book, I documented the characteristics of patterned inequities and provided ample evidence illustrating their existence. In doing so, I aimed to present a comprehensive framework for equity that education stakeholders can use to understand the experiences, opportunities, and rights of dually identified students.

At the beginning of the book, I argued that the problems of practice in the education of MLs with disabilities have a patterned inequity at their core. More than a one-off aberration, patterned inequities are named as such because of their habitual nature. Spanning across sectors—from K–12 classrooms and schools to higher education institutions to state departments of education—the same entangled inequities emerge. Regardless of their respective roles, stakeholders in these varied contexts will inevitably confront these inequities in their daily work to support MLs with disabilities and advocate for their improved education. Taken together, patterned inequities have five core tendencies: they are (1) *repeated* and predictable, (2) *endemic* to most problems of practice, (3) *co-occurring*, reinforcing one another, (4) *pervasive* across education sectors, and (5) *shared,* experienced by all education stakeholders. Because they are foreseeable and formulaic, with awareness, stakeholders can learn to recognize patterned inequities and respond accordingly to mitigate their influence.

In each series of chapters, I presented the case for three routine patterned inequities.

Pattern 1: Language-or-Disability Filter

In this patterned inequity, the difficulties or problems MLs with disabilities experience in their education are inordinately attributed to their language learning or disabilities. With a sustained gaze toward explanations internal to the student (i.e., language or disability), external contributors present in classrooms, systems, and policies go undetected. Used as a sensemaking tool to diagnose the source of problems within children, the language-or-disability filter is a de facto deficit lens that is highly prone to biases.

In systems, the filter is used to determine access to services and placements for dually identified students, guiding educators to encourage monolingual English language services and settings because disability is believed to limit or render improbable their multilingual development. In classrooms, the language-or-disability filter prevents teachers from establishing high expectations and clouds their interpretation of student performance data for MLs with disabilities. In ways that connect deeply to racism and ableism, the filter pathologizes who MLs with disabilities are and what they do—in terms of the language they produce, academic abilities they demonstrate, and behaviors, emotions, and social skills they exhibit. Finally, in policies, thresholds established for academic achievement, such as those in reclassification, deem multilingualism too lofty for MLs with disabilities and the proficiency they attain in English subpar. Across these contexts, while language and disability are blamed, disadvantageous and disabling learning systems, environments, and policies remain intact.

Pattern 2: Unitary Identity

In this second patterned inequity, identity erasure for MLs with disabilities occurs. Although they are a heterogeneous group of students with multiple intersecting identities, they tend to be reduced to a monolithic, singular identity. Commonly, the elision of their fuller identities occurs when they are positioned dichotomously—either as an ML or as a student with a disability. This positioning is predicated on default norms of students in schooling—that is, notions of who students should be. In special education, this default student is a monolingual English-speaking child with a disability, and as such, practices and policies in special education tend to erase multilingualism. In contrast, in ML education, the default norm is a multilingual child without a disability, and thus, disability is commonly overlooked. With unitary identity, the needs of MLs with disabilities remain unaccounted for and unmet, and consequently, they experience a distinct form of double discrimination. Demonstrated throughout the book is the notion that unitary identity is reciprocal with the third patterned inequity: the specialization trap.

Pattern 3: Specialization Trap

In the third patterned inequity, the specialization trap, education stakeholders approach the education of MLs with disabilities through the narrow boundaries of their disciplines. Derived from a medical model, which emphasizes the role of specialists in "treating" individuals, in the specialization trap, education stakeholders address only the needs, issues, and initiatives that pertain to their specialization. The outcome for MLs with disabilities is fractured, disjointed efforts among stakeholders. Further, across these silos, errors and inconsistencies arise in the schooling of dually identified students. In the end, this fragmented, specialist-driven response traps even well-meaning stakeholders' efforts to understand and support the entire child.

Just as with unitary identity, when education stakeholders fall into the specialization trap, they focus on just one set of needs, viewing and responding to MLs with disabilities as though they are solely MLs *or* students with disabilities but not both. In the book, unitary identity and the specialization trap co-occurred in systems, classrooms, and policies.

In systems, when service provision pits language and disability-related services against one another, one service often loses out. As a result, MLs with disabilities are often treated like they have only a set of isolated needs; language specialists only support ELP, and special educators support the academic, behavioral, and socioemotional needs relating to disability. Identity erasure and the specialization trap also manifest in IEPs. Compromising their individualized nature, IEPs are commonly written as if dually identified students only have disabilities. ML families, by extension, experience identity erasure when they attend IEP meetings and are sidelined by a process that is not culturally and linguistically responsive. It is no coincidence that the erasure of language identities occurs in IEP teams and meetings—domains that fall under the purview of special educators and historically have not included other colleagues, such as language specialists. There is little research on ILPs, but these documents could likewise fall short of their potential if they ignore disability and marginalize the expertise of special educators.

In policies, such as reclassification, MLs without disabilities are assumed to be the default norm, and thus disability is profoundly overlooked in the criteria established for reaching English proficient status. Working toward policies that reflect the intersecting needs of dually identified students is a challenging feat because SEA offices are typically organized around specializations, leaving little opportunity for ML and special education state leaders to coordinate and collaborate. Compounding further the interplay between unitary identity and the specialization trap in systems, classrooms, and policies is the highly siloed approach to teacher education programs and professional certification, in which language specialists and special educators are trained to see and respond to bi- and multilingualism or disability, respectively, yet not the intersection of the two.

In all, patterned inequities provide stakeholders with a framework to detect injustice. Even when encountering what seems to be a novel problem of practice in the education of MLs with disabilities, one or several pattern inequities are at the nucleus. Equipped with this awareness, education stakeholders can more readily and effectively respond.

OUR RESPONSE

When we take stock of their pervasiveness across education sectors, patterned inequities can feel insurmountable. Yet they are far from permanent. With strategic and even seemingly small changes in each sector, the eradication of patterned inequities for MLs with disabilities is a goal within our reach. In Chapter 3, I introduced readers to *structuration theory* (Giddens, 1979), which emphasizes the interdependence between institutions and individual agency. The theory asserts that the structures and conditions of institutions influence what people can do as well as their sense of what is possible. But what are institutions made of, if not people? As such, the actions people take can shift the very institutions they inhabit. Applied to education, the inner workings of our institutions (e.g., districts, schools, SEA offices, higher education) can mold us and our actions, but as stakeholders, our actions can mold institutions in turn.

Taking up this understanding, this book emphasized the agentive capacities of critical stakeholders in the education of MLs with disabilities: teachers, educational leaders, state leaders, and the professoriate that train them. Operating as agents of change, these education stakeholders can promote equity for dually identified students in powerful and significant ways. Across the chapters of the book, stakeholders encountered specific recommendations for challenging the patterned inequities they encounter in their work supporting MLs with disabilities, whether in teaching or their leadership at the school, district, higher education, or state levels. The recommendations offered collectively fall under three overarching pathways for promoting equity: (1) dignity and humanistic frames, (2) intersectional approaches, and (3) shared responsibility. Each pathway is needed in the pursuit of an equitable education for dually identified students, and collectively they offer a holistic approach for education stakeholders' efforts. Importantly, these overarching pathways are interrelated and interdependent (see Figure 11.1). Thus, as stakeholders begin to enact one, the others will naturally emerge.

Figure 11.1. Overarching Pathways to Promote Equity

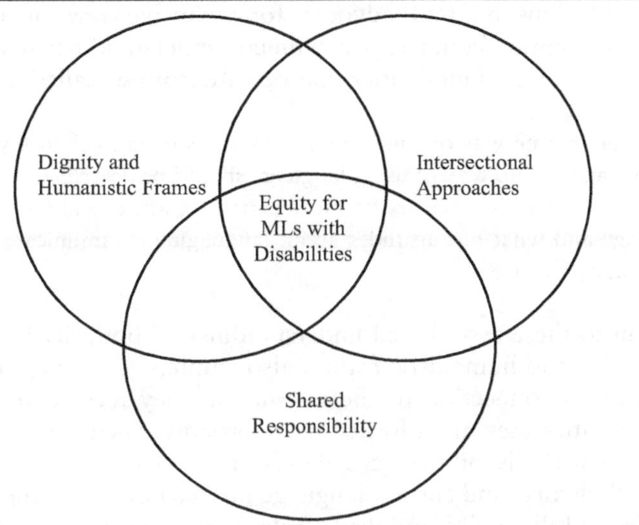

In what follows, I discuss each of these pathways, pulling together the recommendations provided from across the chapters that each stakeholder can enact.

Pathway 1: Dignity and Humanistic Frames

Education scholarship has long called for a reimagining of how we view students, particularly those who have been assigned stigmatizing institutional labels; however, in the past several years, these calls have intensified (see Espinoza et al., 2020; Herrera et al., 2023; Kibler & Valdés, 2016; Martínez-Álvarez, 2023; Poza, 2021). As we reflect on the evidence in this book demonstrating the existence of the language-or-disability filter, a movement toward a more holistic—as opposed to label-driven—understanding of MLs with disabilities is inarguably needed. Scholarship offers us an alternative to the language-or-disability filter and its concomitant preoccupation with deficit-based understandings of disability and language: dignity and humanistic frames (Espinoza et al., 2020; Martínez-Álvarez, 2023; Poza, 2021). These frames offer education stakeholders a lens for seeing and responding to students in ways that affirm the entire person—their inherent value and worth, capabilities, potential, hopes, and dreams.

Dignity and humanistic frames importantly require education stakeholders to take up new and asset-based understandings of both disability and language. Martínez-Álvarez (2023) asserts that a humanistic lens requires "positive views about disability, which are yet to be recognized in today's school and social discourse" (p. 81). Making parallel arguments, Henner and Robinson (2023) advocate for expansive views of language and linguistic capabilities, countering prominent understandings that stigmatize language practices and modalities that deviate from so-called norms:

> We argue that no way of languaging is bad; it is okay to change your own use of language but no way of using language should be described as atypical, disordered, or defective. We need a more expansive attitude about what involves language and what our attitudes about languaging communicate about a person's capacity. (p. 8)

In addition to these asset-based understandings of both disability and language, dignity and humanistic frames also emphasize the potential of each student and its connection to the instruction they receive and the learning opportunities they are afforded more broadly. Such frames help us see how *all* MLs with disabilities, regardless of their identified disabilities, prior educational history, and current language proficiency, can achieve academically, grow multilingually, and thrive holistically—when they are truly given the opportunity to learn.

What does taking up dignity and humanistic frames mean for each stakeholder? For educational leaders of districts and schools, such frames require organizing services and placements to operate from the standpoint that MLs with disabilities are worthy and capable beings. For teachers, such frames inform their pedagogical approaches, evoking them to both *be* and *do* high expectations in the classroom. Dignity and humanistic frames also provide a lens through which teachers can interpret student performance data, understanding that language and disability alone should not be the go-to explanations for the patterns observed in the data. For state leaders, such frames compel state policies, such as those for academic standards, to be predicated on the assumption that *all* MLs with disabilities can grow academically and linguistically, including those with complex support needs. As such, policies should account for the varied ways MLs with disabilities can demonstrate growth in their academic and multilingual skills. Recommendations for enacting dignity and humanistic frames are summarized in Tables 11.1 through 11.4.

Pathway 2: Intersectional Approaches

Scholars who examine the schooling of MLs with disabilities resoundingly argue for *intersectional approaches* (Artiles, 2013; Cioè-Peña, 2017, 2021; Kangas, 2017b, 2018a)—a term I use here to capture practices and policies that account for and respond to students' multiple identities and needs. Intersectional approaches are an antidote to unitary identity, mitigating the tendency in education to reduce students to a single identity, especially according to specific institutional labels. Calling us away from approaches

Table 11.1. Actions for Educational Leaders

	Dignity and Humanistic Frames	Intersectional Approaches	Shared Responsibility
Service Provision and Placements	• Actively debunk myths that limit access to services and programs • Conduct equity audits to examine placements and access to services • Create a policy that allows MLs with disabilities to "try out" higher academic track courses • Develop multiyear equity plan for MLs with disabilities in district/school	• Prioritize MLs with disabilities during master scheduling • Invest in liaison positions, bridging ML and special education • Pilot bilingual special education or integrated ESL–special education programs	• Institute planned collaborative time between ML and special education • Implement professional learning communities focused on MLs with disabilities
Individualized Plans	• Promote IEPs that reflect MLs' strengths and multilingualism • Encourage ILPs to focus on multilingual development and to include multilingual data	• Oversee review of IEPs for MLs to assess their linguistic responsiveness • Initiate revision to IEPs to reflect MLs' multicultural backgrounds and multilingual needs • Adopt EPIC model to promote authentic ML family engagement in IEP meetings	• Implement cross-department training for IEP writing for MLs • Ensure language specialists are members of IEP teams • Support language specialists' participation in IEP team meetings
Teacher Training/ Professional Learning	• Promote professional learning that emphasizes the assets—not deficits—of MLs with disabilities	• Invest in ML–special education joint trainings to support the needs of MLs with disabilities • Form a multiyear professional learning plan centering MLs with disabilities	• Cultivate a culture in which supporting *all* students is the norm • Offer tuition remission or financial incentives for teachers to pursue dual licensure

Table 11.2. Actions for Teachers

	Dignity and Humanistic Frames	Intersectional Approaches	Shared Responsibility
Interactions with Families	• Discover the Funds of Knowledge of ML families • Interact with families regarding positive updates • Conduct informal or formal interviews with families • Participate in family engagement groups	• Secure interpreters for meetings with families and translate correspondence • Utilize the EPIC model to promote authentic family engagement	• Take up the mindset that ML family engagement is for all teachers
Instruction	• Discover the Funds of Knowledge of MLs with disabilities • Provide quality feedback on MLs with disabilities' academic learning • Positively manage and respond to student behavior • Engage MLs with disabilities in higher-order thinking • Position MLs with disabilities as generators of knowledge • Safeguard active engagement in learning for MLs with disabilities	• Implement EBPs that are shared between ML and special education • Expand explicit instruction for MLs with disabilities to support their varied needs • Develop and work toward language objectives • Create classrooms that are linguistically robust • Know and work toward the goals identified in MLs' IEPs • Support the social, emotional, and behavioral needs of MLs with disabilities	• Pursue professional learning that deepens knowledge outside of current specialization • Collaborate with language specialists to understand and support language goals • Partner with special educators and counselors to support MLs with adverse childhood experiences
Data Interpretation and Use	• Seek out and value data and perspectives from family members • Collect ecological data to examine quality of students' learning opportunities • Understand the limitations of standardized assessment data for MLs with disabilities	• Draw upon complementary data to understand student performance • Evaluate whether interventions are culturally and linguistically appropriate • Understand the improbability of disentangling ELP from disability in English-only data	• Ask for and review data from other departments • Ensure all high-stakes decisions are made by teams of educators and parents/families

Table 11.3. Actions for State Leaders

	Dignity and Humanistic Frames	Intersectional Approaches	Shared Responsibility
Teacher Certification	• Ensure teacher certification competencies address deficit-based framing of students	• Launch interdisciplinary teacher certifications, such as bilingual special education • Update teacher certification competencies to include MLs with disabilities	• Incentivize inservice teachers to seek additional certifications in ML and special education
Professional Learning	• Actively debunk myths that limit access to services and programs in trainings • Offer resources and trainings on authentic engagement of ML families	• Identify high priority topics impacting MLs with disabilities • Develop resources for LEAs that are intersectional and interdisciplinary	• Collaborate across departments on professional learning focused on MLs with disabilities • Offer joint ML–special education training that expands teachers' capacities to collaborate
Academic Standard Policies	• Eliminate policies that prohibit MLs with complex support needs from reclassifying • Promote the inclusion of secondary MLs with disabilities in their own reclassification decisions • Include parents/families in reclassification decisions	• Establish reclassification criteria for MLs who take Alt ELP assessments • Broaden the data required and used to make reclassification decisions for MLs with disabilities • Seek guidance on reclassification exemption policies • Evaluate whether academic standard policies overlook MLs with disabilities	• Support LEAs in using team-based approaches for reclassifying MLs with disabilities • Offer guidance to IEP teams regarding their role in reclassification • Partner with special education SEA leaders on academic standard policies
SEA Collaboration	• Advocate the importance of MLs with disabilities with upper-level leadership in states • Raise the awareness of the resources and structures needed for cross-office collaboration	• Invest in liaison positions, bridging ML and special education • Create a cross-office communications plan for sharing resources and guidance with LEAs	• Initiate standing meetings between ML and special education • Create processes for authentic input from other SEA offices • Implement SASSY framework in collaborations

Table 11.4. Actions for Higher Education Faculty

	Dignity and Humanistic Frames	Intersectional Approaches	Shared Responsibility
Teacher Certification and Training	• Promote asset-based lenses of multilingualism and disability • Emphasize the importance of authentic family engagement • Provide teachers with hands-on skills to discover students' Funds of Knowledge	• Create new programming focused on MLs with disabilities • Revise curricula to address mindsets and skills needed to support MLs with disabilities • Expand language specialists' capacity to support the goals in MLs' IEPs • Support special and general educators in creating linguistically rich classrooms	• Work across departments to develop new integrated programs • Recruit bilingual in- and preservice teachers for special education certification • Pursue training grants with a focus on teaching MLs with disabilities
Research	• Partner with districts and schools in conducting equity audits • Conduct research that amplifies voices and perspectives of MLs with disabilities and their families • Challenge myths regarding MLs with disabilities' limited capacity for multilingualism • Examine case studies of MLs with disabilities who are identified as gifted	• Implement studies that attend to heterogeneity of MLs with disabilities • Employ conceptual lenses that reflect the complex identities and needs of students • Interrogate opportunity to learn across elementary and secondary levels • Expand inquiries into outcomes for MLs with disabilities in bilingual schools	• Forge interdisciplinary research collaborations • Attempt to "talk across" disciplinary boundaries in scholarship • Learn about important trends occurring in ML and special education fields • Investigate and disseminate promising cases of effective teacher and school leader collaborations

characterized by erasure and fragmentation, intersectional approaches emphasize the whole child and integrated efforts that encompass both language learning and disability.

Advocating for more expansive responses to students' fuller identities, intersectional approaches dovetail with dignity and humanistic frames that affirm the whole child. In Chapter 3, I argued that the perceived deficits of MLs with disabilities are often the epicenter of institutional and individual responses to these students. However, if stakeholders view MLs with disabilities through a more holistic lens—instead of one focused on alleged deficiencies—their responses can likewise shift to encompass the whole child. Arguing against approaches that isolate and focus on one set of needs, Genesee (1994) asserted that the whole child should be the center of educators' efforts: "The starting point for planning and delivery instruction should be the whole child—instruction for second language children should be first and foremost child-centered" (p. 3). His arguments, I contend, apply to each stakeholder in the education of MLs with disabilities. The starting—and ending—point of education stakeholders' efforts should be in service to the whole child.

Beyond a whole-child stance, intersectional approaches also center integrated responses toward students. Instead of envisaging language learning and disability as isolated, and even at odds with one another, intersectional approaches enable education stakeholders to respond to MLs with disabilities as if these students have both language and disability-related needs and as if these needs interact with one another. Throughout the book, I have shed light on the misconception that education stakeholders can attend to just language or disability alone; language learning and disability needs can be intertwined, influencing one another and together shaping the everyday experiences of students. As such, integrated practices and policies are critical for a more equitable education for dually identified students.

Across the chapters, implementing intersectional approaches in systems entails district and school leaders reimagining service provision through integrated program models, scheduling practices, and staffing positions. Also, as documents with systemic influence, individualized plans require district leaders' and teachers' attention; together they can revamp these documents to reflect the intersecting needs of dually identified students instead of just disability, as in the case of IEPs. In classrooms, intersectional approaches manifest in pedagogical approaches that attend to both language learning and disability simultaneously. To support teachers' pedagogical practices for MLs with disabilities, districts and schools must dedicate resources and time to EBPs that serve these students best. In policies, intersectional approaches require state leaders in both ML and special education offices to reexamine and refine policies, initiatives, and guidance to address the unique needs of MLs with disabilities. All of these efforts necessitate teacher and educational leader training programs to modify curriculum, skills, and competencies to emphasize intersectional views and responses to students. Because state certification policies drive the programs offered in teacher education, implementing intersectional approaches in teacher education involves joint action from higher education faculty and state leaders. Recommendations for implementing intersectional approaches are summarized in Tables 11.1 through 11.4.

Pathway 3: Shared Responsibility

The first two pathways address perceptions of and responses to MLs with disabilities. This third and final pathway—shared responsibility—attends to education stakeholders' efforts to work with and alongside one another, providing a counterapproach to the specialization trap, which is characterized by working in isolation within rigid professional silos. In Chapter 5, readers first encountered the idea of *shared responsibility*. For quite some time, *shared responsibility* has been discussed narrowly in scholarship as a mindset, offered as a solution to improving the collaboration among K–12 teachers. In a recent publication, however, we discussed a more expansive understanding of shared responsibility, proffering that equity in ML education requires shared responsibility in mindsets, norms, and structures across *all* levels of the education system (Weddle et al., 2024). Describing each of these elements, we argue that when there is a sense of shared responsibility in education stakeholders' mindsets, there is an ethos that MLs and the issues they face are not just one person's responsibility; they are for us all to address. In the norms of institutions, when there is shared responsibility, routine ways of working span across siloed departments. Finally, structures within institutions that reflect shared responsibility entail policies, processes, and conditions that reflect and facilitate collective and coordinated efforts across departments. Punctuating this understanding of shared responsibility is the importance of leveraging each stakeholder's expertise to improve the education of MLs.

As we reflect on the multiple needs of MLs with disabilities and the specialization trap's influence on the school-based experiences of these students, there is an urgency for shared responsibility in our systems, classrooms, and policies. In systems such as those for service provision, shared responsibility has implications for modifying existing structures. School and district leaders should prioritize collaborative time among ML and special education teachers for their planning and coordination of services. Further, these parties should be brought together for district-offered professional learning opportunities that center MLs with disabilities. Also, given their systemic influence, IEPs (and other types of individualized plans) require a high level of collaboration across specializations for MLs. To collaborate successfully, language specialists need to be seen as critical members of IEP teams, and new ways of developing IEPs with their input need to be embraced. In classrooms, implementing rigorous instruction for MLs with disabilities requires coordinated services that focus on the whole person. Through professional learning and collaborations between ML and special education, teachers can gain more skills in not only supporting the whole child but also in working together. This is critical, as language specialists and special educators do not have a long history of coteaching, coplanning, and consulting with one another. Such a departure from the specialization trap in K–12 schools involves higher education, specifically teacher preparation programs fostering mindsets of and skills for shared responsibility among all pre- and inservice teachers. In policies, state leaders from across offices and departments need to collaborate on refining state policies, developing initiatives and resources, and offering professional learning for teachers that substantially address the unique needs of dually identified students. Recommendations for enacting shared responsibility are summarized in Tables 11.1 through 11.4.

In sum, the overarching pathways of dignity and humanistic frames, intersectional approaches, and shared responsibility offer a framework for education stakeholders to use across their roles and contexts. By taking these pathways, teachers, educational and state leaders, and university faculty can disrupt the influence of patterned inequities within our sectors that compromise the learning and life opportunities of MLs with disabilities.

FINAL THOUGHTS

In the earliest pages of this book, I offered that promoting equity for MLs with disabilities is not for the faint of heart. It requires a break from the status quo, asking us to think differently, approach our work innovatively, and imagine wholeheartedly an education for MLs with disabilities that offers them access, opportunity, and a promising future. We all as stakeholders can promote this kind of equity. Even small, incremental shifts in our practice today can expand the learning opportunities and rights for these students tomorrow. The recommendations offered in this book are those incremental shifts. Each one individually elevates the needs of MLs with disabilities in our classrooms, schools, and policies, and collectively, they get us closer to that equitable education that we so desire for these students. Given the interdependence of our work across K–12 classrooms and schools, higher education institutions, and state departments of education, safeguarding the learning opportunities and rights of dually identified students cannot be left to one stakeholder group alone. To effect change, promoting equity for MLs with disabilities must be for the now and for us all.

Notes

Chapter 1

1. In this book, I have decided to use the term *multilingual learners with disabilities* for students who have disabilities and are acquiring English as an additional language. No single term is perfect; we know that full well. In education, debates about "disability language" continue. Specifically, person-first (e.g., children with disabilities) and identity-first (e.g., disabled children) language each offer unique affordances and constraints (Andrews et al., 2022; Dunn & Andrew 2015). Likewise, terminology around language learners is in flux, with no consensus. The term *multilingual learner* (or ML) highlights the multilingual identities and capabilities of students, but it does not align with the current term used in federal legislation: *English learner*. In response to this limitation, I will use the term *English learner* when referring to the federal designation or label itself but will continue to use *ML with disabilities* regarding the population overall. This distinction is especially important in Chapter 9, which addresses reclassification from *English learner* status.

Chapter 2

1. *Language services* is used to encompass a range of programming from English-only models (e.g., pull-out, push-in, sheltered) to bilingual models (e.g., transitional, maintenance, two-way, etc.) used to support the emerging English proficiency of MLs.

Chapter 3

1. *Disability-related services* includes both special education and related services (e.g., speech–language, physical, and occupational therapies).

2. *Language specialists* is a term that encompasses certified ESL teachers and bilingual educators or those with substantial expertise in second language acquisition.

Chapter 4

1. *Related services*, according to IDEA (2004), includes services and supports "required to assist a child with a disability to benefit from special education." These services can include but are not limited to speech-language pathology, physical and occupational therapy, and counseling services.

Chapter 8

1. The reclassification study reported in the book was made possible by a grant from the Spencer Foundation (#202100060). The views expressed are those of the authors and do not necessarily reflect the views of the Spencer Foundation.

Chapter 9

1. The policy analysis research reported throughout this chapter was made possible by a grant from the Spencer Foundation (#202300087). The views expressed are those of the authors and do not necessarily reflect the views of the Spencer Foundation.

References

Abedi, J. (2009). English language learners with disabilities: Classification, assessment, and accommodation issues. *Journal of Applied Testing Technology, 10*(2), 1–30. https://www.jattjournal.net/index.php/atp/article/view/48353

Abedi, J., & Ewers, N. (2013). *Accommodations for English language learners and students with disabilities: A research-based decision algorithm.* Smarter Balance Assessment Consortium.

Aceves, T. C., & Kennedy, M. J. (Eds.) (2024). *High-leverage practices for students with disabilities* (2nd ed.) Council for Exceptional Children and CEEDAR Center.

Allday, R. A., Duhon, G. J., Blackburn-Ellis, S., & Van Dycke, J. L. (2011). The biasing effects of labels on direct observation by preservice teachers. *Teacher Education and Special Education, 34*(1), 52–58. https://doi.org/10.1177/0888406410380422

American Educational Research Association/American Psychological Association/National Council on Measurement in Education. (2014). *Standards for educational and psychological testing.* American Educational Research Association. https://www.testingstandards.net/open-access-files.html

Anderson, K. N., Swedo, E. A., Trinh E., Ray, C. M., Krause, K. H., Verlenden, J. V., Clayton, H. B., Villaveches, A., Massetti, G. M., & Holditch Niolon, P. (2022). Adverse childhood experiences during the COVID-19 pandemic and associations with poor mental health and suicidal behaviors among high school students: Adolescent behaviors and experiences survey, United States, January–June 2021. *MMWR Morbidity and Mortality Weekly Report, 71*(41), 1301–1305. https://doi.org/10.15585/mmwr.mm7141a2

Anderson, L. W., & Krathwohl, D. R. (2000). *A taxonomy for learning, teaching, and assessing.* Pearson.

Andrews, E. E., Powell, R. M., & Ayers, K. (2022). The evolution of disability language: Choosing terms to describe disability. *Disability and Health Journal, 15*(3), 101328. https://doi.org/10.1016/j.dhjo.2022.101328

Annamma, S. A., Connor, D., & Ferri, B. (2013) Dis/ability critical race studies (DisCrit): Theorizing at the intersections of race and dis/ability. *Race Ethnicity and Education, 16*(1), 1–31. https://doi.org/10.1080/13613324.2012.730511

Archer, A. L., & Hughes, C. A. (2011). *Explicit instruction: Effective and efficient teaching.* Guilford Press.

Artiles, A. J. (2013). Untangling the racialization of disabilities: An intersectionality critique across disability models. *Du Bois Review, 10*(2), 329–347. https://doi.org/10.1017/S1742058X13000271

Artiles, A. J., & Kozleski, E. B. (2016). Inclusive education's promises and trajectories: Critical notes about future research on a venerable idea. *Education Policy Analysis Archives, 24*(43), 1–25. https://epaa.asu.edu/index.php/epaa/article/view/1919

Artiles, A. J., Kozleski, E. B., Trent, S. C., Osher, D., & Ortiz, A. (2010). Justifying and explaining disproportionality, 1968–2008: A critique of underlying views of culture. *Exceptional Children, 76*(3), 279–299. https://doi.org/10.1177/001440291007600303

Artiles, A. J., & Ortiz, A. A. (Eds.) (2002). *English language learners with special education needs: Identification, assessment, and instruction.* Center for Applied Linguistics.

Artiles, A. J., Rueda, R., Salazar, J. J., & Higareda, I. (2005). Within-group diversity in minority disproportionate representation: English language learners in urban school districts. *Exceptional Children, 71*(3), 283–300. https://doi.org/10.1177/001440290507100305

Assistance to states for the education of children with disabilities and the early intervention program for infants and toddlers with disabilities, 64, Fed. Reg. 12412 (May 11, 1999).

Athanases, S. Z., & de Oliveira, L. C. (2008). Advocacy for equity in classrooms and beyond: New teachers' challenges and responses. *Teachers College Record, 110*(1), 64–104. https://doi.org/10.1177/016146810811000101

Au, W. (2023). *Unequal by design: High-stakes testing the standardization of inequality* (2nd ed.). Routledge.

August, D., & Blackburn, T. (2019). *Promoting success for teachers of English learners through structured observations.* Council of Chief State School Officers.

Baca, L. M., & Amato, C. (1989). Bilingual special education: Training issues. *Exceptional Children, 56*(2), 168–173. https://doi.org/10.1177/001440298905600209

Baca, L. M., & Cervantes, H. T. (2003). *The bilingual special education interface* (4th ed.). Pearson.

Baker, D., Leider, C. M., Kim, H., Rinaldi, C., & Garcia, P. (2024). All over the map: State-level guidance for English learners with disabilities. *Journal of Disability Policy Studies.* Advance online publication. https://doi.org/10.1177/10442073241250276

Barrio, B. L. (2017). Special education policy change: Addressing the disproportionality of English language learners in special education programs in rural communities. *Rural Special Education Quarterly, 36*(2), 64–72. https://doi.org/10.1177/8756870517707217

Batruch, A., Geven., S., Kessenich, E., & van de Werfhorst, H. G. (2023). Are tracking recommendations biased?: A review of teachers' role in the creation of inequalities in tracking decisions. *Teaching and Teacher Education, 123*, 1–18. https://doi.org/10.1016/j.tate.2022.103985

Blad, E. (2024, May 13). Retention is the missing ingredient in special education staffing. *Education Week.* https://www.edweek.org/leadership/retention-is-the-missing-ingredient-in-special-education-staffing/2024/05

Blodgett, C., & Lanigan, J. D. (2018). The association between adverse childhood experience (ACE) and school success in elementary school children. *School Psychology Quarterly, 33*(1), 137–146. https://doi.org/10.1037/spq0000256

Bourdieu, P. (1977). *Outline of a theory of practice* (R. Nice, Trans). Cambridge University Press.

Bourdieu, P. (1990). *The logic of practice* (R. Nice, Trans). Polity Press.

Boveda, M. (2016). *Beyond special and general education as identity markers: The development and validation of an instrument to measure preservice teachers' understanding of the effects of intersecting sociocultural identities* [Doctoral dissertation, Florida International University]. FIU Electronic Theses and Dissertations. http://digitalcommons.fiu.edu/etd/2998

Boveda, M., & Aronson, B. A. (2019). Special education preservice teachers, intersectional diversity, and the privileging of emerging professional identities. *Remedial and Special Education*, *40*(4), 248–260. https://doi.org/10.1177/0741932519838621

Boveda, M., & Weinberg, A. E. (2022). Centering racialized educators in collaborative teacher education: The development of the Intersectionally Conscious Collaboration Protocol. *Teacher Education and Special Education*, *45*(1), 8–26. https://doi.org/10.1177/08884064211062874

Brandmiller, C., Dumont, H., & Becker, M. (2020). Teacher perceptions of learning motivation and classroom behavior: The role of student characteristics. *Contemporary Educational Psychology*, *63*, 1–11. https://doi.org/10.1016/j.cedpsych.2020.101893

Bray, L. E., & Russell, J. L. (2018). The dynamic interaction between institutional pressures and activity: An examination of the implementation of IEPs in secondary inclusive settings. *Educational Evaluation and Policy Analysis*, *40*(2), 243–266. https://doi.org/10.3102/0162373718756189

Brooks, M. D. (2022). What does it mean?: EL-identified adolescents' interpretations of testing and course placement. *TESOL Quarterly*, *56*(4), 1218–1241. https://onlinelibrary.wiley.com/doi/full/10.1002/tesq.3099

Brooks, M. D. (2023). What does ESL mean to her? An analysis of women of color recounting their attempts to exit EL instructional services. *AERA Open*, *9*. https://doi.org/10.1177/23328584231195878

Brosnan, F. L. (1983). Overrepresentation of low-socioeconomic minority students in special education programs in California. *Learning Disability Quarterly*, *6*(4), 517–525. https://doi.org/10.2307/1510540

Brown, C. G., Hess, F. M., Lautzenheiser, D. K., & Owen, I. (2011). *State education agencies as agents of change: What it will take for the states to step up on education reform*. Center for American Progress. https://files.eric.ed.gov/fulltext/ED522627.pdf

Burho, J., & Thompson, K. (2021). Parent engagement in reclassification of English learner students with disabilities. *Journal of Family Diversity in Education*, *4*(1), 20–41. https://familydiversityeducation.com/index.php/fdec/article/view/155

Burke, A. M., Morita-Mullaney, T., & Singh, M. (2016). Indiana emergent bilingual student time to reclassification: A survival analysis. *American Educational Research Journal*, *53*(5), 1310–1342. https://doi.org/10.3102/0002831216667481

Burke, M. M., Rossetti, Z., Aleman-Tovar, J., Rios, K., Lee, J., Schraml-Block, K., & Rivera, J. (2021). Comparing special education experiences among Spanish- and English-speaking parents of children with disabilities. *Journal of Developmental and Physical Disabilities*, *33*, 117–135. https://doi.org/10.1007/s10882-020-09736-y

Byrd, D. (2019). Uncovering hegemony in higher education: A critical appraisal of the use of "institutional habitus" in empirical scholarship. *Review of Educational Research*, *89*(2), 171–210. https://doi.org/10.3102/0034654318812915

California Department of Education. (2024). *Alternate assessment IEP team guidance*. https://www.cde.ca.gov/ta/tg/ca/caaiepteamrev.asp

Callahan, R. M. (2005). Tracking and high school English learners: Limiting opportunity to learn. *American Educational Research Journal*, *42*(2), 305–328. https://doi.org/10.3102/00028312042002305

Callahan, R. M., & Shifrer, D. (2016). Equitable access for secondary English learner students: course taking as evidence of EL program effectiveness. *Educational Administration Quarterly*, *52*(3), 463–496. https://doi.org/10.1177/0013161X16648190

Campbell, S. L. (2012). For colored girls?: Factors that influence teacher recommendations into advanced courses for Black girls. *The Review of Black Political Economy*, *39*(4), 389–402. https://doi.org/10.1007/s12114-012-9139-1

Capin, P., Miciak, J., Bhat, B. H., Roberts, G., Steinle, P. K., Fletcher, J., & Vaughn, S. (2024). An extensive reading intervention for emergent bilingual students with significant reading difficulties in middle school. *Remedial and Special Education*, *45*(4), 230–246. https://doi.org/10.1177/07419325231213876

Carrizales, D., Greenlees, L., & Lara, D. (2022). The effects of teacher preparation special population courses for multispecialty certification. *Educational Research and Development Journal*, *25*(1), 26–46.

Center on Positive Behavioral Interventions and Support. (2024). *Classroom PBIS*. Center on PBIS, University of Oregon. https://www.pbis.org/classroom-pbis

Chang, Y. C., Avila, M., & Rodriguez, H. (2022). Beyond the dotted line: Empowering parents from culturally and linguistically diverse families to participate. *Teaching Exceptional Children*, *55*(2), 132–140. https://doi.org/10.1177/00400599221099868

Chang., S., Lozano, M., Neri, R., & Herman, J. (2017). *High-leverage principles of effective instruction for English learners*. WestEd & the National Center for Research, Evaluation, Standards, and Student Testing, University of California Los Angeles. https://csaa.wested.org

Christensen, L. L., Albus, D. A., Liu, K. K., Thurlow, M. L., & Kincaid, A. (2013). *Accommodations for students with disabilities on state English language proficiency assessments: A review of 2011 state policies*. National Center on Educational Outcomes. https://files.eric.ed.gov/fulltext/ED545326.pdf

Cioè-Peña, M. (2017). The intersectional gap: How bilingual students in the United States are excluded from inclusion. *International Journal of Inclusive Education*, *21*(9), 906–919. https://doi.org/10.1080/13603116.2017.1296032

Cioè-Peña, M. (2020). Planning inclusion: The need to formalize parental participation in individual education plans (and meetings). *Educational Forum*, *84*(4), 377–390. https://doi.org/10.1080/00131725.2020.1812970

Cioè-Peña, M. (2021). *(M)othering labeled children: Bilingualism and disability in the lives of Latinx mothers*. Multilingual Matters.

Cioè-Peña, M. (2022). TrUDL, a path to full inclusion: The intersectional possibilities of translanguaging and universal design for learning. *TESOL Quarterly*, *56*(2), 799–812. https://doi.org/10.1002/tesq.3074

Closson, T. (2023, March 13). Regents exams may become optional for high school graduation in New York. *The New York Times*. https://www.nytimes.com/2023/11/13/nyregion/regents-exams-new-york.html

Cobb-Clark, D. A., Harmon, C., & Staneva, A. (2021). The bilingual gap in children's language, emotional, and pro-social development. *Journal of Labor Economics*, *10*(1), 1–41. https://doi.org/10.2478/izajole-2021-0001

Coleman, H., Boit, R., Butterworth, L., La Paro, K., Ricks, T., Hestenes, L., Ozdemir, M., & Aal-Anubia, A. J. (2023). Effective teaching strategies: Pre-service teachers' experiences in team taught courses in an interdisciplinary early childhood teacher education program. *Teaching and Teacher Education*, *121*, 1–10. https://doi.org/10.1016/J.TATE.2022.103937

Collier, C. (2011). *Seven steps to separating difference from disability*. Corwin.

Colón, G., & Alsace, T. (2022). *Bilingual special education for the 21st century: A new interface*. IGI Global.

Conderman, G., Bresnahan, V., & Pedersen, T. (2009). *Purposeful co-teaching: Real cases and effective strategies*. Corwin.

Cooc, N. (2023). National trends in special education and academic outcomes for English learners with disabilities. *The Journal of Special Education*, *57*(2), 106–117. https://doi.org/10.1177/00224669221147272

Council for Exceptional Children. (2022). *Co-teaching*. https://exceptionalchildren.org/topics/co-teaching

Council of Chief State School Officers. (2014). *English language proficiency (ELP) standards*. https://www.elpa21.org/wp-content/uploads/2023/02/1.2.2-ELP-Standards-2014.pdf

Crawford, J., & Reyes, S. A. (2015). *The trouble with SIOP®: How a behaviorist framework, flawed research, and clever marketing have come to define—and diminish—sheltered instruction for English language learners: Featuring an alternative approach to sheltered instruction and a sample unit applying that framework*. Institute for Language and Education Policy.

Crenshaw, K. (1989). Demarginalizing the intersection of race and sex: A Black feminist critique of antidiscrimination doctrine, feminist theory and antiracist politics. *University of Chicago Legal Forum*, *1*, 138–167. https://chicagounbound.uchicago.edu/cgi/viewcontent.cgi?article=1052&context=uclf

Crenshaw, K. (1991). Mapping the margins: Intersectionality, identity politics, and violence against women of color. *Stanford Law Review*, *43*(6), 1241–1299. https://doi.org/10.2307/1229039

Crockett, J. B., & Kauffman, J. M. (2013). *The least restrictive environment: Its origins and interpretations in special education*. Lawrence Erlbaum. https://doi.org/10.4324/9781410603722 (Originally published 1999)

Crouch, E., Probst, J. C., Radcliff, E., Bennett, K. J., & McKinney, S. H. (2019). Prevalence of adverse childhood experiences (ACEs) among US children. *Child Abuse & Neglect*, *92*, 209–218. https://doi.org/10.1016/j.chiabu.2019.04.010

Cruze, A., & López, F. (2020). Equity and excellence among Arizona school leaders: encouraging integration within a segregative policy context. *Leadership and Policy in Schools*, *19*(1), 81–103. https://doi.org/10.1080/15700763.2020.1714058

Cruze, A., Holmes, S., López, F., Kelsey, I., & Campuzano, C. (2020). Inclusive leadership and multilingual learners. In G. Theoharis & M. Scanlan (Eds.), *Leadership for increasingly diverse schools* (pp. 109–134). Routledge.

Cuba, M. J., & Tefera, A. A. (2024). Contextualizing multilingual learner disproportionality in special education: A mixed-methods approach. *Teachers College Record, 126*(1), 29–60. https://doi.org/10.1177/01614681241233877

Cummins, J. (1981). *Bilingualism and special education: Issues in assessment and pedagogy*. Pro Ed.

Cummins, J. (1989). A theoretical framework for bilingual special education. *Exceptional Children, 56*(2), 111–119. https://doi.org/10.1177/001440298905600203

Dabach, D. B. (2014). "I am not a shelter!": Stigma and social boundaries in teachers' accounts of students' experience in separate "sheltered" English learner classrooms. *Journal of Education for Students Placed at Risk, 19*(2), 98–124. https://doi.org/10.1080/10824669.2014.954044

Daniel, S. M., & Conlin, L. (2015). Shifting attention back to students within the sheltered instruction observation protocol. *TESOL Quarterly, 49*(1), 169–187. https://doi.org/10.1002/tesq.213

Danielson, C. (2013). *The Framework for Teaching*. The Danielson Group. https://www.danielsongroup.org/framework/

Davison, C. (2006). Collaboration between ESL and content teachers: How do we know when we are doing it right? *International Journal of Bilingual Education and Bilingualism, 9*(4), 454–475. http://dx.doi.org/10.2167/beb339.0

de Jong, E., & Harper, C. A. (2005). Preparing mainstream teachers for English-language learners: Is being a good teacher good enough? *Teacher Education Quarterly*, 32, 101–124. https://files.eric.ed.gov/fulltext/EJ795308.pdf

de Valenzuela, J. S., Pacheco, R., & Shenoy, S. (2022). Current practices and challenges in language proficiency assessment for English learners with complex support needs. *Research and Practice for Persons With Severe Disabilities, 47*(1), 6–21. https://doi.org/10.1177/15407969221075848

Demie, F. (2022). Tackling teachers' low expectations of Black Caribbean students in English schools. *Equity in Education & Society, 1*(1), 32–49. https://doi.org/10.1177/27526461211068511

Domina, T., Penner, A. M., & Penner, E. K. (2023). *Schooled and sorted: How educational categories create inequality*. The Russell Sage Foundation.

Dove, M. G, & Honigsfeld, A. (2010). ESL coteaching and collaboration: Opportunities to develop teacher leadership and enhance student learning, *TESOL Journal, 1*(1), 3–22. https://doi.org/10.5054/tj.2010.214879

Doyle, L., Easterbrook, M. J., & Harris, P. R. (2023). Roles of socioeconomic status, ethnicity and teacher beliefs in academic grading. *British Journal of Educational Psychology*, 93, 91–112. https://doi.org/10.1111/bjep.12541

Dunn, D. S., & Andrews, E. E. (2015). Person-first and identity-first language: Developing psychologists' cultural competence using disability language. *The American Psychologist, 70*(3), 255–264. https://doi.org/10.1037/a0038636

Echevarría, J., Vogt, M., Short, D. J., & Toppel, K. (2024). *Making content comprehensible for multilingual learners: The SIOP model* (6th ed.). Pearson.

Education for All Handicapped Children Act. Pub. L. No. 94–142, 89 Stat. 773. (1975).

Ellis, N. C. (2011). Implicit and explicit SLA and their interface. In C. Sanz & R. P. Leow (Eds.), *Implicit and explicit language learning: Conditions, processes, and knowledge in SLA and bilingualism* (pp. 35–48). Georgetown University Press.

Ellis, R. (2002). Does form-focused instruction affect the acquisition of implicit knowledge?: A review of the research. *Studies in Second Language Acquisition, 24*(2), 223–236. https://doi.org/10.1017/S0272263102002073

Ellis, R. (2008). Explicit form-focused instruction and second language acquisition. In B. Spolsky & F. M. Hult (Eds.). *The handbook of educational linguistics* (pp. 437–455). Blackwell Publishing.

Erickson, F. (1986). Qualitative methods in research on teaching. In W. C. Wittrock (Ed.), *Handbook of research on teaching* (3rd ed.) (pp. 119–161). Macmillan.

Ertanir, B., Cobb, C. L., Unger, J. B., Celada-Dalton, T., West A. E., Zeledon, I., Perazzo, P. A., Cano, M. A., Des Rosiers, S. E., Duque, M. C., Ozer, S., Cruz, N., Scaramutti, C., Vos, S. R., Salas-Wright, C. P., Maldonado-Molina, M. M., Nehme, L., Martinez, C. R., Zayas, L. H., & Schwartz, S. J. (2023). Crisis migration adverse childhood events: A new category of youth adversity for crisis migrant children and adolescents. *Research on Child and Adolescent Psychopathology, 51*(12), 1871–1882. https://doi.org/10.1007/s10802-022-01016-x

Esparza Brown, J., & Ault, P. C. (2015). Disentangling language differences from disability: A case study of district-preservice collaboration, *Journal of Multilingual Education Research*, 6(7), 111–136. https://research.library.fordham.edu/jmer/vol6/iss1/7

Esparza Brown, J., & Doolittle, J. (2008). A cultural, linguistic, and ecological framework for response to intervention with English language learners. *Teaching Exceptional Children, 40*(5), 66–72. https://doi.org/10.1177/004005990804000509

Espinoza, M. L., Vossoughi, S., Rose, M., & Poza, L. E. (2020). Matters of participation: Notes on the study of dignity and learning. *Mind, Culture, and Activity, 27*(4), 325–347. https://doi.org/10.1080/10749039.2020.1779304

Estrada, P., & Wang, H. (2018). Making English learner reclassification to fluent English proficient attainable or elusive: When meeting criteria is and is not enough. *American Educational Research Journal, 55*(2), 207–242. https://doi.org/10.3102/0002831217733543

Every Student Succeeds Act, 20 U.S.C. § 6301 (2015).

Exceptional Children's Assistance Center. (n.d.). *Person centered planning fact sheet.* https://www.ecac-parentcenter.org/resource-documents/person-centered-planning-fact-sheet/

Ferrero, M., Konstantinidis, E., & Vadillo, M. A. (2020). An attempt to correct erroneous ideas among teacher education students: The effectiveness of refutation texts. *Frontiers in Psychology, 11*(577738). https://doi.org/10.3389/fpsyg.2020.577738

Figueroa, R. A. (1989). Psychological testing of linguistic-minority students: Knowledge gaps and regulations. *Exceptional Children, 56*(2), 145–152. https://doi.org/10.1177/001440298905600206

Finn, C. E., Jr., & Petrilli, M. J. (2014). Foreword. In A. Smarick & J. Squire, *The state education agency: At the helm, not the oar* (pp. 1–2). Thomas B. Fordham Institute.

Finn, J. D., & Zimmer, K. S. (2012). Student engagement: What is it? Why does it matter? In S. L. Christenson, A. L. Reschly, & C. Wylie (Eds.), *Handbook of research on student engagement* (pp. 97–131). Springer Science + Business Media. https://doi.org/10.1007/978-1-4614-2018-7_5

Flores, N., & Rosa, J. (2015). Undoing appropriateness: Raciolinguistic ideologies and language diversity in education. *Harvard Educational Review, 85*(2), 149–171. https://doi.org/10.17763/0017-8055.85.2.149

Friedrick, A., Flunger, B., Nagengast, B., Jonkmann, K., & Trautwein, U. (2015). Pygmalion effects in the classroom: Teacher expectancy effects on students' math achievement. *Contemporary Educational Psychology*, *41*, 1–12. https://doi.org/10.1016/j.cedpsych.2014.10.006

Friend, M., Cook, L., Hurley-Chamberlain, L., & Shamberger, C. (2010). Co-teaching: An illustration of the complexity of collaboration in special education. *Journal of Educational and Psychological Consultation, 20*(1), 9–27. http://dx.doi.org/10.1080/10474410903535380

Gage, N., Gersten, R., Sugai, G., & Newman-Gonchar, R. (2013). Disproportionality of English learners with emotional and/or behavioral disorders: A comparative meta-analysis with English learners with learning disabilities. *Behavioral Disorders*, *38*(3), 123–136. https://doi.org/10.1177/019874291303800302

Gamoran, A. (2009). *Tracking and inequality: New directions for research and practice* [WCER Working Paper No. 2009-6]. University of Wisconsin–Madison, Wisconsin Center for Education Research.

Gamoran, A. (2021). *President's comment: Effective programs are not enough, we need structural change to reduce inequality.* William T. Grant Foundation. https://wtgrantfoundation.org/presidents-comment-effective-programs-are-not-enough-we-need-structural-change-to-reduce-inequality

Gándara, P., & Orfield, G. (2012). Segregating Arizona's English learners: A return to the "Mexican room"? *Teachers College Record, 114*(9), 1–27. https://doi.org/10.1177/016146811211400905

Gándara, P., Rumberger, R., Maxwell-Jolly, J., & Callahan, R. (2003). English learners in California schools: Unequal resources, unequal outcomes. *Education Policy Analysis Archives*, *11*(36), 1–54. https://doi.org/10.14507/epaa.v11n36.2003

Garcia, D. (2021). *Teach truth to power: How to engage in education policy*. MIT Press.

García, S. B., & Ortiz, A. A. (1988). *Preventing inappropriate referrals of language minority students to special education.* The National Clearinghouse for Bilingual Education.

García, S. B., & Tyler, B.-J. (2010). Meeting the needs of English language learners with learning disabilities in the general curriculum. *Theory into Practice*, *49*(2), 113–120. http://www.jstor.org/stable/40650724

Garver, R., & Hopkins, M. (2020). Segregation and integration in the education of English learners: Leadership and policy dilemmas. *Leadership and Policy in Schools*, *19*(1), 1–5. https://doi.org/10.1080/15700763.2019.1711133

Genesee, F. (1994). Introduction. In F. Genesee (Ed.), *Educating second language children: The whole child, the whole curriculum, the whole community* (pp. 1–12). Cambridge University Press.

Genesee, F. (2015). Myths about early childhood bilingualism. *Canadian Psychology, 56*(1), 6–15. http://dx.doi.org/10.1037/a0038599

Gentrup, S., Lorenz, G., Kristen, C., & Kogan, E. (2020). Self-fulfilling prophecies in the classroom: Teacher expectations, teacher feedback and student achievement. *Learning and Instruction, 66*, 1–17. https://doi.org/10.1016/j.learninstruc.2019.101296

Gershenson, S., Holt, S. B., & Papageorge, N. W. (2016). Who believes in me? The effect of student–teacher demographic match on teacher expectations. *Economics of Education Review, 54*, 209–224. https://doi.org/10.1016/j.econedurev.2016.03.002

Gibbons, P. (2014). *Scaffolding language, scaffolding learning: Teaching English language learners in the mainstream classroom* (2nd ed.). Heinemann.

Giddens, A. (1979). *Central problems in social theory*. University of California Press.

Gill, M. G., Trevors, G., Greene, J. A., & Algina, J. (2022). Don't take it personally?: The role of personal relevance in conceptual change. *The Journal of Experimental Education, 90*(1), 1–22. https://doi.org/10.1080/00220973.2020.1754152

González, N., Moll, L. C., & Amanti, C. (Eds.). (2005). *Funds of knowledge: Theorizing practices in households, communities, and classrooms*. Lawrence Erlbaum Associates Publishers.

González, N., Moll, L. C., Tenery, M. F., Rivera, A., Rendon, P., Gonzales, R., & Amanti, C. (1995). Funds of knowledge for teaching in Latino households. *Urban Education, 29*(4), 443–470. https://doi.org/10.1177/0042085995029004005

González, T., Artiles, A. J., Martínez-Álvarez, P., & Salinas, S. M. (2024). Towards the full potential of Lau: Interrogating the intersectional nuances of language, disability, & race. *Bilingual Research Journal, 47*(4), 421–437. https://doi.org/10.1080/15235882.2024.2412541

Gonzalez-Barrero, A. M., & Nadig, A. (2018). Bilingual children with autism spectrum disorders: The impact of amount of language exposure on vocabulary and morphological skills at school age. *Autism Research, 11*(12), 1667–1678. https://doi.org/10.1002/aur.2023

Greenberg Motamedi, J., Cox, M., Williams, J., & Deussen, T. (2016). *Uncovering diversity: Examining the representation of English learners in special education in Washington State*. Education Northwest, Regional Educational Laboratory Northwest. https://files.eric.ed.gov/fulltext/ED570981.pdf

Groen, M. M. (2012). NCLB: The educational accountability paradigm in historical perspective. *American Educational History Journal, 39*(1), 1–14. https://www.infoagepub.com/american-educational-history-journal.html

Haas, E. M., & Esparza Brown, J. E. (2019). *Supporting English learners in the classroom: Best practices for distinguishing language acquisition from learning disabilities*. Teachers College Press.

Han, W., & Huang, C. (2010). The forgotten treasure: Bilingualism and Asian children's emotional and behavioral health. *American Journal of Public Health, 100*(5), 831–838. https://doi.org/10.2105/AJPH.2009.174219

Hanover Research (2023). *District leaders' guide for developing a K–12 professional learning plan*. https://www.hanoverresearch.com/reports-and-briefs/k-12-education/district-leaders-guide-for-developing-k-12-professional-learning-plan/

Harris, A., & Jones, M. (2010). Professional learning communities and system improvement. *Improving Schools*, *13*(2), 172–181. https://doi.org/10.1177/1365480210376487

Harry, B., & Klingner, J. K. (2005). *Why are so many students of color in special education? Understanding race and disability in schools.* (1st ed.). Teachers College Press.

Harry, B., & Klingner, J. K. (2022). *Why are so many students of color in special education? Understanding race and disability in schools.* (3rd ed.). Teachers College Press.

Hart, J. E., Cheatham, G., & Jimenez-Silva, M. (2012). Facilitating quality language interpretation for families of diverse students with special needs. *Preventing School Failure: Alternative Education for Children and Youth*, *56*(4), 207–213. https://doi.org/10.1080/1045988x.2011.645910

Henner, J., & Robinson, O. (2023). Unsettling languages, unruly bodyminds: A crip linguistics manifesto. *Journal of Critical Study of Communication and Disability*, *1*(1), 7–37. https://doi.org/10.48516/jcscd_2023vol1iss1.4

Herrera, S. G., Rodríguez, D., Cabral, R. M., & Holmes, M. A. (2023). *Equitable and inclusive teaching for diverse learners with disabilities: A biography-driven approach.* Teachers College Press.

Hibel, J., & Jasper, A. D. (2012). Delayed special education placement for learning disabilities among children of immigrants. *Social Forces*, *91*(2), 503–529. http://www.jstor.org/stable/23361099

Hill, L. E., Weston, M., & Hayes, J. M. (2014). *Reclassification of English learner students in California.* Public Policy Institute of California. https://www.ppic.org/publication/reclassification-of-english-learner-students-in-california/

Hodge, E. M., Salloum, S. J., & Benko, S. L. (2024). How state educational agency coordinators navigate logics of local control in standards implementation. *Educational Policy*, *38*(2), 391–420. https://doi.org/10.1177/08959048231153595

Honigsfeld, A., & Dove, M. G. (2010). *Collaboration and co-teaching: Strategies for English learners.* SAGE Publications.

Honigsfeld, A., & Dove, M. G. (2021). *Co-planning: 5 essential practices to integrate curriculum and instruction for English learners.* Corwin.

Hoover, J. J. (2008). Data-driven decision making in a multi-tiered model. In J. K. Klingner, J. J. Hoover, & L. M. Baca (Eds.), *Why do English language learners struggle with reading? Distinguishing language acquisition from learning disabilities* (pp. 75–92). Corwin.

Hoover, J. J., Baca, L. M., & Klingner, J. K. (2016). *Why do English learners struggle with reading?: Distinguishing language acquisition from learning disabilities.* Corwin Press.

Hoover, J. J., Erickson, J. R., Patton, J. R., Sacco, D. M., & Tran, L. M. (2019). Examining IEPs of English learners with learning disabilities for cultural and linguistic responsiveness. *Learning Disabilities Research and Practice*, *34*(1), 14–22. https://doi.org/10.1111/ldrp.12183

Hoover, J. J., & Patton, J. R. (2017). *IEP for ELs and other diverse learners.* Corwin.

Hopkins, M., Weddle, H., Castillo, M., Costa, J., Edwards, K., Elliot, S., Gautsch, L., Lowenhaupt, R., & Salas, V. (2022). Upholding multilingual learners' civil rights under ESSA: State education agency leaders and the contextual factors shaping their work. *American Journal of Education*, *128*(4), 591–616. https://doi.org/10.1086/720362

Hord, S. M. (1997). *Professional learning communities: Communities of continuous inquiry and improvement.* Southwest Educational Development Laboratory, U.S. Department of Education.

Horn, R. A., & Carr, A. A. (2000). Providing systemic change for schools: Towards professional development through moral conversation. *Systems Research and Behavioral Science*, *17*(3), 255–272. https://doi.org/10.1002/(SICI)1099-1743(200005/06)17:3<255::AID-SRES318>3.0.CO;2-Z

Hott, B. L., Jones, B. A., Rodriguez, J., Brigham, F. J., Martin, A., & Mirafuentes, M. (2021). Are rural students receiving FAPE?: A descriptive review of IEPs for students with social, emotional, or behavioral needs. *Behavior Modification*, *45*(1), 13–38. https://doi.org/10.1177/0145445518825107

Hott, B. L., Morano, S., Peltier, C., Pulos, J., & Peltier, T. (2020). Are students with mathematics learning disabilities receiving FAPE?: Insights from a descriptive review of individualized education programs. *Learning Disabilities Research and Practice*, *35*(4), 170–179. https://doi.org/10.1111/ldrp.12231

Hughes, C. A., Morris, J. R., Therrien, W. J., & Benson, S. K. (2017). Explicit instruction: Historical and contemporary contexts. *Learning Disabilities Research & Practice*, *32*(3), 140–148. https://doi.org/10.1111/ldrp.12142

Illinois State Board of Education. (n.d.). *Educator licensure: Educator licensure approval requirements.* https://www.isbe.net/Pages/educator-licensure-approvals.aspx

Individuals with Disabilities Education Act. 20 U.S.C.§ 1400 (2004).

IRIS Center. (n.d.). *What is the transition planning process for students with disabilities?* The IRIS Center, Peabody College, Vanderbilt University. https://iris.peabody.vanderbilt.edu/module/cou2/cresource/q1/p02/

Jackson, L., Fitzpatrick, H., Alazemi, B., & Rude, H. (2018). Shifting gears: Reframing the international discussion about inclusive education. *Journal of International Special Needs Education*, *21*(2), 11–22. https://doi.org/10.9782/2159-4341-21.2.01

Jamil, F. M., Stephan, A. T., & Bennett, A. E. (2024). Exploring longitudinal associations between teacher expectancy effects and reading achievement among a U.S. nationally representative sample of K–8 students. *The Elementary School Journal*, *125*(1), 52–76. https://doi.org/10.1086/731256

Jonson, J. L., Trantham, P., & Usher-Tate, B. J. (2019). An evaluative framework for reviewing fairness standards and practices in educational tests. *Educational Measurement: Issues and Practice, 38*(3), 6–19. https://doi.org/10.1111/emip.12259

Jung, A. W. (2011). Individualized education programs (IEPs) and barriers for parents from culturally and linguistically diverse backgrounds. *Multicultural Education*, *19*(3), 21–25. https://eric.ed.gov/?id=EJ955935

Kangas, S. E. N. (2014). When special education trumps ESL: An investigation of service delivery for ELLs with disabilities. *Critical Inquiry in Language Studies*, *11*(4), 273–306. https://doi.org/10.1080/15427587.2014.968070

Kangas, S. E. N. (2017a). A cycle of fragmentation in an inclusive age: The case of English learners with disabilities. *Teaching and Teacher Education*, *66*, 261–272. doi:10.1016/j.tate.2017.04.016

Kangas, S. E. N. (2017b). "That's where the rubber meets the road": The intersection of special education and dual language education. *Teachers College Record, 119*(7), 1–36. https://doi.org/10.1177/016146811711900701

Kangas, S. E. N. (2018a). Breaking one law to uphold another: How schools provide services to English learners with disabilities. *TESOL Quarterly, 52*(4), 877–910. https://doi.org/10.1002/tesq.431

Kangas, S. E. N. (2018b). Why working apart doesn't work at all: Special education and English learner teacher collaborations. *Intervention in School and Clinic, 54*(1), 31–39. https://doi.org/10.1177/1053451218762469

Kangas, S. E. N. (2020). Counternarratives of English learners with disabilities. *Bilingual Research Journal, 43*(3), 267–285. https://doi.org/10.1080/15235882.2020.1807424

Kangas, S. E. N. (2021). "Is it language or disability?': Confronting an ableist and monolingual filter for English learners with disabilities. *TESOL Quarterly, 55*(3), 673–683. https://doi.org/10.1002/tesq.3029

Kangas, S. E. N. (2024). *Promoting equitable reclassification of English learners with disabilities.* The Center for Promoting Research to Practice. College of Education. Lehigh University.

Kangas, S. E. N., & Cioè-Peña, M. (2024). Individualized language plans: Promises and pitfalls. *TESOL Quarterly, 58*(1), 522–536. https://doi.org/10.1002/tesq.3283

Kangas, S. E. N., & Cook, M. (2020). Academic tracking of English learners with disabilities in middle school. *American Educational Research Journal, 57*(6), 2415–2449. https://doi.org/10.3102/0002831220915702

Kangas, S. E. N., & Cook, M. (2023). Navigating competing policy demands: Dual service provision for English learners with disabilities in middle school. *Language Policy, 22,* 315–341. https://doi.org/10.1007/s10993-023-09653-8

Kangas, S. E. N., & Ruiz, M. (in press). Data skepticism and capacity for data-based decisions: The case of reclassifying English learners with disabilities. *Studies in Second Language Acquisition.*

Kangas, S. E. N., & Schissel, J. L. (2021). Holding them back or pushing them out?: Reclassification policies for English learners with disabilities. *Linguistics and Education, 63*, 1–11. https://doi.org/10.1016/j.linged.2021.100927

Kanno, Y. (2021). *English learners' access to postsecondary education: Neither college nor career ready*. Multilingual Matters.

Kanno, Y., & Kangas, S. E. N. (2014). "I'm not going to be, like, for the AP": English language learners' limited access to advanced college-preparatory courses in high school. *American Educational Research Journal, 51*(5), 848–878. https://doi.org/10.3102/0002831214544716

Kanno, Y., & Kangas, S. E. N. (2024). English learner as an intersectional identity. *Journal of Language, Identity, and Education, 23*(2), 320–326. https://doi.org/10.1080/15348458.2023.2275280

Kay-Raining Bird, E., Cleave, P., Trudeau, N., Thordardottir, E., Sutton, A., & Thorpe, A. (2005). The language abilities of bilingual children with Down syndrome. *American Journal of Speech-Language Pathology, 14*(3), 187–199. http://doi.org/10.1044/1058-0360(2005/019)

Kerr, E., & Wood, S. (2023, September 23). A look at 20 years of tuition costs at national universities. *U.S. News & World Report*. https://www.usnews.com/education/best-colleges/paying-for-college/articles/see-20-years-of-tuition-growth-at-national-universities

Kibler, A. K., & Valdés, G. (2016). Conceptualizing language learners: Socioinstitutional mechanisms and their consequences. *Modern Language Journal, 100*(S1), 96–116. https://doi.org/10.1111/modl.12310

Kieffer, M. J., & Parker, C. E. (2016). *Patterns of English learner student reclassification in New York City public schools*. U.S. Department of Education, Institute of Education Science, National Center for Education Evaluation and Regional Assistance. https://ies.ed.gov/use-work/resource-library/report/descriptive-study/patterns-english-learner-student-reclassification-new-york-city-public-schools

Klingner, J. K. (n.d.). *Distinguishing language acquisition from learning disabilities*. Division of Specialized Instruction and Student Support Office of English Language Learners. New York City Department of Education. http://whenl.weebly.com/uploads/4/9/5/2/49524833/language_acquisition_vs_learning_disability.pdf

Klingner, J. K., Artiles, A. J., Kozleski, E., Harry, B., Zion, S., Tate, W., Zamora Durán, G., & Riley, D. (2005). Addressing the disproportionate representation of culturally and linguistically diverse students in special education through culturally responsive educational systems. *Education Policy Analysis Archives, 13*(38), 1–40. https://doi.org/10.14507/epaa.v13n38.2005

Klingner, J. K., & Edwards, P. A. (2006). Cultural considerations with response to intervention models. *Reading Research Quarterly, 41*(1), 108–117. https://doi.org/10.1598/RRQ.41.1.6

Klingner, J. K., & Eppolito, A. M. (2014). *English language learners: Differentiating between language acquisition and learning disabilities*. Council for Exceptional Children.

Klingner, J. K., & Geisler, D. (2008). Helping classroom reading teachers distinguish between language acquisition and learning disabilities. In J. K. Klingner, J. J. Hoover, & L. M. Baca (Eds.), *Why do English language learners struggle with reading?: Distinguishing language acquisition from learning disabilities* (pp. 57–73). Corwin.

Krashen, S. D. (1985). *The input hypothesis: Issues and implications*. Addison-Wesley Longman Ltd.

Kuklinski, M., & Weinstein, R. (2000). Classroom and grade level differences in the stability of teacher expectations and perceived differential teacher treatment. *Learning Environments Research, 3*(1), 1–34. https://doi.org/10.1023/A:1009904718353

Landmark, L. J., & Zhang, D. (2013). Compliance and practices in transition planning: A review of individualized education program documents. *Remedial and Special Education, 34*(2), 113–125. https://doi.org/10.1177/0741932511431831

Lasswell, H. D. (1951). The policy orientation. In S. Braman (Ed.), *Communication researchers and policy-making* (pp. 85–104). MIT Press Sourcebooks.

Lasswell, H. D. (1956). The political science of science: An inquiry into the possible reconciliation of mastery and freedom. *The American Political Science Review, 50*(4), 961–979. https://www.jstor.org/stable/1951330

Learning Disabilities Association of America. (n.d.). *The role of parents/family in Response to Intervention*. https://ldaamerica.org/info/the-role-of-parentsfamily-in-response-to-intervention/

Link, B. G., & Phelan, J. (2010). Social conditions as fundamental causes of health inequalities. *Handbook of Medical Sociology*, 6, 3–17.

Linquanti, R. (2001). *The redesignation dilemma: Challenges and choices in fostering meaningful accountability for English learners*. Linguistic Minority Research Institute. University of California.

Linquanti, R., Cook, H. G., Bailey, A. L., & MacDonald, R. (2016). *Moving toward a more common definition of English learner: Collected guidance for states and multi-state assessment consortia*. Council of Chief State School Officers. https://www.academia.edu/115355470/Moving_Toward_a_More_Common_Definition_of_English_Learner_Collected_Guidance_for_States_and_Multi_State_Assessment_Consortia

Lipsky, M. (2010). *Dilemmas of the individual in public service*. Russell Sage Foundation (30th Ann. Ed). http://www.jstor.org/stable/10.7758/9781610446631

Liu, K. K., Lazarus, S., Thurlow, M. L., Stewart, J., & Larson, E. (2020). *A summary of the research on test accommodations for English learners and English learners with disabilities: 2010–2018*. Improving Instruction Project, National Center on Instructional Outcomes. https://nceo.umn.edu/docs/OnlinePubs/ImpInst_LitAccommodations.pdf

Liu, Y.-J., Ortiz, A. A., Wilkinson, C. Y., Robertson, P., & Kushner, M. I. (2008). From early childhood special education to special education resource rooms: Identification, assessment, and eligibility determinations for English language learners with reading-related disabilities. *Assessment for Effective Intervention, 33*(3), 177–187. https://doi.org/10.1177/1534508407313247

Lo, L. (2008). Chinese families' level of participation and experiences in IEP meetings. *Preventing School Failure: Alternative Education for Children and Youth, 53*(1), 21–27. https://doi.org/10.3200/psfl.53.1.21-27

Luevano, C., & Collins, T. A. (2020). Culturally appropriate math problem-solving instruction with English language learners. *School Psychology Review*, *49*(2), 144–160. https://doi.org/10.1080/2372966X.2020.1717243

Macswan, J., & Rolstad, K. (2006). How language proficiency tests mislead us about ability: Implications for English language learner placement in special education. *Teachers College Record*, *108*(11), 2304–2328. https://doi.org/10.1111/j.1467-9620.2006.00783.x

Martínez-Álvarez, P. (2023). *Teaching emergent bilingual students with dis/abilities: Humanizing pedagogies to engage learners and eliminate labels*. Teachers College Press.

Massanari, C. (2001). *Leadership and general supervision of the education of children and youth with disabilities: Responsibilities, skills, and requirements*. Mountain Plains Regional Resource Center. https://files.eric.ed.gov/fulltext/ED461239.pdf

Mavrogordato, M., & White, R. S. (2017). Reclassification variation: How policy implementation guides the process of exiting students from English learner status. *Educational Evaluation and Policy Analysis*, *39*(2), 281–310. https://doi.org/10.3102/0162373716687075

Mayer, S., LeChasseur, K., & Donaldson, M. (2018). The structure of tracking: Instructional practices of teachers leading low- and high-track classes. *American Journal of Education*, *124*(4), 383–520. https://doi.org/10.1086/698453

Mayes, T. A., & Zirkel, P. A. (2000). State educational agencies and special education: Obligation and liabilities. *Boston University Public Interest Law Journal*, *10*(1), 62–90.

McCain, G. & Farnsworth, M. (2018). *Determining difference from disability: What culturally responsive teachers should know*. Routledge.

McConnochie, M. (2024). "Needs to put in more effort": How teacher deficit beliefs frame the moral worth of Latinx children and families in school-based discourses. *Journal of Latinos and Education*, *23*(1), 132–148. https://doi.org/10.1080/15348431.2022.2114906

McKown, C., & Weinstein, R. S. (2002), Modeling the role of child ethnicity and gender in children's differential response to teacher expectations. *Journal of Applied Social Psychology*, *32*(1), 159–184. https://doi.org/10.1111/j.1559-1816.2002.tb01425.x

McKown, C., & Weinstein, R. S. (2003), The development and consequences of stereotype consciousness in middle childhood. *Child Development*, *74*(2), 498–515. https://doi.org/10.1111/1467-8624.7402012

McLaughlin, M. (1987). Learning from experience: Lessons from policy implementation. *Policy Analysis*, *9*(2), 171–178. https://doi.org/10.2307/1163728

Menken, K. (2008). *English learners left behind: Standardized testing as language policy*. Multilingual Matters.

Menken, K., Kleyn, T., & Chae, N. (2012). Spotlight on "long-term English language learners": Characteristics and prior schooling experiences of an invisible population. *International Multilingual Research Journal*, *6*(2), 121–142. https://doi.org/10.1080/19313152.2012.665822

Merriam, S. B. (1995). What can you tell from an N of 1?: Issues of validity and reliability in qualitative research. *AACE Journal of Lifelong Learning*, *4*, 51–60.

Michigan Department of Education. (2024). *Read by grade 3 guide*. https://www.michigan.gov/-/media/Project/Websites/mde/OEAA/Early-Literacy-and-Mathematics/Read_Grade_3_Guide.pdf

Migliarini, V., & Stinson, C. (2021). Inclusive education in the (new) era of anti-immigration policy: Enacting equity for disabled English language learners. *International Journal of Qualitative Studies in Education*, *34*(1), 72–88. https://doi.org/10.1080/09518398.2020.1735563

Minnema, J. E., Thurlow, M. L., VanGetson, G. R., & Jimenez, R. (2006). *Including English language learners with disabilities in large-scale assessments: A case study of linguistically-diverse populations* (ELLs with Disabilities Report 14). National Center on Educational Outcomes. https://rtc3.umn.edu/docs/OnlinePubs/ELLsDisRpt14.pdf

Moll, L. C., Amanti, C., Neff, D., & González, N. (1992). Funds of knowledge for teaching: Using a qualitative approach to connect homes and classrooms. *Theory Into Practice*, *31*(2), 132–141. http://www.jstor.org/stable/1476399?origin=JSTOR-pdf

Montoya, C., Gilson, C., & Yllades, V. (2022). *Experiences of Latinx immigrant parents of children with developmental disabilities in the IEP process.*

https://www.researchgate.net/publication/367331502_Experiences_of_Latinx_Immigrant_Parents_of_Children_with_Developmental_Disabilities_in_the_IEP_Process

Morgan, P. L., Farkas, G., Cook, M., Strassfeld, N. M., Hillemeier, M. M., Pun, W. H., Wang, Y., & Schussler, D. L. (2018). Are Hispanic, Asian, Native American, or language-minority children overrepresented in special education? *Exceptional Children*, *84*(3), 261–279. https://doi.org/10.1177/0014402917748303

Morgan, P. L., Woods, A. D., Wang, Y., & Gloski, C. A. (2023). Texas special education cap's associations with disability identification disparities of racial and language minority students. *Exceptional Children*, *89*(2), 125–141. https://doi.org/10.1177/00144029221109849

MTSS for English Learners. (2022). *Multitiered system of supports for English learners: Model demonstration research sponsored by the Office of Special Education Programs.* U.S. Department of Education. https://www.mtss4els.org

Muller, C., Riegle-Crumb, C., Schiller, K. S., Wilkinson, L., & Frank, K. A. (2010). Race and academic achievement in racially diverse high schools: Opportunity and stratification. *Teachers College Record*, *112*(4), 1038–1063. https://doi.org/10.1177/016146811011200406

Myat Zaw, A. M., Win, N. Z., & Thepthien, B. (2022). Adolescents' academic achievement, mental health, and adverse behaviors: Understanding the role of resilience and adverse childhood experiences. *School Psychology International*, *43*(5), 516–536. https://doi.org/10.1177/01430343221107114

Najarro, I. (2023, February 21). The English learner population is growing: Is teacher training keeping pace? *Education Week*. https://www.edweek.org/teaching-learning/the-english-learner-population-is-growing-is-teacher-training-keeping-pace/2023/02

National Association of State Directors of Special Education (n.d.). *State director of special education: success profile.* https://www.nasdse.org/docs/NASDSE_State_Director_Success_Profile_2021.pdf

National Center for Education Statistics. (2024). *English language learners in public schools. Condition of Education.* U.S. Department of Education, Institute of Education Sciences. https://nces.ed.gov/programs/coe/indicator/cgf/english-learners-in-public-schools

National Center for Educational Outcomes. (n.d.). *Alt-ELP participation.* https://nceo.info/Assessments/alternate_elp_assessment/participation

National Center for Learning Disabilities. (2011). *A parent's guide to Response to Intervention (RTI).* https://www.advocacyinstitute.org/resources/ParentRTIGuide.pdf

National Center for Systemic Improvement. (2018). *Three circles of evidence-based decision-making in early childhood.* https://files.eric.ed.gov/fulltext/ED591450.pdf

National Center for Systemic Improvement. (2021). *Equity-driven systems coherence: Important questions to ask.* https://onlinelearning.cadreworks.org/resources/ncsi-equity-driven-systems-coherence-important-questions-ask

National Clearinghouse for English Language Acquisition (NCELA). (2021). *Profile of English learners in the United States.* U.S. Department of Education, Office of

English Language Acquisition. https://ncela.ed.gov/resources/fact-sheet-profile-of-english-learners-in-the-united-states-january-2021

National Clearinghouse for English Language Acquisition (NCELA). (2023). *English learners with disabilities.* U.S. Department of Education, Office of English Language Acquisition. https://ncela.ed.gov/resources/infographic-english-learners-with-disabilities-october-2023

National Parent Center on Transition and Employment. (2023). *Person-centered planning.* https://www.pacer.org/transition/learning-center/independent-community-living/person-centered.asp

Nebraska Department of Education. (2019). *Individual reading improvement plans (IRIPs): Guidance for districts.* https://www.education.ne.gov/wp-content/uploads/2019/08/Individualized-Reading-Plan-DRAFT-guidance-doc.pdf

New Mexico Public Education Department. (2023). *English learner students with disabilities guidance manual.* https://webnew.ped.state.nm.us/wp-content/uploads/2023/10/Identifying_Serving_ELs_Disabilities_Guidance_FINAL.pdf

Noddings, N. (2006). What does it mean to educate the whole child? *Educational Leadership, 63*(1), 8–13. https://www.ascd.org/el/articles/what-does-it-mean-to-educate-the-whole-child

Oakes, J. (2005). *Keeping track: How schools structure inequality* (2nd ed.). Yale University Press.

Ochoa, S. H., Riccio, C., Jimenez, S., Garcia de Alba, R., & Sines, M. (2004). Psychological assessment of English language learners and/or bilingual students: An investigation of school psychologists' current practices. *Journal of Psychoeducational Assessment, 22*(3), 185–208. https://doi.org/10.1177/073428290402200301

Orosco, M. J., & Klingner, J. K. (2010). One school's implementation of RTI with English language learners: "Referring into RTI." *Journal of Learning Disabilities, 43*(3), 269–288. https://doi.org/10.1177/0022219409355474

Ortiz, A. A., Fránquiz, M. E., & Lara, G. P. (2020). The education of emergent bilinguals with disabilities: State of practice. *Bilingual Research Journal, 43*(3), 245–252. https://doi.org/10.1080/15235882.2020.1823734

Ortiz, A. A., Robertson, P. M., Wilkinson, C. Y., Liu, Y. J., McGhee, B. D., & Kushner, M. I. (2011). The role of bilingual education teachers in preventing inappropriate referrals of ELLs to special education: Implications for response to intervention. *Bilingual Research Journal, 34*(3), 316–333. https://doi.org/10.1080/15235882.2011.628608

Ortiz, S. O., Piazza, N. N., Ochoa, S. H., & Dynda, A. M. (2018). Testing with culturally and linguistically diverse populations: New directions in fairness and validity. In D. P. Flanagan & E. M. McDonough (Eds.), *Contemporary intellectual assessment: Theories, tests, and issues* (pp. 684–714). Guilford Press.

Padía, L., Cioè-Peña, M., & Phuong, J. (2024). Mending the intersectional gap: Supporting emergent multilinguals labeled as disabled through translanguaging and Universal Design for Learning. *Theory Into Practice, 63*(4), 438–456. https://doi.org/10.1080/00405841.2024.2355843

Padilla, A. M., Chen, X., Song, D., Swanson, E., & Peterson, M. (2022). Mindset, stereotype threat and the academic achievement gap between Chinese and

Latinx English learners (ELs). *International Journal of Educational Research, 112*, 1–16. https://doi.org/10.1016/j.ijer.2021.101916

Paradis, J., Genesee, F., & Crago, M. F. (2021). *Dual language development and disorders: A handbook on bilingualism and second language learning* (3rd ed). Brookes.

Park, S. (2019). Disentangling language from disability: Teacher implementation of tier 1 English language development policies for ELs with suspected disabilities. *Teaching and Teacher Education, 80*, 227–240. https://doi.org/10.1016/j.tate.2019.02.004

Park, S. (2020). Demystifying disproportionality: Exploring educator beliefs about special education referrals for English learners. *Teachers College Record, 122*(5), 1–40. https://doi.org/10.1177/016146812012200510

Park, S. (2023). Thickening borders through least restrictive environment: The case of an Immigrant kindergartner with autism. *Multiple Voices for Ethnically Diverse Exceptional Learners, 23*(1), 4–19. https://doi.org/10.56829/2158-396X-23.1.4

Park, S., & Chou, F. (2019). *CCSSO framework on supporting educators to prepare and successfully exit English learners with disabilities from EL status.* Council of Chief State School Officers. https://files.eric.ed.gov/fulltext/ED593499.pdf

Peltier, T. K., Heddy, B. C., & Peltier, C. (2020). Using conceptual change theory to help preservice teachers understand dyslexia. *Annals of Dyslexia, 70*(1), 62–78. https://doi.org/10.1007/s11881-020-00192-z

Pennsylvania Department of Education. (2020). *Standards align systems: Standard area—CC.1.4.* https://pdesas.org/Standard/Detail?linkStandardId=0&standardId=160118

Perlstein, L. (2007). *Tested: One American school struggles to make the grade.* Henry Holt & Company.

Phuong, J., & Cioè-Peña, M. (2022). Perfect or mocha: Language policing and pathologization. In S. Annamma, B. A. Ferri, & D. J. Connor (Eds.), *DisCrit expanded: Reverberations, ruptures, and inquiries* (pp. 129–143). Teachers College Press.

Phuong, J., DiPasquale, K., & Rivera, N. (2021). "If you're gonna be inclusive, you have to be inclusive on all levels": Ableism in teacher collaboration. *TESOL Quarterly, 55*(3), 684–693. https://doi.org/10.1002/tesq.3032

Powell, S. R., Berry, K. A., & Tran, L. M. (2020). Performance differences on a measure of mathematics vocabulary for English learners and non-English learners with and without mathematics difficulty. *Reading & Writing Quarterly, 36*(2), 124–141. https://doi.org/10.1080/10573569.2019.1677538

Poza, L. E. (2021). Adding flesh to the bones: Dignity frames for English learner education. *Harvard Educational Review, 91*(4), 482–510. https://doi.org/10.17763/1943-5045-91.4.482

Project ELITE, Project ESTRE²LLA, & Project REME. (2015). *Effective practices for English learners: Brief 2, Assessment and data-based decision-making.* U.S. Department of Education, Office of Special Education Programs. https://www.mtss4els.org/files/resource-files/Brief2.pdf

Project LEE, Project ELLIPSES, & Project ELITE. (2021). *Meeting the needs of English learners with and without disabilities: Brief 4, Fostering collaborative partnerships with families of English learners within a multitiered system of supports*. U.S. Department of Education, Office of Special Education Programs. https://www.mtss4els.org/files/resource-files/Series2-Brief4.pdf

Pryzmus, S. D., & Alvarado, M. (2019). Advancing bilingual special education: Translanguaging in content-based story retells for distinguishing language difference from disability. *Multiple Voices for Ethnically Diverse Exceptional Learners, 19*(1), 23–43. https://doi.org/10.56829/2158-396X.19.1.23

Randez, R. A., & Cornell, C. (2023). Advancing equity in language assessment for learners with disabilities. *Language Testing, 40*(4), 984–999. https://doi.org/10.1177/02655322231169442

Rios, J. A., Ihlenfeldt, S. D., & Chavez, C. (2020). Are accommodations for English learners on state accountability assessments evidence-based?: A multistudy systematic review and meta-analysis. *Educational Measurement: Issues and Practice, 39*(4), 65–75. https://doi.org/10.1111/emip.12337

Robinson-Cimpian, J. P., & Thompson, K. D. (2016). The effects of changing test-based policies for reclassifying English learners. *Journal of Policy Analysis and Management, 35*(2), 279–305. https://doi.org/10.1002/pam.21882

Rosa, J., & Flores, N. (2017). Unsettling race and language: Toward a raciolinguistic perspective. *Language in Society, 46*(5), 621–647. https://doi.org/10.1017/S0047404517000562

Roseberry-McKibbin, C. (2021). Utilizing comprehensive preassessment procedures for differentiating language difference from language impairment in English learners. *Communication Disorders Quarterly, 42*(2), 93–99. https://doi.org/10.1177/1525740119890314

Rosenthal, R. (2002). The Pygmalion effect and its mediating mechanisms. In J. Aronson (Ed.), *Improving academic achievement: Impact of psychological factors on education* (pp. 25–36). Academic Press.

Rosenthal, R., & Jacobson, L. (1966). Teachers' expectancies: Determinants of pupils' IQ gains. *Psychological Reports, 19*(1), 115–118. https://doi.org/10.2466/pr0.1966.19.1.115

Rosenthal, R., & Jacobson, L. (1968). Pygmalion in the classroom. *The Urban Review, 3*, 16–20. https://doi.org/10.1007/BF02322211

Rossetti, Z., Sauer, J. S., Bui, O., & Ou, S. (2017). Developing collaborative partnerships with culturally and linguistically diverse families during the IEP process. *TEACHING Exceptional Children, 49*(5), 328–338. https://doi.org/10.1177/0040059916680103

Rubie-Davies, C. M. (2007). Classroom interactions: Exploring the practices of high- and low-expectation teachers. *British Journal of Educational Psychology*, 77(2), 289–306. https://doi.org/10.1348/000709906X101601

Rubie-Davies, C. M. (2014). *Becoming a high expectation teacher: Raising the bar*. Routledge.

Ruble, L. A., McGrew, J., Dalrymple, N., & Jung, L. A. (2010). Examining the quality of IEPs for young children with autism. *Journal of Autism and Developmental Disorders, 40*(12), 1459–1470. https://doi.org/10.1007/s10803-010-1003-1

Russell Valezy, J., & Spada, N. (2006). The effectiveness of corrective feedback for the acquisition of L2 grammar: A meta-analysis of the research. In J. M. Norris & L. Ortega (Eds.), *Synthesizing research on language learning and teaching* (pp. 133–164). John Benjamins Publishing Company.

Sahakyan, N., & Ryan, S. (2018). *Long-term English learners across 15 WIDA states: A research brief* [WIDA Research Brief No. RB-2018-1]. https://wida.wisc.edu/resources/long-term-english-learners-across-15-wida-states

Sailor, W. (2008). Access to the general curriculum: Systems change or tinker some more? *Research & Practice for Persons with Severe Disabilities, 33*(4), 249–257. http://dx.doi.org/10.2511/rpsd.33.4.249

Salas, L. (2004). Individualized educational plan (IEP) meetings and Mexican American parents: Let's talk about it. *Journal of Latinos and Education, 3*(3), 181–192. https://doi.org/10.1207/s1532771xjle0303_4

Samson, J. F., & Lesaux, N. K. (2009). Language-minority learners in special education: Rates and predictors of identification for services. *Journal of Learning Disabilities, 42*(2), 148–162. https://doi.org/10.1177/0022219408326221

Sanford, A. K., Pinkney, C. J., Esparza Brown, J., Elliott, C. G., Rotert, E. N., & Sennott, S. C. (2020). Culturally and linguistically responsive mathematics instruction for English learners in multitiered support systems: PLUSS enhancements. *Learning Disability Quarterly, 43*(2), 101–114. https://doi.org/10.1177/0731948719836173

Scanlan, M. & López, F. A. (2015). *Leadership for culturally and linguistically responsive schools*. Routledge.

Schalock, R. L., & Luckasson, R. (2005). *Clinical judgment*. American Association on Mental Retardation.

Schissel, J. L. (2019). *Social consequences of testing for language-minoritized bilinguals in the United States*. Multilingual Matters.

Schissel, J. L., & Kangas, S. E. N. (2018). Reclassification of emergent bilinguals with disabilities: The intersectionality of improbabilities. *Language Policy, 17*(4), 567–589. https://doi.org/10.1007/s10993-018-9476-4

Scruggs, T. E. & Mastropieri, M. A. (2017). Making inclusion work with co-teaching. *TEACHING Exceptional Children, 49*(4), 284–293. https://doi.org/10.1177/0040059916685065

Scudella, V. (2013). *State education governance models*. Education Commission of the States. https://www.ecs.org/clearinghouse/01/08/70/10870.pdf

Servage, L. (2008). Critical and transformative practices in professional learning communities. *Teacher Education Quarterly, 35*(1), 63–77. http://www.jstor.org/stable/23479031

Shenoy, S., de Valenzuela, J. S., & Pacheco, R. (2022). Reimagining language proficiency assessment for English learners with significant cognitive disabilities. *Research and Practice for Persons with Severe Disabilities, 47*(3), 176–183. https://doi.org/10.1177/15407969221119137

Shifrer, D. (2013). Stigma of a label: Educational expectations for high school students labeled with learning disabilities. *Journal of Health and Social Behavior, 54*(4), 462–480. https://doi.org/10.1177/0022146513503346

Shin, N. (2020). Stuck in the middle: Examination of long-term English learners. *International Multilingual Research Journal, 14*(3), 181–205. https://doi.org/10.1080/19313152.2019.1681614

Simon-Cereijido, G., & Gutiérrez-Clellen, V. F. (2013). Bilingual education for all: Latino dual language learners with language disabilities. *International Journal of Bilingual Education and Bilingualism, 17*(2), 235–254. https://doi.org/10.1080/13670050.2013.866630

Skrla, L. E., McKenzie, K. B., & Scheurich, J. J. (2009). *Using equity audits to create equitable and excellent schools*. Corwin.

Slama, R., Brodziak de los Reyes, I., Molefe, R. A., August, D., Gerdeman, D., Cavazos, L., & Herrera, A. (2017). *Time to proficiency for Hispanic English learner students in Texas*. https://ies.ed.gov/use-work/resource-library/report/descriptive-study/time-proficiency-hispanic-english-learner-students-texas

Slanda, D. D., & Pike, L. (Eds.). (2022). *Handbook of research on interdisciplinary preparation for equitable special education*. IGI Global.

Smarick, A., & Squire, J. (2014). *The state education agency: At the helm, not the oar* [Report]. Thomas B. Fordham Institute. https://fordhaminstitute.org/national/research/state-education-agency-helm-not-oar

Smylie, M. A., Bay, M., & Tozer, S. E. (1999). Preparing teachers as agents of change. *Teachers College Record, 100*(5), 29–62. https://doi.org/10.1177/016146819910000502

Sotelo-Dynega, M., Ortiz, S. O., Flanagan, D. P., & Chaplin, W. F. (2013). English language proficiency and test performance: An evaluation of bilingual students with the Woodcock-Johnson III tests of cognitive abilities. *Psychology in the Schools, 50*(8), 781–797. https://doi.org/10.1002/pits.21706

Spies, T. G., & Cheatham, G. A. (2018). Introduction to the special issue: Successful inclusion for students with disabilities who are learning English. *Intervention in School and Clinic, 54*(1), 3–5. https://doi.org/10.1177/1053451218762580

Stelitano, L., Russell, J. L., & Bray, L. E. (2020). Organizing for meaningful inclusion: Exploring the routines that shape student supports in secondary schools. *American Educational Research Journal, 57*(2), 535–575. https://doi.org/10.3102/0002831219859307

Stinson, C., Migliarini, V. & Miller, A. L. (2025). 'We persist in this cycle': A critical disability sociolinguistic analysis of behavioral policies for emergent bilinguals labeled as disabled. *Urban Review, 57*, 239–262. https://doi.org/10.1007/s11256-024-00719-3

Stoll, L., & Luis, K. S. (2007). Professional learning communities: Elaborating new approaches. In L. Stoll & K. S. Luis (Eds.), *Professional learning communities: Divergence, depth, and dilemmas* (pp. 1–14). Open University Press.

Stoll, L., Bolam, R., McMahon, A., Wallace, M., & Thomas, S. (2006). Professional learning communities: A review of the literature. *Journal of Educational Change, 7*, 221–258. https://doi.org/10.1007/s10833-006-0001-8

Stolz, S. (2021). Time for critical reimagining and breaking of silos in teacher education. *Teacher Education Quarterly, 48*(4), 97–100. https://www.jstor.org/stable/27099524

Stutzman, B., & Lowenhaupt, R. (2022). At the intersection: Examining teacher and administrator perceptions of ELs and special education. *International Journal of Disability, Development and Education, 69*(3), 1047–1064. https://doi.org/10.1080/1034912X.2020.1749240

Sullivan, A. L. (2011). Disproportionality in special education identification and placement of English language learners. *Exceptional Children, 77*(3), 317–334. https://doi.org/10.1177/001440291107700304

Sullivan, A. L., Artiles, A. J., & Hernandez-Saca, D. I. (2015). Addressing special education inequity through systemic change: Contributions of ecologically based organizational consultation. *Journal of Educational and Psychological Consultation, 25*(2–3), 129–147. https://doi.org/10.1080/10474412.2014.929969

Swain, M. (1985). Communicative competence: Some roles of comprehensible input and comprehensible output in its development. In S. Gass & C. Madden (Eds.), *Input in second language acquisition* (pp. 235–253). Newbury House.

Swanson, H. L., Kong, J., Petcu, S. D., & Asencio Pimentel, M. F. (2020). Can difficulties in language acquisition and specific learning disabilities be separated among English learners? *Exceptional Children, 86*(3), 293–309. https://doi.org/10.1177/0014402919893931

Tannenbaum, M., & Berkovich, M. (2005). Family relations and language maintenance: Implications for language educational policies. *Language Policy, 4*, 287–309. https://doi.org/10.1007/s10993-005-7557-7

TESOL International. (2018). *The 6 principles for exemplary teaching of English learners*. TESOL Press.

Texas Education Code § 21.04891 (2021). Bilingual special education certification.

Thomas, W., & Collier, V. P. (2012). *Dual language education for a transformed world*. Dual Language Education of New Mexico—Fuente Press.

Thompson, K. D. (2015). Questioning the long-term English learner label: How categorization can blind us to students' abilities. *Teachers College Record, 117*(12), 1–50. https://doi.org/10.1177/016146811511701203

Thompson, K. D., & Rodriguez-Mojica, C. (2023). Individualized language plans: A potential tool for collaboration to support multilingual students. *Journal of Education for Students Placed at Risk (JESPAR), 28*(1), 97–121. https://doi.org/10.1080/10824669.2022.2123330

Thorius, K. A. K., Waitoller, F. R., Cannon, M. A., & Moore, T. S. (2018). Responsive to what?: Conceptualizations of "culture" and "culturally responsive" in *Multiple Voices. Multiple Voices for Ethnically Diverse Exceptional Learners, 18*(1), 3–21. https://doi.org/10.56829/2158-396X.18.1.3

Trainor, A. A., Newman, L., Garcia, E., Woodley, H. H., Traxler, R. E., & Deschene, D. N. (2019). Postsecondary education–focused transition planning experiences of English learners with disabilities. *Career Development and Transition for Exceptional Individuals, 42*(1), 43–55. https://doi.org/10.1177/2165143418811830

U.S. Centers for Disease Control and Prevention. (2024). *About adverse childhood experiences*. https://www.cdc.gov/aces/about/index.html

U.S. Department of Education (2007). *Questions and answers on highly qualified teachers serving children with disabilities*. https://sites.ed.gov/idea/files/07-0006.HQT_.pdf

U.S. Department of Education (n.d.). *Our nation's English learners*. https://www2.ed.gov/datastory/el-characteristics/index.html

U.S. Department of Justice & U.S. Department of Education. (2015, January 5). *Dear colleague letter: English learner students and limited English proficient parents*. https://www2.ed.gov/about/offices/list/ocr/letters/colleague-el-201501.pdf

U.S. Office of Special Education Programs. (2022). *OSEP fast facts: Students with disabilities who are English learners (ELs) served under IDEA Part B*. https://sites.ed.gov/idea/osep-fast-facts-students-with-disabilities-english-learners

Umansky, I. M. (2016). Leveled and exclusionary tracking: English learners' access to academic content in middle school. *American Educational Research Journal, 53*(6), 1792–1833. https://doi.org/10.3102/0002831216675404

Umansky, I. M., & Avelar, J. D. (2023). Canaried in the coal mine: What the experiences and outcomes of students considered long-term English learners teach us about pitfalls in English learner education . . . and what we can do about it. *Journal of Education for Students Placed at Risk (JESPAR)*, *28*(1), 122–147. https://doi.org/10.1080/10824669.2022.2123326

Umansky, I. M., & Dumont, H. (2021). English Learner labeling: How English learner classification in kindergarten shapes teacher perceptions of student skills and the moderating role of bilingual instructional settings. *American Educational Research Journal*, *58*(5), 993–1031. https://doi.org/10.3102/0002831221997571

Umansky, I. M., Hopkins, M., Dabach, D. B., Porter, L., Thompson, K., & Pompa, D. (2018). *Understanding and supporting the educational needs of recently arrived immigrant English learner students: Lessons for state and local education agencies.* The Council of Chief State School Officers. https://eric.ed.gov/?id=ED586975

Umansky, I. M., Thompson, K. D., & Díaz, G. (2017). Using an ever–English learner framework to examine disproportionality in special education. *Exceptional Children*, *84*(1), 76–96. https://doi.org/10.1177/0014402917707470

Valencia, R. R. (1997). *The evolution of deficit thinking: Educational thought and practice.* Routledge.

van den Bergh, L., Denessen, E., Hornstra, L., Voeten, M., & Holland, R. W. (2010). The implicit prejudiced attitudes of teachers: Relations to teacher expectations and the ethnic achievement gap. *American Educational Research Journal*, *47*(2), 497–527. https://doi.org/10.3102/0002831209353594

VanPatten, B., & Cadierno, T. (1993). Explicit instruction and input processing. *Studies in Second Language Acquisition*, *15*(2), 225–243. https://doi.org/10.1017/S0272263100011979

Vaughn, S., Martinez, L. R., Williams, K. J., Miciak, J., Fall, A.-M., & Roberts, G. (2019). Efficacy of a high school extensive reading intervention for English learners with reading difficulties. *Journal of Educational Psychology, 111*(3), 373–386. https://doi.org/10.1037/edu0000289

Voulgarides, K. (2018). *Does compliance matter in special education?: IDEA and the hidden inequities of practice.* Teachers College Press.

Walker, T. (2023, November 3). *Teacher 'pay penalty' reaches record high.* National Education Agency (NEA) Today. https://www.nea.org/nea-today/all-news-articles/teacher-pay-penalty-reaches-record-high

Wallace, D. (2023). *The culture trap: Ethnic expectations and unequal schooling for Black children.* Oxford University Press.

Walqui, A. (1992). *Sheltered instruction: Doing it right.* San Diego County Office of Education.

Walqui, A. (2006). Scaffolding instruction for English language learners: A conceptual framework. *International Journal of Bilingual Education and Bilingualism*, 9(2), 159–180. https://doi.org/10.1080/13670050608668639

Walqui, A., & Bunch, G. C., & Mueller, P. (Eds.). (2025). *Amplifying the curriculum: Designing quality learning opportunities for English learners* (2nd ed.). Teachers College Press.

Weddle, H. (2023). Developing a research–practice partnership with policy intermediaries: An examination of collaboration with state education agency leaders. *Educational Evaluation and Policy Analysis*. https://doi.org/10.3102/01623737231213082

Weddle, H., Hopkins, M., Lowenhaupt, R., & Kangas, S. E. N. (2024). Fostering shared responsibility for multilingual learners across levels of the education system. *Educational Researcher*, *53*(4), 252–261. https://doi.org/10.3102/0013189X241227913

Whittaker, M. (2023). High standards & innovative solutions: How some states are addressing the special educator shortage crisis. *Office of Special Education and Rehabilitative Services Blog*. U.S. Department of Education. https://sites.ed.gov/osers/2023/05/high-standards-innovative-solutions-how-some-states-are-addressing-the-special-educator-shortage-crisis/

WIDA. (2020). *WIDA English language development standards framework, 2020 edition: Kindergarten–grade 12*. Board of Regents of the University of Wisconsin System.

WIDA. (2022). *Accessibility and accommodations manual*. https://wida.wisc.edu/sites/default/files/resource/Accessibility-Accommodations-Manual.pdf

WIDA. (2024). *WIDA alternate ACCESS*. https://wida.wisc.edu/assess/alt-access

WIDA. (2025). *ACCESS for ELLs interpretive guide for score reports grades K–12*. Board of Regents of the University of Wisconsin System. https://wida.wisc.edu/sites/default/files/resource/Interpretive-Guide.pdf

Wilkinson, C. Y., & Ortiz, A. A. (1986). *Characteristics of limited English proficient and English proficient learning disabled Hispanic students at initial assessment and at reevaluation*. U.S. Department of Education.

Williams, K. J., & Vaughn, S. (2020). Effects of an intensive reading intervention for ninth-grade English learners with learning disabilities. *Learning Disability Quarterly*, *43*(3), 154–166. https://doi.org/10.1177/0731948719851745

Wu, Y. C., Thurlow, M., & Johnson, D. (2022). Parent's post-school goal expectations for English learners with disabilities. *Exceptionality*, *31*(4), 275–290. https://doi.org/10.1080/09362835.2022.2156868

Xin, Y. P., Kim, S. J., Lei, Q., Wei, S., Liu, B., Wang, W., Kastberg, S., Chen, Y., Yang, X., Ma, X., & Richardson, S. E. (2020). The effect of computer-assisted conceptual model-based intervention program on mathematics problem-solving performance of at-risk English learners. *Reading & Writing Quarterly*, *36*(2), 104–123. https://doi.org/10.1080/10573569.2019.1702909

Yamasaki, B. L., & Luk, G. (2018). Eligibility for special education in elementary school: The role of diverse language experiences. *Language, Speech, Hearing Services in Schools*, *49*(4), 889–901. https://doi.org/10.1044/2018_LSHSS-DYSLC-18-0006

Zehler, A. M., Fleischman, H. L., Hopstock, P. J., Stephenson, T. G., Pendzick, M. L., & Sapru, S. (2003). *Descriptive study of services to LEP students and LEP students with disabilities*. Office of English Language Acquisition, U.S.

Department of Education. https://www.ncela.ed.gov/files/rcd/BE021199/special_ed4.pdf

Zhang, C., & Bennett, T. (2003). Facilitating the meaningful participation of culturally and linguistically diverse families in the IFSP and IEP process. *Focus on Autism and Other Developmental Disabilities, 18*(1), 51–59. https://doi.org/10.1177/108835760301800107

Zirkel, P. (2021). English learners in K–12 schools at the perilous intersection with disability laws: The need for guardias bilingües. *Boston University Public Interest Law Journal, 30*, 59–88. https://www.bu.edu/pilj/files/2021/04/Zirkel.pdf

Index

Page numbers followed by *f* or *t* refer respectively to a figure or a table on that page. Page numbers followed by "n" and another number refer to an endnote that is referenced on that page.

About the Author

Sara E. N. Kangas is an associate professor in the College of Education at Lehigh University in Bethlehem, Pennsylvania. Her research explores the everyday beliefs, conditions, and policies in K–12 education that shape the learning opportunities of multilingual learners (MLs) with disabilities. Dr. Kangas utilizes critical frameworks in her research to promote more inclusive and socially just school-based experiences for students at the nexus of ML and special education. For her work in this intersection, she has received the James E. Alatis Prize from the TIRF Foundation and the Wilga Rivers Award from the American Association for Applied Linguistics. Kangas's research has been funded by the Spencer Foundation and has been published in scholarly venues such as *American Educational Research Journal*, *Educational Researcher*, *The Journal of Special Education*, and *TESOL Quarterly*, among other journals.